# THE FALL OF FRANCE

**Julian Jackson** is Professor of Modern History at Queen Mary and
Westfield, University of London, and the author of several books on
twentieth-century France, including *France: The Dark Years 1940–1944*
(OUP, 2001), and editor of *Europe 1900–1945* (OUP, 2002).

# THE FALL OF FRANCE
## *The Nazi Invasion of 1940*

JULIAN JACKSON

OXFORD
UNIVERSITY PRESS

# OXFORD

UNIVERSITY PRESS

Great Clarendon Street, Oxford, OX2 6DP,
United Kingdom

Oxford University Press is a department of the University of Oxford.
It furthers the University's objective of excellence in research, scholarship,
and education by publishing worldwide. Oxford is a registered trade mark of
Oxford University Press in the UK and in certain other countries

© Julian Jackson 2003

The moral rights of the authors have been asserted

First published 2003
First published as an Oxford University Press paperback 2004

Published in the United States of America by Oxford University Press
198 Madison Avenue, New York, NY 10016, United States of America

British Library Cataloguing in Publication Data

Data available

ISBN 978-0-19-280550-8

Links to third party websites are provided by Oxford in good faith and
for information only. Oxford disclaims any responsibility for the materials
contained in any third party website referenced in this work.

*To Douglas*

# THE MAKING OF THE MODERN WORLD

This group of narrative histories focuses on key moments and events in the twentieth century to explore their wider significance for the development of the modern world.

PUBLISHED:

*The Fall of France: The Nazi Invasion of 1940*, Julian Jackson

FORTHCOMING:

*A Bitter Revolution: China's Struggle with the Modern World*, Rana Mitter
*The Vietnam Wars: A Global History*, Mark Bradley
*Algeria: The Undeclared War*, Martin Evans
*The Burning of Louvain*, Alan Kramer

SERIES ADVISERS:

PROFESSOR CHRIS BAYLY, University of Cambridge
PROFESSOR RICHARD J. EVANS, University of Cambridge
PROFESSOR PAUL PRESTON, London School of Economics
PROFESSOR DAVID REYNOLDS, University of Cambridge
PROFESSOR MEGAN VAUGHAN, University of Cambridge

# Acknowledgements

Most of this book was written in a sabbatical semester in the autumn of 2001, and I would like to thank my Head of Department, Professor Noel Thompson, for granting me this leave. In some form or other I have taught a Special Subject on the Fall of France in Swansea History Department for the last fifteen years. Some years have worked better than others, but overall I have learnt a lot from the experience and enjoyed it (as I hope the students have as well). I have profited enormously from conversations, electronic or otherwise, with Martin Alexander, Peter Jackson, and Talbot Imlay. Talbot Imlay was kind enough to show me some sections of his forthcoming book on the Phoney War. I am grateful to Katharine Reeve, my editor at OUP, for her comments and advice. I am grateful also to Patrick Higgins for taking the time to read the whole manuscript with great care. This is certainly a much better book as a result of his criticisms and suggestions. Perhaps it would be a better one still if I had listened to all of them. Finally, I would like to thank Eleanor Breuning who generously gave up hours of her time to read through the proofs. Her heroic labours and vigilant eye saved me from more than mere typographical errors.

J.J.

# Contents

CONTENTS

# List of Illustrations

The publisher and the author apologize for any errors or omissions in the above list. If
contacted they will be pleased to rectify these at the earliest opportunity.

# List of Maps

# Brief Chronology

**1934**
6 February: Stavisky riots in Paris

**1935**
11–14 April: Stresa Conference
18 June: Anglo-German Naval Agreement
2 October: Italian invasion of Abyssinia

**1936**
7 March: Germany reoccupies Rhineland
3 May: Popular Front wins French elections
September: French rearmament programme approved
14 October: Belgium ends military alliance with France

**1938**
10 April: Daladier becomes premier
28–30 September: Munich agreement signed
30 November: General strike protesting against end of 40-hour week

**1939**
15–16 March: Germany occupies the rest of Czechoslovakia
31 March: Anglo-French guarantee to Poland
23 August: Nazi-Soviet Non-Aggression Pact concluded
3 September: France and Britain declare war on Germany
30 November: Soviet invasion of Finland

**1940**
10 January: Mechelen incident
12 March: Soviet-Finnish Armistice

9 April: Germany invades Norway
10 May: Germany invades the Netherlands, Belgium, and Luxembourg
13 May: German troops cross Meuse at Sedan
15 May: Anglo-French forces in Belgium begin retreat
16 May: Churchill in Paris
18 May: Reynaud reshuffles government and brings in Pétain
19 May: Weygand replaces Gamelin as Commander-in-Chief
20 May: German troops reach Channel at Abbeville
21 May: Weygand visits Ypres
22 May: French and British leaders accept 'Weygand Plan'
25 May: Armistice first mentioned in French War Committee
26 May: Reynaud visits London; Gort decides to withdraw towards Channel
28 May: Capitulation of Belgium
26 May–4 June: Dunkirk evacuation
5 June: Reynaud reshuffles government; Daladier goes and de Gaulle comes in
5–7 June: German army breaks through Somme/Aisne line
10 June: French government leaves Paris; Italy declares war on France
12 June: Weygand asks the government to request an armistice
13 June: Last Franco-British war council meets at Tours
14 June: German troops enter Paris; French government heads for Bordeaux
15 June: Chautemps proposes the government ask conditions for an armistice
16 June: Offer of Anglo-French Union; Reynaud resigns; Pétain becomes premier
17 June: Pétain's radio speech announcing need for armistice
22 June: Signature of Franco-German armistice

# Abbreviations

AASF   Advanced Air Strike Force
BEF    British Expeditionary Force
CGT    Conféderation Générale du Travail/General Confederation of
       Labour
CIGS   Chief of the Imperial General Staff
DCR    Division Cuirassée de Réserve/Reserve Armoured Division
DI     Division d'Infanterie/Infantry Division
DIM    Division d'Infantrie Motorisée/Motorized Infantry Division
DLM    Division Légère Méchanique/Light Mechanized Division
RI     Régiment d'Infanterie/Infantry Regiment
RPF    Rassemblement du Peuple Français/Gathering of French People
SWC    Supreme War Council

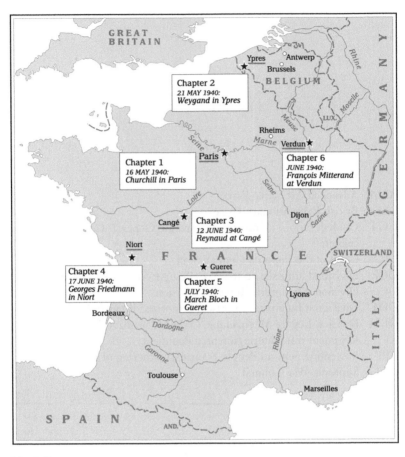

**Map I** France 1940

# INTRODUCTION

January 1940. Sir Edmund Ironside, Chief of the Imperial General Staff, summed up his impressions of the French army after a visit to France:

I must say that I saw nothing amiss with it on the surface. The Generals are all tried men, if a bit old from our view-point. None of them showed any lack of confidence. None of the liaison officers say that they have seen any lack of morale after the long wait they have had, after the excitement of mobilisation. I say to myself that we shall not know till the first clash comes. In 1914 there were many officers and men who failed but old Joffre handled the situation with great firmness. Will the Blitzkrieg when it comes allow us to rectify things if they are the same? I must say I don't know. But I say to myself that we must have confidence in the French army. It is the only thing in which we can have confidence. Our own army is just a little one and we are dependent upon the French. We have not even the same fine army we had in 1914. All depends on the French army and we can do nothing about it.[1]

When Ironside wrote these cautious words, France and Britain had already been at war with Germany for just over three months, but there had been almost no fighting thus far. The Allies' plan was to strangle the German war economy by imposing a blockade while meanwhile building up their own military strength. The intention was to mount an offensive in 1941 or 1942 once the British and French armies were fully prepared. If the Germans attacked in the meantime, the Allies had to be able to hold them off. The border between France and Germany was protected by the fortifications of the Maginot Line, but the French border with Belgium and Luxembourg was unprotected. Here almost everything would depend on the fighting quality of the French army.

On 10 May the Germans launched their offensive in the west, invading Holland, Belgium, and France. Holland capitulated in six days. On 13 May the Germans succeeded in crossing the River Meuse at Sedan, and forged ahead towards the Channel, threatening to cut off the British, French, and

Belgian forces in Belgium. On 28 May, the Belgians surrendered. Between 26 May and 4 June, the bulk of the British forces were successfully evacuated from the French Channel port of Dunkirk before they could fall into German hands. There was now almost no British military presence left on the Continent. Now the Germans were free to turn south, into the heart of France. They broke through the French defences on the rivers Aisne and Somme. The French government evacuated Paris on 10 June, and the Germans arrived in the city four days later. On 22 June, the French government signed an armistice with Germany. In only six weeks the French had been defeated. This was the most humiliating military disaster in French history.

General Ironside's questions about the French army seemed to have been answered with a finality that must have surpassed even his worst nightmares. In mid-June, one French observer, caught up in the huge wave of people fleeing south from Paris to escape the Germans, encountered a very different army from the one that Ironside had seen five months earlier:

I came upon some isolated soldiers, without arms, eyes cast down, their shoes scraping the grass at the road side. They avoided a cyclist, then brushed past a stationary car without seeming to see either of them. They walked like blind men, like dishevelled ghosts. Keeping apart from the peasants on their carts, from the city people in their cars . . . they moved on alone, like beggars who have even given up begging. We were witnessing the start of the rout, but we did not yet know it. We took them for laggards, we thought their regiments were far in front.[2]

The immediate consequences of the defeat were devastating for France. Half the country was occupied by German troops. In an unoccupied Zone in the south an authoritarian regime, with its capital at the spa town of Vichy, was set up under the leadership of the First World War hero Marshal Pétain. Democracy was dead in France. The country was liberated by the British and Americans in 1944 and a democratic Republic was set up again. But the trauma of the defeat of 1940 continued to mark the French people. In the words of the historian René Remond, who was a young man in 1940:

There is probably no more terrible trial for a people than the defeat of its armies: in the scale of crises, this is the supreme catastrophe. It scarcely matters whether one was formerly a pacifist or a militarist, whether one hated war or resigned oneself to it . . . defeat creates a deep and lasting traumatism in everyone. It wounds something essential in each of us: a certain confidence in life, a pride in oneself, an indispensable self-respect.[3]

The Fall of France was an event that resonated throughout the world. For Rebecca West, writing soon after the event, it was a tragedy that 'ranks as supreme in history as Hamlet and Othello and King Lear rank in art'.[4] As the *New York Times* observed a few days before the final French capitulation, Paris was seen throughout the world as 'a stronghold of the human spirit... when Paris is bombed, the civilized world is bombed'. In Australia the *Sydney Morning Herald* proclaimed: 'One of the lights of world civilisation is extinguished.' On 19 June the Canadian Prime Minister, Mackenzie King, declared: 'It is midnight in Europe.' There was panic in Moscow, where Stalin was only too aware that the defeat of France made it possible for Hitler to turn his attention to the east. As Khrushchev recalled in his memoirs: 'Stalin let fly with some choice Russian curses and said that now Hitler was sure to beat our brains in.'[5] He was right. Hitler invaded the Soviet Union in June 1941. In the Far East, the collapse of French power created a power vacuum in the French colony of Indo-China, and excited the expansionist ambitions of Japan. In short, the defeat of France set in motion a massive escalation of the war: it helped to turn what had been so far a limited European conflict into a world war.

The rapidity and totality of France's collapse has remained puzzling ever since. The British Foreign Secretary, Lord Halifax, wrote on 25 May 1940: 'the mystery of what looks like the French failure is as great as ever. The one firm rock on which everybody had been willing to build for the last two years was the French Army, and the Germans walked through it like they did through the Poles.' Later, in his memoirs, Halifax wrote that the Fall of France was an 'event which at the time seemed something so unbelievable as to be almost surely unreal, and if not unreal then quite immeasurably catastrophic'.[6] The French writer Antoine de Saint-Exupéry (author of the celebrated *Little Prince*), who was a pilot in 1940 and viewed much of the catastrophe from the air, begins his memoir of the events with the words: 'Surely I must be dreaming.'[7]

Within France the search for scapegoats began at once. The immediate aftermath of defeat saw the emergence of a whole literature of accusation and self-flagellation with titles such as *The Gravediggers of France* (by André Géraud), *J'Accuse! The Men Who Betrayed France* (by André Simon), *The Truth about France* (by Louis Lévy). One book, published in 1941, was even entitled *Dieu a-t-il puni la France?* [Has God Punished France?]. The answer was, of course, yes. Depending on ideological preference, people blamed politicians or generals, Communist agitators or Fascist fifth columnists, school-teachers or industrialists, the middle classes or the working classes. They blamed individualism, materialism, feminism, alcoholism, *dénatalité*, dechristianization, the break-up of the family, the decline of patriotism, treason, Malthusianism, immoral literature.

3

1. This 1941 cartoon mocks some of the more moralistic explanations for 1940. Two bemused French peasants are being told: 'How can you be surprised [about the defeat]? You gorged yourselves on the works of Proust, Gide and Cocteau.' All these writers shared in common the fact that they were homosexual.

The debate on the Fall of France has gone on ever since 1940, but now at least it is possible to view the event with greater serenity, and abandon the tone of polemic and accusation. That will be the purpose of this book: to tell the story of the defeat, explain why it occurred, and reflect on its consequences both for France and the world. The first part of the book provides a narrative of the defeat; the second part reflects on the causes, and the consequences, of that defeat in the light of the narrative that has gone before.

There are many strands to the Fall of France: it was a military defeat, the collapse of a political system, the breakdown of an alliance between two countries, and in its final stages, almost the complete disintegration of a society. Thus, each of the four narrative chapters in Part I will approach the events from a different angle. The first chapter looks at the military aspects of the defeat: French military doctrine, rearmament, the strategy of the High Command, the conduct of the military operations. The second looks at the relations between France and its allies: why France had so few allies in 1939, the way the British and French viewed each other, the way they cooperated during the fighting, and the relations between the leading personalities. The third looks at the political aspects of the defeat: the French political background, France's political structures and leadership, the relations between the politicians and the military. The fourth chapter looks at the morale of the French people: French inter-war pacifism, the attitude of

4

the French population towards the war, the training of the French army, and the way the soldiers fought once the Germans attacked.

In Part II we examine how these different narratives fit together. Is one of these four factors—military planning, allied relations, politics, morale—more important than any other? How are they related to each other? Was such a catastrophic defeat the indictment of an entire nation, or was it due merely to miscalculations by military leaders? Does an event of this magnitude necessarily have momentous causes stretching far back in French history? The answers to these questions will of course depend partly on the facts of the case; partly upon one's own philosophical assumptions. The British military historian Basil Liddell Hart once wrote that 'war is not a game which is won by sheer weight, but by the intelligence and finesse of its leaders'. Leo Tolstoy, on the other hand, famously believed that victory in a battle depended on massive historical forces outside the control of any individual. He scoffed at the idea that Napoleon had any control over events at the Battle of Borodino. This leads Tolstoy to the following conclusion: '[I]f in the descriptions given by historians we find their wars and battles carried out in accordance with previously formed plans, the only conclusion to be drawn is that these descriptions are false.'[8] This pessimistic conclusion at least has the merit of reminding us that the smooth narratives of military history are prone to iron out the true messiness of battle. Tolstoy gives us Pierre Bezukhov wandering lost on the field of Borodino in search of a battle and finding only confusion; Stendhal gives us Fabrice del Dongo who only discovers subsequently that he has participated in the 'Battle of Waterloo'. For this reason, I have tried in the narrative that follows to allow the ordinary soldier to be heard as well as the generals, the diplomats, and the politicians.

# PART I

## The Story

'A skilful commander?' replied Pierre. 'Why, one who foresees all contingencies . . . and foresees the adversary's intentions.'

'But that's impossible,' said Prince Andrew as if it were a matter settled long ago. Pierre looked at him with surprise.

'And yet they say that war is like a game of chess,' he remarked.

'Yes,' replied Prince Andrew, 'but with this little difference, that in chess you may think over each move as long as you please and are not limited for time, and with this difference too, that a knight is always stronger than a pawn, and two pawns are always stronger than one, while in war a battalion is sometimes stronger than a division and sometimes weaker than a company. The relative strengths of bodies of troops can never be known to anyone.'

(Tolstoy, *War and Peace*)

# 1

# 'WE ARE BEATEN'

## 16 May 1940: Churchill in Paris

EARLY in the morning of 15 May 1940, five days after the Germans had launched their offensive in the west, Winston Churchill was woken by a telephone call from Paul Reynaud, the French Prime Minister:

He spoke in English, and evidently under stress. 'We have been defeated.' As I did not immediately respond he said again: 'We are beaten; we have lost the battle.' I said: 'Surely it can't have happened so soon?' But he replied: 'The front is broken near Sedan; they are pouring through in great numbers with tanks and armoured cars.'

Reynaud's call was not a complete surprise. Already on the previous evening he had wired Churchill that the situation was 'very serious' and requested ten additional British fighter squadrons. Churchill did what he could to reassure Reynaud, reminding him that there had been moments in 1914 and 1918 that seemed equally desperate.

By the end of the day the gravity of the crisis became even more apparent. General Gamelin, the Commander-in-Chief, informed the Defence Minister, Édouard Daladier, that the situation was catastrophic. Daladier shouted down the phone that it was necessary to counterattack. 'With what?' replied Gamelin, 'I have no more reserves.' 'Then it means the destruction of the French armies.' 'Yes, between Laon and Paris I do not have a single corps of soldiers at my disposal.' Nothing stood between the German armies and the French capital.

On the morning of 16 May, Reynaud and other political leaders debated whether the government should evacuate Paris as recommended by the city's governor, General Héring. For the moment they decided against this in case it caused a civilian panic. Within the administration, however, panic had already taken hold. While the politicians talked, thick smoke rose above the city as officials of the Quai d'Orsay, the French Foreign Ministry, began burning papers to prevent their falling into German hands. Files were thrown out of the windows and heaped on to a bonfire on the lawns of the Quai. One senior official, Jean Chauvel, tried to burn some papers in the fireplace of his office, but only managed to set fire to the chimney.[1]

The smoke could be seen from the parliament building next door where, at 3.30 p.m., Reynaud made a defiant but hollow speech, which was greeted by an ovation. At 5.30 Churchill arrived at the Quai d'Orsay for a meeting with French leaders. He remembered:

At no time did we sit down around a table. Utter dejection was written on every face. In front of Gamelin on a student's easel was a map, about two yards square purporting to show the Allied front. In this line there was drawn a small but sinister bulge at Sedan.... The General talked perhaps five minutes without anyone saying anything. When he stopped there was a considerable silence. I then asked: 'Where is the strategic reserve?' and breaking into French, which I used indifferently (in every sense): 'Où est la masse de manoeuvre?' General Gamelin turned to me and with a shake of the head and a shrug, said: 'Aucune.'

There was another long pause. Outside in the garden of the Quai d'Orsay clouds of smoke arose from large bonfires, and I saw from the window venerable officials pushing wheelbarrows of archives on to them.... Presently I asked General Gamelin when and where he proposed to attack the flanks of the Bulge. His reply was 'Inferiority of numbers, inferiority of equipment, inferiority of method'—and then a hopeless shrug of the shoulders.

Now Churchill too was convinced of the seriousness of the situation. Returning to the British Embassy, he wired London that in his opinion the French should, as they requested, be sent six more squadrons of fighters. He warned that 'French resistance may be broken up as early as that of Poland' and ended: 'I again emphasize the mortal gravity of the hour.' Later he wrote of these dramatic days: 'I was dumbfounded. What were we to think of the great French army and its highest chiefs?'[2]

## The Mysterious General Gamelin

How was it possible that only six days after the German attack, the great French army seemed on the verge of collapse? Had not General Weygand proclaimed in a speech at Lille on 14 July 1939: 'I believe that the French army is a more effective force than at any other time in its history; it possesses equipment and fortifications of first class quality, excellent morale and a remarkable high command.' Even if such a morale-boosting public statement should not be taken at face value, it reflected a general optimism on the part of the French High Command. On 10 May 1940, when the normally reserved General Gamelin received the news that the German attack had started, he was seen 'striding up and down the corridor in his fort, humming, with a pleased and martial air'; another observer commented that 'he was in excellent form with a large smile'.[3] Perhaps Gamelin was relieved that after so many false alarms the long-awaited offensive had arrived, but his good spirits also reflected genuine confidence in France's prospects.

It was Gamelin who had informed the government at a meeting on 23 August 1939 that the army was 'ready for war'. The meeting had been called immediately after France heard the news that the Soviet Union had signed a non-aggression pact with Germany. This made it almost inevitable that Hitler would move against France's ally Poland within days. All the service chiefs were present. Daladier asked them whether France could stand by while Poland was wiped off the map of Europe and what measures France should take. Gamelin was unequivocal that France had 'no choice' but to honour its commitments to Poland. This did not mean, however, that he was ready to take the offensive. His strategy was to prepare for a long war (*guerre de longue durée*). The French, with their British allies, would asphyxiate the German economy with a blockade, while at the same time building up their armed forces in order to be able to mount an offensive in 1941 or 1942. Ultimately, it was believed, the superior economic potential of the Allies would give them the military advantage; in the meantime they were defensively prepared to meet any German offensive. Gamelin's counsel on 23 August 1939 carried all the more weight because it contrasted strikingly with his attitude one year earlier, at the time of the Munich crisis, when he had done everything possible to dissuade the government from going to war. He had warned that war would bring a 'modernized battle of the Somme'. Similarly in 1936 he had poured cold water on the idea of a military response to the German reoccupation of the Rhineland.

Gamelin's advice in 1939 was telling also because he had the reputation of being an exceptionally cautious and level-headed individual. In other respects, it has to be said, his personality is elusive. The best biography of him is appropriately called 'The Gamelin Mystery'.[4] The mystery is thickened by the fact that so much written about him is inevitably coloured by 1940: 'a beaten leader is a discredited leader' in the words of France's First World War leader Marshal Foch.

Born into a military family in 1872, Gamelin had quickly come to the attention of his superiors as a man of outstanding intelligence. After the outbreak of war in 1914 he was appointed to the staff of General Joffre.

Although later in the war he went on to give distinguished service in the field, it was as a staff officer that he made his reputation. He was credited with an important role in planning the Battle of the Marne, which had halted the German advance in September 1914. Joffre and Gamelin could not have been more different, but they had worked very effectively together. It was on Joffre that Gamelin was believed to have modelled his air of laconic unflappability. But if Joffre was silent because he often had nothing to say, this was not true of Gamelin, a cultivated intellectual who enjoyed nothing more than talking about painting or philosophy. Many observers thought Gamelin resembled a prelate or an academic more than a soldier. People often commented on his 'soft' handshake.

The dismissal of Joffre after the Battle of Verdun in 1916 had taught Gamelin the importance of cultivating politicians. Indeed he owed his rapid rise after 1918 partly to his success in doing this. It also helped his career that he was one of the few leading generals who was not suspected of harbouring anti-Republican sympathies. In 1935, after the retirement of General Weygand, Gamelin became the senior figure in the French army. He was Commander-in-Chief designate for time of war and also Chief of Staff—that is, he was both in charge of preparing the military establishment for war and commanding if war broke out. The last person to combine both these posts had been Joffre in 1911.

Politicians found Gamelin much more agreeable to deal with than the splenetic and irascible General Weygand, who relished confrontation. Gamelin always avoided it. When a subordinate asked him to choose between two suggestions he would sometimes put 'agreed' in the margin. This could be unsettling. Daladier, who generally got on well with him, complained on one occasion that a conversation with Gamelin was like sand slipping through one's fingers. It was difficult to be sure if Gamelin was so evasive because he was so intelligent that he could always see several possibilities, or because he did not like to take personal responsibility. His slipperiness is displayed to great effect in his memoirs, where he often demonstrates that what he had said on a particular occasion meant quite the opposite of what it had seemed to mean at the time. Thus, his claim on 23 August that France was ready for war was subsequently shown to have meant only that the army was ready 'for mobilisation and concentration'.

## 'Ready for War': Tanks and Guns

Gamelin's confidence in 1939 was sustained by the massive achievement of French rearmament during the second half of the 1930s, after a faltering start. There had been severe cuts in military spending in the first half of the decade, when faith in disarmament was at its height and the Depression had imposed budgetary economies. France's first rearmament plan was adopted in 1934, only to be followed by a cutback in expenditure in the next year. Rearmament only became a priority after Germany's reoccupation of the Rhineland in March 1936. This event prompted the newly elected left-wing Popular Front government to announce in September 1936 a 14-billion-franc rearmament programme to include the production of 3,200 tanks. In March 1938, after the Anschluss, another four-year programme (12 billion francs) was approved (concentrating especially on artillery and anti-aircraft guns). In 1934, military spending had accounted for one-fifth of all government expenditure; by 1938 it accounted for over one-third.

Although the decision to rearm dated back to 1934, the results were slow to emerge. Production was initially hampered by a whole series of obstacles. After years of retrenchment and under-investment the French armaments industry was unable to meet the new demands made of it. In 1934 machine tools in French factories were on average 13 years older than those in Germany (20 years as opposed to 7). In the Hotchkiss factory, pieces were hand-finished with files as they might have been in the 1890s. To make matters worse, the army had little understanding of the economics of arms production. It demanded the submission of numerous prototypes before approving mass production of a selected design. For example, prototypes of the 47mm anti-tank gun—one of the best on any side in 1940—had existed since 1935. But endless discussions in the army as to whether such a big gun was necessary, and then innumerable changes in specifications, meant that the first ones were not ready before January 1939. The replacement of the old Lebel rifle had been under discussion since 1926 but a decision on a substitute was taken only in 1936. Such perfectionism unsettled manufacturers, who had little incentive to modernize plant without the guarantee of a steady stream of orders. Production was also disrupted by labour disturbances and strikes under the Popular Front (1936–7). In 1936 the Popular Front government nationalized a number of armaments producers (mainly in the aircraft industry), and if in the long run this contributed to the modernization of plant, in the short term it caused further disruption. Despite increased spending, the number of tanks produced actually *fell* between 1936 and 1938.

It was only from the start of 1939 that the results of the arms spending started to show. In that year 1,059 tanks were produced, and 854 in the first six months of 1940. The rearmament achieved was in the end quite remarkable. There were about 2,900 modern tanks available to the French army in

**French tank production**

| Year | B1 | Total |
|---|---|---|
| 1934 | 3 | 3 |
| 1935 | – | 50 |
| 1936 | 27 | 467 |
| 1937 | 35 | 482 |
| 1938 | 25 | 403 |
| 1939 | 100 | 1,059 |
| 1940 (Jan.–June) | 187 | 854 |

*Source:* Robert Frankenstein, *Le Prix du réarmament français (1935–1939)* (1982), 228.

north-eastern France in 1940. This was slightly more than those on the German side (including Czech tanks which Germany had seized).

Qualitatively also the French tanks were more than a match for the German. Comparisons of quality are difficult to make because there are so many different criteria to consider—size, speed, armour thickness, firepower, manoeuvrability—and a tank has to be judged according to the role it is intended to perform. Nonetheless, it is generally agreed that in terms of all-round performance the best armoured vehicle in 1940 was the French SOMUA S35, a medium tank that was fast, well protected, and with greater firepower than its German equivalent (the Panzer III).

2. After a slow start, French industrial mobilization was a success, especially in the production of tanks. This picture shows a factory producing light tanks in February 1940.

The French also had the best heavy tank—the B1 and B1bis[5]—whose combination of firepower and protection made it more formidable than its German equivalent, the Panzer IV. Its armour was twice as thick as any German tank, and it was armed with a turret-mounted 47mm gun and a hull-mounted 75mm. The B1 did have some shortcomings. It was slower than the Panzer IV (25 kph as opposed to 40 kph), and because of its size, it consumed a lot of fuel. This meant that it could operate only for between three and five and a half hours. The tanks were supposed to be accompanied by tracked fuel tankers capable of operating in any terrain, but there were not enough of these, and refuelling had sometimes to be done by civilian tankers. This proved to be a major problem in 1940. Both the SOMUA and the B1 had another disadvantage. Their turret guns were operated by only one man who had to load, aim, and fire. In the German tanks these tasks were performed by two or three men, which meant they could fire three or four times as fast. Finally, because the B1's main gun was in the hull not the turret, it could only be directed by turning the entire vehicle. In short, the B1 was powerful, but less manoeuvrable than the Panzer IV.

If the French and Germans were more or less equally matched in tank numbers, the French artillery significantly outnumbered the German— 11,200 guns to 7,710—and contained a higher proportion of large-calibre heavy guns. The French were, however, much less well supplied with anti-tank guns than the Germans. The delays in producing the 47mm gun meant that only 270 of these were ready by mobilization. This was far short of the number necessary if each infantry division was to receive its quota of 12. Less powerful, but also effective, was the 1934 25mm gun. These were less scarce but still not sufficient. Many divisions still had to use the 37mm model that dated from the previous war and was not effective against modern tanks. All these guns had the disadvantage of mostly relying on horse transport or converted tractors. Even more serious were France's deficiencies in anti-aircraft guns, with only about 3,800 medium and heavy French guns to 9,300 German ones. The most powerful French gun—the 90mm gun—was in very short supply. Many units were reduced to using 75mm guns left over from 1918 or even light machine-guns.

France's rearmament was certainly not complete in September 1939, but if Gamelin was ready to accept war, it was because the growing pace of arms production suggested that, where deficiencies did still exist, they could soon be overcome. Only a few days after the declaration of war, the government had for the first time created an armaments ministry headed by Raoul Dautry, one of those remarkable technician-administrators that

**Main features of French and German tanks**

FRENCH

| Name | Weight (tons) | Speed (km/h) | Armour | Armament (n × n mm cannon/n machine gun) | Crew |
|---|---|---|---|---|---|
| B1bis | 32 | 28 | 60mm | 1 × 75 (hull), 1 × 47 (turret)/2 | 4 |
| SOMUA S35 | 20 | 40 | 50mm | 1 × 47/1 | 3 |
| Hotchkiss H39 | 12.5 | 20 | 40mm | 1 × 37/2 | 2 |
| Hotchkiss H35 | 11 | 25 | 40mm | 1 × 37/2 | 2 |
| Renault R35 | 10.5 | 19 | 30mm | 1 × 37/1 | 2 |

GERMAN

| Name | Weight (tons) | Speed (km/h) | Armour | Armament (n × n mm cannon/n machine gun) | Crew |
|---|---|---|---|---|---|
| Panzer IV | 25 | 40 | 30mm | 1 × 75/2 | 5 |
| Panzer III | 20 | 40 | 30mm | 1 × 37/2 | 5 |
| Panzer II | 15 | 27 | 30mm | 1 × 20/1 | 3 |
| Panzer I | 6 | 39 | 13mm | 0/2 | 2 |

France has always been particularly good at producing. Dautry, a graduate of the elite École Polytechnique, had spent most of his career running the French railways. But there were limits to what one man's prodigious energy and organizational flair could achieve, and during the Phoney War French rearmament was bedevilled by problems. Tens of thousands of skilled workers had been called up into the armies: at the huge Renault plant near Paris, the workforce dropped from 35,000 to 12,000 in a few days. Even once the chaos had been sorted out and the conscripted workers sent back to their factories, it took months for production to recover. The output of some tanks, including the B1s, actually fell in the last quarter of 1939.

By the spring of 1940, the situation was improving. A lot had been achieved also to overcome the shortage of anti-tank guns: the monthly production of 47mm guns doubled between September 1939 and April 1940. There were about 1,000 of these guns by May. When the Germans attacked, there should have been enough of these guns for every division to receive its quota, but many of them were so recently out of the factories that they had not yet all been distributed to the armies.

## The Air Force

The worst problems were experienced in the air force. Rearmament had started in 1934 with the so-called Plan I, which envisaged the production of 1,343 planes. The aircraft industry, scattered among some 40 quasi-artisanal firms, was thrown into complete chaos by this sudden flood of orders. In fact the planes were obsolete as soon as they were delivered because the Plan was launched just as major advances in technology were about to occur. The problem was compounded because the models ordered under Plan I were multi-purpose aircraft capable of serving as bombers, fighters, and reconnaissance planes (BCR). As a result they were outstanding in no single category. The decision to build BCRs was an unhappy compromise arising out of long-standing disputes over the appropriate role of the air force. Many aviators were seduced by the ideas of the Italian theorist Giulio Douhet, who believed that the air force could win wars on its own through 'strategic' bombing—that is, destroying the enemy's economic strength by bombing industrial targets. The army, however, wanted the air force to operate primarily in support of land operations.

A new plan (Plan II) was launched in September 1936 with priority being given to bombers—1,339 bombers to 756 fighters—because the new Air Minister, Pierre Cot, was a convert to the strategic bombing theory. The fate of Plan II was no more glorious than its predecessor's. The chaos in the factories was exacerbated by the Popular Front's nationalization programme. Between the last quarter of 1937 and the first quarter of 1938 average monthly production of aircraft fell from 40 planes to 35. It was in 1936 that the Luftwaffe overtook the French air force in terms of both quality and quantity. When the French premier visited London in November 1937, the British Prime Minister taxed him about the lamentable state of the French air force. A few months later, General Vuillemin, France's Chief of Air Staff, warned the government that in a war the French air force would be destroyed in a few days. He kept up these warnings throughout the year, especially after a visit to Germany in 1938 from which he returned very impressed by the strength of the Luftwaffe (as he had been meant to be). When Daladier set off for Munich he was armed with a letter from Vuillemin warning him that France had no air force.

Urgent improvements were obviously needed, and so in March 1938 the government decided to give priority to air rearmament. In that year for the first time the Air Ministry took the largest proportion of arms spending (42 per cent). A new plan (Plan V)[6] aimed nearly to double existing production, with the majority of (41 per cent) new planes being fighters and 34 per cent of them bombers. This change in priorities occurred largely because fighters were faster and cheaper to build (and because it was known that the British had bombers). But it was also the case that the French air force was moving away from its doctrinaire commitment to strategic bombing, and becoming more open to the idea of air–army cooperation. French observers had noted the effective way in which the German air force had been able to support land operations in the Spanish Civil War. The French air force, however, was slow to translate this into new operational doctrines. For example, nothing was done to produce dive bombers, which had in been used in Spain to support offensive operations by ground troops. When the French air force thought in terms of cooperation with the army, its perspective was defensive: producing fighters to deny French air space to enemy aircraft.

**Air rearmament**

| Plan name | Date | Total |
|---|---|---|
| Plan I | Apr. 1934 | 1,343 |
| Plan II | Sept. 1936 | 2,851 |
| Plan V | Mar. 1938 | 4,739 |
| Plan V (revision) | Mar. 1939 | 5,133 |
| Plan V (revision) | Sept. 1939 | 8,176 |

Plan V was twice scaled upwards between Munich and the declaration of war. It was also accompanied by huge investment in plant modernization: 4 billion francs between January 1938 and June 1940. After Munich Albert Caquot, an effective industrial administrator, was appointed to run the nationalized aircraft companies. At last, in 1939, these efforts began to pay dividends. Monthly production of planes now rose steadily from 41 in November 1938 to 298 in September 1939. In effect, a modern aircraft industry had been created almost from scratch within two years, as is shown by the striking increase in the workforce employed in the aircraft factories.

At the meeting of 23 August, where Gamelin declared himself ready for war, the Air Minister, Guy La Chambre, also spoke. Although not as confident as Gamelin, he agreed that the situation of the air force was improving. There would be a desperate shortage of bombers until 1940, but this could be made good in the short term by Britain. He concluded: 'the situation of our air force no longer needs to weigh on the government's decisions as it did in 1938.' General Vuillemin did not speak, and in a note for La Chambre three days later he was more cautious, pointing out that France's stock of bombers had hardly improved since Munich. But even Vuillemin believed that within six months the Allies' combined air strength could match that of the Axis'. This might not seem like a ringing endorsement of war, but it contrasted with his gloomy assessments in the previous year.

After the declaration of war, Plan V's targets were revised upwards yet again, but the aircraft industry was badly affected by the industrial problems caused by mobilization. In two months production actually fell, and Caquot resigned in despair in January 1940.

What made matters worse was that industry was now producing planes at such a rate that the producers of spare parts and accessories could not keep up. Then tests and final adjustments needed to be carried out, which

**Size of the workforce in aircraft industry**

| Date | Workforce |
| --- | --- |
| Nov. 1934 | 21,500 |
| Dec. 1936 | 35,200 |
| May 1938 | 48,000 |
| Jan. 1940 | 171,000 |
| May 1940 | 250,000 |

Source: P. Facon, L'Armée de l'air dans la tourmente: La Bataille de France 1939–1940 (1997), 133.

**Aircraft production in the Phoney War**

| Month | Planned production | Actual production |
|-------|-------------------|-------------------|
| Oct.  | 422   | 254 |
| Nov.  | 615   | 296 |
| Dec.  | 640   | 314 |
| Jan.  | 805   | 358 |
| Feb.  | 1,066 | 279 |
| Mar.  | 1,185 | 364 |
| Apr.  | 1,375 | 330 |
| May   | 1,678 | 434 |

Source: Facon, L'Armée de l'air, 134.

could take weeks. Thus, the monthly production figures overestimate the actual number of planes with the army and ready for combat.

The situation was so worrying that after Munich Daladier had sent the French banker Jean Monnet to compensate for French deficiencies by buying aircraft in the United States. Daladier was prepared to resort to almost any financial expedient to achieve this. Five hundred and fifty planes were ordered by Monnet at the beginning of 1939. After the declaration of war, Monnet, now head of the Anglo-French Purchasing Committee, negotiated an agreement for the purchase of another 4,500 aircraft, but deliveries of these were only to begin in October 1940. When the Germans attacked, only about 200 of the American planes were on the French mainland and ready for immediate use.

Vuillemin's hope in August 1939 that the Allies might reach parity with the Germans within six months was nowhere near being met either quantitatively or qualitatively. Most French bombers were still obsolete, and the newer models were only just starting to arrive. The best French fighter, the Dewoitine D520, with a maximum speed of up to 600 kph, was as good as any German plane, but the prototypes were only finalized in the autumn of 1939. Production had begun in December, but there were only 80 of them available in May 1940. By the armistice there were another 430 ready—and the Germans used them on the Eastern Front in 1941.

As for overall numbers of planes, there are numerous estimates of the respective strengths of the French and German air forces in May 1940, and the differences partly depend on what is being counted. Does one include the total number of planes, the number of battle-ready planes, or only those planes already integrated into squadrons? Does one count both modern and old planes? Does one count all planes with the air force or just

**Plane type**

| Plane type | French | German |
|---|---|---|
| Fighters | 632 | 1,210 |
| Bombers | 262 | 1,680 |
| Reconnaissance | 392 | 640 |
| TOTAL | 1,286 | 3,530 |

Source: Facon, L'Armée de l'air, 169.

those on the north-eastern front? Whatever principle is adopted, there is no dispute about the rough balance of forces between France and Germany. The most recent estimate of the total number of planes with the air force, on French soil, and ready for immediate action on 10 May 1940, as compared with the German equivalents, is shown in the table above. Even with the 416 British planes stationed in France, the Allies were far from matching German numbers. Allied inferiority in bombers was particularly dramatic. In the race against the clock to match Germany, the French air force was still far behind when the fighting started on 10 May 1940.

## French Military Doctrine: 'Retired on Mount Sinai'?

What kind of war was the French army expecting and how was it intending to use its arms? It is commonly asserted that, through a mixture of complacency, conservatism, and intellectual laziness, the French had failed to modernize their military thinking and were preparing to fight the previous war again. In 1950, the parliamentary inquiry into the causes of France's defeat concluded: '[T]he General Staff, retired on its Mount Sinai among its revealed truths and the vestiges of its vanished glories, devoted all its efforts to patching up an organization outmoded by the facts.'[7] Was this true?

The main charge is that the French military had not adapted to the idea of mobile warfare and had neglected the possibility of grouping tanks together so that they could be deployed offensively and autonomously rather than playing an infantry support role as in the Great War. One of the earliest advocates of using tanks like this was General Jean-Baptiste Estienne, the so-called 'father of the tank', who started in 1919 to argue for the development of heavy breakthrough tanks that could be deployed independently of the infantry. As Inspector of Tanks between 1921 and 1927, Estienne instigated studies of the development of armour. Although he had a decreasing influence on military policy, the prototype heavy tanks that he commissioned in 1921 were the ancestor of the B1. Without him, France would probably not have had a heavy tank ready at the start of the 1930s.

The modernization of the army started at the beginning of the 1930s under the inspiration of General Weygand, even before the first rearmament programmes had been adopted. In 1930 Weygand launched a programme to motorize seven infantry divisions and he initiated the creation of an armoured division in the cavalry in October 1933. The setting up of this 'light mechanized division' (DLM) meant that, far from being mired in the past, France had the world's first standing armoured division (two years before Germany). At this stage, however, the cavalry lacked a really powerful combat vehicle and the DLM sounded more impressive on paper than it was in reality. The SOMUA tank was developed precisely to meet this need, and once these started to come off the production lines the DLMs had powerful armour at their disposal.[8] Even so, the first DLM was not fully operational until the start of 1938. A second DLM was created in 1937 and a third in February 1940.[9] In addition, the five remaining cavalry divisions had been partially motorized and consisted of a mixture of horse and motorized vehicles ('oil and oats'). These developments did meet with some resistance from traditionalists like General René Altmayer, who thought that the cavalry could best carry out its tasks with horse units, and worried about an excessive dependence on petrol. But there were ardent advocates of modernization like General Jean Flavigny, who had been involved in the development of the SOMUA tanks and became the commander of the first DLM when it was set up.

The DLMs were designed to carry out the cavalry's traditional tasks of reconnaissance, screening operations, and forward delaying actions. They were not intended to be able to break through the enemy lines. For this task it was necessary to establish more heavily armoured divisions, capable of acting autonomously. But progress towards this objective was very slow. In September 1932 experimental manoeuvres took place to study the possibility of developing heavy armoured divisions. The problem was that since at this time the army only possessed three heavy (B1) tanks, the manoeuvres had to be carried out by combining these with lighter infantry accompanying tanks (H35, R35). These two different kinds of tanks could not really be used together, and the exercise was considered to have been a failure. Thus, for the moment, the army abandoned the attempt to develop heavy divisions and concentrated mainly on the production of light infantry support tanks. On the other hand, the B1S still continued to roll slowly off the production lines, even if there was no clear idea how they were to be deployed. Given that the French military had at this stage no doctrine for the use of heavy tanks, it is a testimony to the continuing legacy of Estienne that any were being produced at all. But this was also a drawback. It meant that the specifications of these vehicles had not been drawn up to meet the requirements of evolving military doctrine, but that the doctrine would have to adapt itself to the tanks that were being produced (the opposite of the situation of the cavalry where the SOMUA had been designed to meet specific requirements).

The most eloquent and public plea for the development of independent armoured divisions came in 1934 with the publication of the book *Vers une armée de métier* [Towards a Professional Army] by the relatively unknown Colonel Charles de Gaulle. In 1940 this book was translated into English with the title *The Army of the Future*. The cover bore the words: 'A 1934 Prophecy! France disregarded it! Germany worked on it!' In many respects, de Gaulle's book was prescient, but it probably did little to advance the cause he was advocating. Indeed de Gaulle possibly even harmed his case by linking the technical issue of tank deployment to the politically sensitive issue of the professional army. While the modernization of the army might have required the recruitment of some specialized personnel—radio operators, mechanics—it did not necessarily imply full professionalization. By making this point the centre of his argument, de Gaulle was bound to antagonize politicians who were suspicious of professional armies for political reasons. De Gaulle's book is indeed suffused with a romantic and almost mystical celebration of the military vocation and the role it could play in national regeneration. This was not the best way to win converts.

Within the High Command, however, there were others pushing more discreetly, and more effectively, for armoured divisions. The keenest advocates were Generals Pierre Héring and Gaston Billotte; the most sceptical was General Dufieux, Inspector of Infantry. The slow production of B1S continued to hinder the holding of trials, and provided arguments for the conservatives. As Dufieux said after the war: '[W]e were able to lay down our regulations only ... according to the number and possibility of tanks which we possessed.' It is difficult to say where Gamelin stood. He was to be found arguing for armoured divisions from 1936, but other comments he made underplayed their importance. In 1939 he remarked that 'armoured divisions ... can handle local operations, like reducing a pocket, but not an offensive action'. He told the army commissions of the Chamber and

Senate in July 1939: 'One must not exaggerate the importance of mechanized divisions. They can play an auxiliary role in enlarging a breach, but not the major role that the Germans seem to expect of them.' Nonetheless in December 1938 the Army War Council (CSG) finally decided to establish two heavy armoured divisions known as DCRs (Divisions Cuirassées de Réserve [Reserve Armoured Divisions]). Continued bottlenecks in production meant that this order could not immediately be translated into reality, and as a result little was done to disseminate information on the employment of tanks. The contents of the 'provisional notice on the use of tanks' that had been drafted in 1938 was kept so secret that General Georges felt compelled to write to the General Staff in January 1940: '[T]hey cannot remain secret indefinitely if one wants them to become sufficiently known.'[10]

At the declaration of war, the first DCR was still not ready. But in the light of the German use of tanks in Poland, it was decided in December 1939, on Billotte's initiative, to create two more. By the start of May 1940, three DCRs were in existence, although the shortage of B1bis tanks meant that they had to be partially equipped with less powerful vehicles that had been designed to accompany the infantry. A fourth DCR was created in the heat of battle on 15 May. Even if one includes this fourth unit, the result was that, of the 2,900 French tanks in 1940, only about 960 were organized in armoured divisions (3 DLMs and 4 DCRs). The others were dispersed through the rest of the army in infantry support roles. The Germans, on the other hand, concentrated all their 2,900 tanks into ten Panzer divisions grouped into Panzer Corps. The DCRs and the DLMs comprised each on average about 160 tanks (about half of them light infantry tanks); a Panzer division averaged about 270 tanks.

Despite the decision to establish the DCRs, French army doctrine allotted them only a limited role. They could launch blows against an enemy that was not well organized defensively or had already been undermined by other action, they could operate in conjunction with the DLMs in counterattacks, and they could exploit a successful offensive. But whatever kind of operations they undertook, they were always to function under corps or army control—that is, as part of larger infantry units. In other words, they had to fit into the army's prevailing doctrine, which was encapsulated by the idea of the 'methodical battle' (*bataille conduite*). The 'methodical battle' started from the premiss that in modern warfare the strength of firepower bestowed an immense advantage upon the defender. Massing the amount of material necessary to carry out a successful offensive was a complex logistical operation that required meticulous preparation. What the army wanted to avoid above all were improvised 'encounter battles' where moving armies came upon each other without having prepared their positions. Instead the emphasis of French doctrine was on a tightly controlled battle where decision-making was centralized at the highest levels. This was in stark contrast to German doctrine, which encouraged initiatives by lower-level commanders.

If the enemy managed to break through the front, the French response was known as *colmatage*, plugging the gap by moving reserves into the path of the attacking troops in order to slow down their advance and restore a continuous front. Infantry remained the key to victory: '[P]rotected and accompanied by its own guns and by the guns of the artillery, and occasionally preceded by combat tanks and aviation ... the infantry conquers the ground, occupies it, organizes it and holds it.' These were the words of the 1921 Provisional Instruction on the Tactical Employment of Large Units. This famous document, which codified French doctrine, was revised in 1936, but this new draft asserted that the 1921 version, 'fixed by our eminent leaders' must 'remain our charter'. Having establised this, it did go on to offer some qualifications. It noted the 'acceleration of battle' and affirmed that 'the offensive is the pre-eminent mode of action' and the defensive the 'attitude momentarily chosen by a commander who does not feel able to take the offensive'. The document concluded: '[H]owever strong fortified fronts, the decision ... will only be obtained by manoeuvre in which speed and mobility are essential.' All this seemed to embody a characteristically Gamelinesque tension between two positions, between the overwhelming imperative of attack and the inherent superiority of defence. The circle was squared by the concept of 'methodical battle', which described the conditions in which a successful offensive might occur but set almost impossibly tough prerequisites for success.

In the end, then, while it would not be true to say that the French army in 1940 had learnt nothing and was planning to fight the last war again— the French army of 1940 was very different from that of 1918—or that the military were not engaged in intensive discussions about the most appropriate ways of modernizing the army, the changes which had occurred were basically incremental adjustments, albeit important ones, of a corpus of doctrine that had not fundamentally altered.

## Fighting in Belgium: The Dyle Plan

The French military knew what kind of war they expected to fight. They also knew where they expected (and wanted) to fight it: in Belgium. This seemed almost certain as a result of the fortifications that the French had built along their border with Germany. These fortifications, known as the Maginot Line (after the name of the Minister of War at the time that construction started), stretched from Basle on the Swiss frontier up to Longwy on the frontier with Luxembourg. They left France's frontier with Belgium unfortified, and the assumption was that the Germans would attack, as in 1914, through north and central Belgium.

The idea of fortifying France's frontiers had been under discussion since the early 1920s. The First World War had been fought on French soil, and the constant preoccupation of French military planners since 1918 was to ensure that this would not happen again by guaranteeing the 'inviolability of the national territory'. Some people advocated building fortifications all the way along the Belgian frontier up to the Channel, but the waterlogged terrain of north-east France would have made this expensive and technically difficult. Furthermore it made no sense to seal off France's frontier with Belgium, given that the two countries had signed a military alliance in 1920. The French military therefore considered that France's northern military frontier should be considered to lie on the border between Belgium and Germany. This had the advantage of keeping the next war off French

3. An above-ground view of the Maginot Line. Its fortresses were serviced by a highly sophisticated system of underground railways and power stations. As in today's nuclear submarines, the soldiers manning the forts could live like troglodytes without seeing daylight for weeks on end

soil and protecting a region in which most of France's heavy industry was concentrated. In 1932, by a majority of one vote, the Army War Council (CSG) decided not to fortify the north-eastern frontier. At various times there were discussions about financing fortifications on the Belgian–German frontier, but this was rejected as too expensive.

Work on the 140 km of the Maginot Line started in 1930 and finished in 1937. This system of fortifications, linked by underground railways and served by vast underground power stations, was a considerable feat of technology. It has often been alleged that the Maginot Line contributed to France's defeat by making the military too complacent and defence-minded. Such accusations are unfounded. Certainly the Maginot Line was constructed in the service of a defensive strategy. When in 1935 Parliament debated a proposal based on de Gaulle's ideas, the War Minister, General Maurin, defended the status quo in these words: '[H]ow could one think that we are still thinking about an offensive when we have spent billions to establish a fortified barrier? Would we be mad enough to advance beyond this barrier to undertake some adventure?' Such remarks were all right for the debating chamber, but the Maginot Line had never been conceived as a sort of Great Wall of China sealing France off from the outside world. Its purpose was to free manpower for offensive operations elsewhere—especially important given France's demographic inferiority to Germany—and to protect the forces of manoeuvre. The logic behind Weygand's support for the mechanization and modernization of the army in the 1930s was to permit a rapid advance by the French army into Belgium. French strategy was based on the idea of forward defence in Belgium. Having set up positions in Belgium, the army would prepare for the offensive which would ultimately win the war.

This strategy was dealt a terrible blow in 1936 when the Belgian government cancelled its military agreement with France and declared neutrality. Since financial resources were now fully committed to rearmament, it was not possible to think of fortifying the Belgian frontier. Although some light fortifications were undertaken in the north-east to provide a second line of defence, the French remained committed to fighting in Belgium. Since Gamelin wanted to avoid an encounter battle, Belgian neutrality badly complicated his plans. It was no longer possible for the French and Belgian military to coordinate their defensive plans in advance. But Gamelin hoped to overcome this problem by retaining secret informal contacts with his Belgian opposite number, General van den Bergen.

There were three possible lines of defence in Belgium. The first was on the Albert Canal near the Belgian frontier with Germany. But there was no chance of being able to prepare this position unless the Belgians were willing to invite the French in well before a German attack. Since this seemed unlikely, two other options remained. One was to defend a line along the River Scheldt (called Escaut by the French) through Ghent to Antwerp. This became known as the E (Escaut) Plan. The other was to defend a line running from the French frontier at Givet along the Meuse to Namur, and then along the Dyle River to Antwerp. This became known as the D (Dyle) Plan. Because it involved moving less far from the French frontier, the former was less risky than the latter. The Dyle River was some 96 km from the frontier, and it would have required about eight days to reach this line and prepare it. The Escaut was also a more formidable obstacle than the Dyle, which was hardly more than a wide stream. The final disadvantage of the D Plan was the existence of 40 km of open plain between Wavre, where the Dyle ended, and Namur, on the River Meuse. This 'Gembloux gap', so called because the small town of Gembloux lay at its centre, contained no natural defensive positions. But the D Plan also had many advantages. The line to be defended was about 70–80 km shorter than the E Plan and it kept more Belgian territory, including the main industrial regions, out of enemy hands. It also increased the chance of linking up with Belgian units defending the Albert Canal.

In the first weeks of the war, Gamelin's preference was for the E Plan, but information that the Belgians were fortifying the Gembloux gap encouraged him (with British approval) to adopt the D Plan instead, providing conditions permitted. This also opened up the possibility of advancing north of Antwerp to join up with the Dutch forces. In March 1940, Gamelin therefore decided to exploit this possibility by modifying the D Plan. On the extreme left flank of the Allied forces, he placed an army that would advance to Breda in Holland, link up with the Dutch forces, and secure the estuary of the Scheldt. This mission was confided to the Seventh Army of General Giraud, which contained some of the most mobile divisions in the French army. Speed was essential if the move into Holland was to occur fast enough. Previously Giraud's seven divisions had been part of the central reserve, whose role was to cope with unexpected contingencies. Gamelin's deputy, General Georges, who had been sceptical about the D Plan, was even more so about this 'Breda variant', as were Billotte and Giraud himself. Georges warned against 'committing the major part of our reserves in this part of the theatre in the face of a German action which could be nothing more than a feint. For example, in the event of an attack ... in the centre or on our front between the Meuse and the

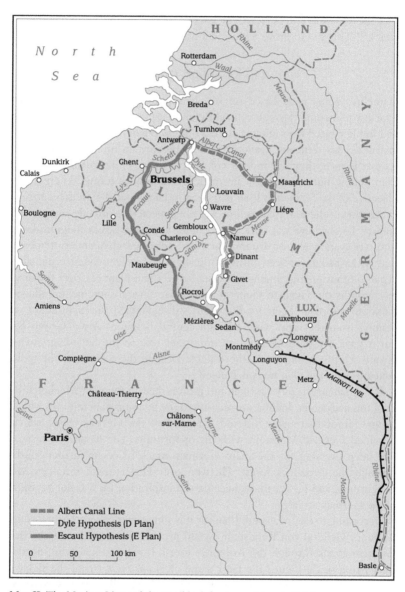

**Map II** The Maginot Line and the possible defensive positions in Belgium

29

Moselle we could find ourselves lacking the necessary means for a counter-attack.'[11] This was to prove a prescient warning.

## The Matador's Cloak

Gamelin's plans were based on the assumption that the main German attack would come through central Belgium, as in 1914 when the Germans had implemented the famous Schlieffen Plan. When in October 1939 Hitler instructed his reluctant General Staff to prepare an immediate offensive against France, they did indeed come up with a similar plan, christened Plan Yellow, but conceived it in much less ambitious terms. Whereas the objective of the Schlieffen Plan had been to knock out the French entirely at the start of the war, Plan Yellow was not expected to provide an outright victory. Its objective was only to secure air and sea bases in Belgium for a future operation against Britain. The plan's relative lack of ambition meant that Hitler had never been enthusiastic about it. As a consequence, and also because of misgivings among some senior German planners, over the next few months the German General Staff made several incremental adjustments to the plan. Their modifications still envisaged the main attack as coming from the right wing through central Belgium (Army Group B), but it gave a progressively more important role to the left wing (Army Group A), protecting its southern flank. Despite these changes, the basic conception of the plan was unchanged.

On 10 January 1940 a German aircraft crashed in fog near Mechelen in Belgium and secret documents relating to the invasion plan fell into Allied hands. Hitler thereupon ordered a review of the German plan, which provided General Manstein with his opportunity. For months Manstein had been pressing for the main German attack to occur further south, through the Ardennes forest. He won over Hitler at an interview on 17 February, and his idea now became the inspiration for a major revision of the German strategy.

According to the 'Manstein Plan', as it is sometimes called, Army Group A, under General von Rundstedt, would provide the central thrust of the German attack through the Ardennes forest. It would then swing north-west like a sickle (hence the later name of *Sichelschnitt:* cut of the sickle), cutting off the Allied armies in Belgium. Meanwhile Army Group B, advancing into northern Belgium, was, in the words of Liddell Hart, to play the role of the 'matador's cloak', luring the unsuspecting Allies northwards. The size of Army Group A was increased from 22 divisions to 45 divisions (7 of them to be armoured Panzer divisions), while Army Group B was reduced from 43 divisions to 29 (3 of them Panzers). A third Army Group (17 divisions) under General Leeb was to push against the Maginot Line in order to keep French divisions pinned down there. The new plan was a mirror image of the Schlieffen Plan, which had been like a revolving door through which the German armies advancing through Belgium swung south-east behind the French marching eastwards into Lorraine. This time the rotation operated clockwise, with the Germans swinging north-west behind the French moving into Belgium.

Success depended on the ability of the German armoured forces to crash through the Ardennes before the French had time to respond. Although the Maginot Line stopped short of the Ardennes, much of this area consisted of steep hills covered by thick forest, and its western extremity was protected by the deep and wide River Meuse with its steeply escarped banks. Manstein himself was not a tank expert, but he had been persuaded by General Heinz Guderian that it would be possible to break

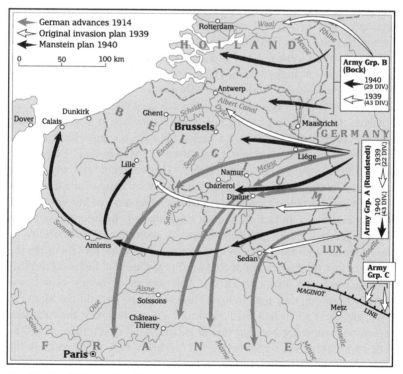

**Map III** The Schieffen Plan, Plan Yellow, and the Manstein Plan

through the Ardennes with a sufficient concentration of armour. In his book *Achtung Panzer* (1937) Guderian, who had studied the use of tanks in the Great War and read the works of British military writers like Liddell Hart and Fuller, argued for the creation of mechanized and fully integrated Panzer divisions powerful enough to break through the enemy lines, and rapid enough to exploit that breakthrough before the enemy could react.

The greatest risk of the German plan lay in sending the tanks across the Meuse before the bulk of the infantry had caught up with them, and then dispatching them towards the Channel despite the vulnerability of their unprotected flanks. Many German experts had reservations. General von Rundstedt's own Chief of Staff, General Soderstern, preferred allowing the infantry to lead and have the tanks come up afterwards despite the extra time this would involve. Even Guderian had his moments of doubt. General Halder noted in his Journal on 14 February 1940: 'Guderian has lost confidence.' These moments of doubt were understandable. Transporting a massive army across this area, with its limited road network, was a hugely complex logistical operation. Two German map exercises in February 1940 concluded that a concerted attack across the Meuse would not be possible before the ninth day of the offensive, whereas Guderian envisaged it on the fourth day. The German plan was a gamble with high stakes. The German Chief of General Staff, General Halder, wrote to Rundstedt on 12 March: '[E]ven if the operation were to have only a 10% chance of success, I would stick with it. For only this can lead to the defeat of the enemy.'[12]

Given that such nerves existed on the German side, it is not surprising that the French did not expect a major offensive through the Ardennes. Addressing the Senate Army Committee in March 1934, Pétain had declared the area to be 'impenetrable'. He went on: '[I]f any enemy attacked he would be pincered as he left the forest. This is not a dangerous sector.' Gamelin himself said in 1937 that the Ardennes had 'never favoured large operations'.[13] In fact the French were not as complacent as is sometimes suggested. Pétain qualified his remark about the 'impenetrability' of the Ardennes with the words 'as long as we make special provisions'. In the spring of 1938 the French conducted a map exercise that had the Germans moving armoured forces across the Ardennes in 60 hours—which was roughly how long they took in 1940. However, there was still the Meuse to cross, and the French remained convinced not so much that the Ardennes region was 'impenetrable', but that, if an attack did occur, there would be time to reinforce the sector before the Germans were ready to cross the river.

## The Allied Order of Battle

When Gamelin distributed his forces for the advance into Belgium, his assumption therefore was that the Ardennes area was the least vulnerable sector of the line. Moving from left to right, the Allied forces were to be disposed as follows:

(1) On the extreme left, Giraud's Seventh Army was to advance up the Channel coast to Breda.

(2) The Dyle River between Antwerp and Louvain would be covered by 22 Belgian divisions, which would fall back to this position once they were no longer able to hold off the Germans on the Albert Canal.

(3) The nine divisions of the British Expeditionary Force (BEF) would defend the Dyle from Louvain to Wavre.

(4) The ten infantry divisions of the First Army under General Blanchard were to cover the Gembloux gap in central Belgium.

(5) The Ninth Army of General André Corap was to move into the Belgian Ardennes and occupy positions along the Meuse from Namur to just north of Sedan.

(6) Finally, the Second Army of General Charles Huntziger was to stay put along the Meuse at the point it entered France just north of Sedan and cover the front down to the point where the Maginot Line ended.

The hinge of the French advance therefore lay at the junction between the Ninth and Second Armies. All these French armies formed part of the First Army Group under the overall command of General Billotte. Further south lay the Second and Third Army Groups behind the Maginot Line and in Alsace-Lorraine; and a Fourth Army Group guarded the Alps and the Italian frontier.

On the eve of the German attack the total forces of the two sides were more or less evenly matched. The French had 79 divisions and 13 fortress divisions. Of these 79 divisions, there were 35 in Army Group I in Belgium and facing the Ardennes; and 17 were in the general reserve (including the three DCRs); 27 divisions were in Army Group II, 7 in Army Group III, and 3 in Army Group IV. With the 10 British, 22 Belgian, and 12 Dutch divisions, this made a total of 136 divisions facing 135 German ones. On the German side there were 10 Panzer divisions; on the French side 3 DCRs and 3 DLMs.

The best French forces were those advancing into central and northern Belgium, while the weakest were those covering the Ardennes. Giraud's Seventh Army included the First DLM and two motorized infantry

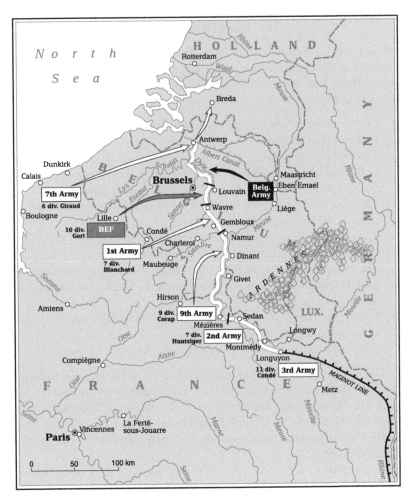

**Map IV** The planned positions of the Allied Armies

divisions. As for Blanchard's First Army, three of its infantry divisions were fully motorized, and five partially so. Blanchard also had at his disposal the two other DLMs which were grouped in a cavalry corps commanded by General René Prioux. Owing to the vulnerability of the Gembloux gap, Prioux's mission was to advance ahead of the body of the army and hold off the Germans while Blanchard set up his positions on the Dyle. The armies of Corap and Huntziger, covering the Ardennes sector, were much weaker. Corap's nine divisions had to cover a front of approximately 80 km as the crow flies, but more in reality because of the sinuous course of the Meuse. Two of them were light cavalry, which were supposed to advance beyond the river and delay any German advance while the infantry moved into position. Of Corap's seven infantry divisions only two were regular units; one was a fortress division; and two were Series-B reservists (61 and 53DI), who were at least 35 years old and had performed their military service up to 20 years earlier. Huntziger's nine divisions, which covered the 75 km of the French Ardennes, included two Series-B infantry divisions (55DI and 71DI). General Baudet, commander of 71DI, was known to be no longer up to the job and was about to be replaced when the Germans attacked on 10 May. Since Huntziger's army was not intended to move forward—unlike the armies to his north—but was defending an unfortified area—unlike the armies to his south behind the Maginot Line—he had his troops spend most of their time building fortifications. He succeeded in increasing the density of blockhouses in the sector, but the soldiers spent so much time digging and pouring cement that they had little time to update their training. They were also hampered by the fact that, like all Series-B reserves, they came lowest in the pecking order for the allocation of new equipment.

Corap complained to Gamelin on numerous occasions about the inadequacies of his troops and their insufficient number. But he was not listened to. Huntziger was more complacent. In March 1940, the parliamentary Army Committee visited the front, and its rapporteur, Pierre Taittinger, sent an alarmist report to Daladier and Gamelin pointing out the 'grave insufficiencies' at Sedan, which he described as a 'particularly weak point' in the French defences. Huntziger sent a furious reply that concluded: 'I believe that no urgent measures are necessary to reinforce the Sedan front.'[14]

As overall Commander-in-Chief Gamelin had installed his headquarters at the fortress of Vincennes just outside Paris, preferring not to be too far from the government. This led to accusations after the defeat that Gamelin had been too cut off from his troops and subordinate commanders. De Gaulle's memoirs contain a celebrated description of Gamelin holed up in his headquarters like 'a scientist locked up in his laboratory, experimenting in search of a magic formula for victory'. In fact Gamelin did emerge quite frequently from his Vincennes hideout to visit the front, but the impression that he was rather remote is confirmed by many other witnesses. Gamelin's deputy, General Georges, was Commander-in-Chief of the north-east theatre of operations—that is the armies in the First, Second, and Third Army Groups. He set up his headquarters at La

Ferté-sous-Jouarre 70 km east of Vincennes. Many people felt that Georges would have made a better choice for Commander-in-Chief than Gamelin, even if he lacked Gamelin's intellectual brilliance. In 1934 he had been badly injured in the assassination attempt on King Alexander of Yugoslavia who was on a visit to France. After the French defeat, it was often claimed that Georges had never fully recovered from his injuries. But this does not seem to have been felt at the time, and if Georges was passed over in favour of Gamelin the reasons were primarily political. Georges, whose career had been in the entourage of Weygand, was suspected of having right-wing sympathies, although he was not an open reactionary like Weygand.

In January 1940, Gamelin had decided to move part of the General Staff from La Ferté to Montry, which was midway between Vincennes and La Ferté, about 40 km from each of them. At the same time he appointed a new Chief of Staff in the person of General Aimé Doumenc, an expert in logistics and communications who had made his reputation organizing the supply of Verdun in 1916. This complicated structure, which created three centres of control—Vincennes (Gamelin), Montry (Doumenc), La Ferté (Georges)—was probably designed to weaken Georges's influence. Gamelin's biographer comments: 'Gamelin chose a compromise which gave him all the advantages in case of success and all the disadvantages to Georges in case of failure.'[15] The relations between Georges and Gamelin became very

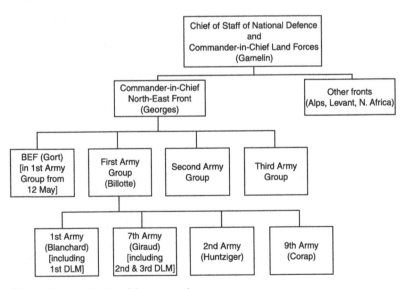

Chart of the organization of the command structure

strained. Gamelin assured Georges that he was on his side and that it was Daladier who hated him. Georges felt sure Gamelin was trying to undermine him.

## 10–15 May: Into Belgium

On the evening of 9 May, troops facing the German frontier from Holland to Luxembourg could hear a 'vast murmuring'. At 4.35 a.m. (French time) the German invasion commenced. German airborne units began landing in Holland, and German land forces crossed the frontiers of Luxembourg and Belgium. From about 1 a.m. information was coming in from Brussels and Luxembourg that an invasion was imminent, and this was passed on to Vincennes and Montry from about 3 a.m. But the army intelligence services were sceptical, having already been taken in by a number of false alarms, and were wary of falling into the same trap again. Only at 6.30 a.m.—two hours after the invasion had started and over five hours after the first serious information had been received—was Gamelin woken to be told that the attack had started and that the Belgian government had called on the French to help them. He ordered the Dyle Plan to be put into action.

Most accounts of the Fall of France concentrate on the German breakthrough on the Meuse, but even in Belgium and Holland where the French expected the attack, events did not proceed as planned. Giraud's Seventh Army rushed forwards and his first forces reached Breda on 11 May. But German airborne troops had seized the Moerdijk causeway (on the Meuse estuary) cutting Holland in two, and therefore the Dutch army withdrew northwards towards Amsterdam and Rotterdam. This made it impossible for Giraud to link up with the Dutch forces—which had been the purpose of the Breda operation—and on the afternoon of 12 May he was ordered to abandon the plan and redeploy his troops further south towards Antwerp. The Dutch held out for two more days, but capitulated on 14 May after the bombing of Rotterdam.

The key to the Belgian defence along the Albert Canal was the supposedly impregnable fortress of Eben-Emael. In a brilliant tactical stroke, German gliders landed troops on the fortress and captured it by midday on 11 May, as well as capturing two bridges at Maastricht. The Belgians decided they could not hold the Albert Canal line any longer and would have to fall back on the Dyle River immediately. This severely compromised the French plan, which required the Belgians to hold off the Germans long enough to allow Blanchard's First Army to set up its positions. Reaching the Gembloux gap on 11 May, General Prioux, commanding the

4. Gamelin decided on the D Plan partly because he had information that the Belgians had built anti-tank defences on the plain leading to Gembloux. These so-called 'Cointet' defences proved totally inadequate and hardly delayed the Germans. Here tanks are passing through a defence which has been blown up

advance force of cavalry of Blanchard's army, was shocked to discover how little the Belgians had done to fortify the area. In the afternoon he sent an urgent message to Billotte and Georges pleading for the D Plan to be abandoned in favour of the less ambitious E Plan. He was overruled because the BEF and the Seventh Army were already well on their way, but it was decided to speed up Blanchard's advance by 24 hours so that he would be in position by 14 May.

Meanwhile Prioux had to delay the Germans, although his force was very exposed owing to the collapse of Belgian resistance. Between 12 May and 14 May, Prioux's two DLMs held off two Panzer divisions[16] near the village of Hannut, a few kilometres forward of the Gembloux gap. Finally, on the afternoon of 14 May, Prioux was able to fall back behind Blanchard, whose army had now reached its positions. In the 'Battle of Hannut', which was the first tank battle in history (in the First World War there had only been tanks on the Allied side), Prioux successfully accomplished his mission. The SOMUA tanks had stood up to all but the heaviest German cannon. Overall the French lost 105 tanks, and the Germans 165. But because the Germans remained in occupation of the terrain, they were able to recover and repair about 100 of these, while the French ones were definitively lost. On the next day (15 May), Blanchard's First Army confronted the German attack on the Dyle. This was just the kind of encounter battle Gamelin had wished to avoid, though the French line held. But at about the same moment, it became apparent that the key events had really been taking place further south. The French tactical victory in Belgium threatened to turn into strategic disaster: while the French were holding out on the Dyle, the Germans were breaking through on the Meuse. On 16 May, Blanchard was ordered to draw back towards the French frontier.

## 10–12 May: Through the Ardennes

The main thrust of the Panzer advance through the Ardennes was to come from the 'Kleist Group', under the overall command of General Ewald von Kleist. This comprised five Panzer divisions divided into two corps: the XIX Corps, under Guderian, consisting of three divisions,[17] headed for Sedan (defended by the Second Army), and the XLI Corps of General Reinhardt consisting of two divisions,[18] headed for Monthermé (defended by the Ninth Army). Further north, coming through the upper Ardennes, was the XV Corps of General Hoth, which consisted of two divisions[19] heading for Dinant (also defended by the Ninth Army). Originally intended primarily to offer flanking cover to the main assault, it ended up playing a much more important role, largely because of the actions of General Rommel, commanding the 7th Division. Transporting von Kleist's huge force of 134,000 soldiers and 1,600 vehicles (1,222 of them tanks) across the tortuous road network of the Ardennes was an extraordinary logistical operation. It was the 'greatest traffic jam known to that date in Europe'.[20] The first German units reached the Meuse at 2 p.m. on 12 May. As one German general said after the war, it was 'not really an operation in the tactical sense but an approach march. In making the plan, we had reckoned it unlikely we should meet any serious resistance before reaching the Meuse.'[21] On the whole this confidence was justified, and before they reached the Meuse most of this German force had not seen an enemy soldier.

Those Germans who did come upon the French were not much troubled by them. On 10 and 11 May, advance elements of Guderian's army encountered Huntziger's cavalry, which had been sent forward into the Ardennes, although the rest of his army was required to stay put. On both days, after chaotic fighting the French fell back, not having expected to come upon such significant forces. But still they had no idea that they had stumbled upon the main German attack. Further north, Corap's two cavalry divisions had also advanced beyond the Meuse, but on 12 May

5. Line of German vehicles heading for the French frontier. In the words of one German general: 'If the line of tanks had advanced on a single road its tail would have stretched back to Koenigsberg in East Prussia when its head was at Treves.'

Corap pulled them back before they had even had a chance to engage with the enemy. Thus, he lost an opportunity to delay the advance of Rommel's 7th Panzer Division. Corap took this decision partly because the withdrawal of Huntziger's cavalry had potentially exposed the right flank of his cavalry. In addition, he was worried by the fact that not all his infantry had yet reached their positions on the Meuse, and he felt it necessary to employ the expedient of using the cavalry to reinforce a line that would have been thinly stretched even if all the forces had already been in place. This does not mean that Corap feared any immediate danger on the Meuse. It was assumed that the Germans encountered in the Ardennes were running far ahead of the main force and would certainly not attempt an immediate crossing.

If only the French High Command had realized what was happening, the huge concentration of German armour moving through the tangled roads of the Ardennes would have offered an easy target to Allied bombers. As it was, most bombers were being dispatched to northern Belgium to impede the German advance there, while Blanchard moved into position. During these raids, which concentrated especially on the bridges at Maastricht,

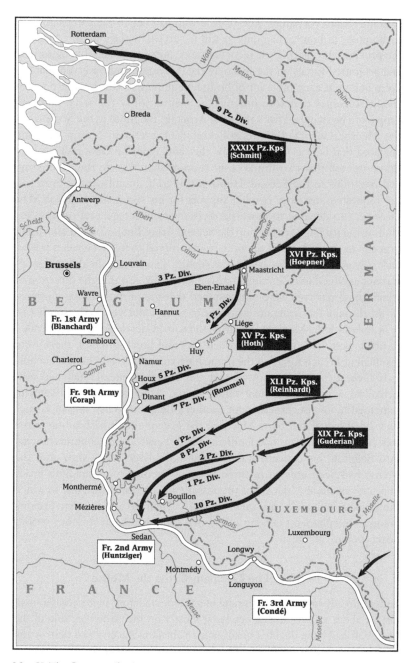

**Map V** The German offensive

casualties were very high. The British, who had begun the campaign with 135 bombers in France, had only 72 still in service by the end of 12 May. On the previous day, French air reconnaissance noted 'considerable motorized and armoured forces on the move' in the Ardennes, and observed that the Germans were carrying a lot of bridging equipment. On the afternoon of 12 May Georges therefore ordered the main priority for aerial bombing support to be switched from the First Army (in Belgium) to the Second (on the Meuse). General Billotte, still fixated on events in central Belgium, declared that he was 'astonished' by this, and, ignoring Georges's instructions, ordered that two-thirds of air support should go to the First Army and one-third to the Second. Huntziger himself, complacent as ever, had not requested any extra bomber support for his sector. On 11 and 12 May, Georges also decided to move six divisions from the general reserve (including the 3rd DCR) to back up the Second Army. But he did not attach any urgency to the order, and the units were ordered to move between 11 May and 13 May as transport became available. The danger in the Ardennes was not assumed to be imminent. It is noteworthy also that the direction in which these reserves were sent assumed that the purpose of any German thrust through the Ardennes would be to swing clockwise to the south-east in order attack the Maginot Line from the rear. In fact the Germans intended to pivot west. This meant that when they did break through, there were insufficient French forces in the immediate vicinity to respond fast enough.

If Georges's actions showed that the French General Staff had now perceived a possible tactical threat in the Ardennes, he and Gamelin remained more concerned about northern Belgium. When one of Gamelin's aides speculated on 12 May that the French might be heading into a trap since the Germans had hardly bombed the advancing columns moving into Belgium, his concern was brushed aside. Even on 13 May, after the Meuse had been crossed in three places, a report from Gamelin's headquarters concluded: '[I]t is not yet possible to determine the zone in which the enemy will make his main attack.'[22] Then at 9.25 on that evening Georges telephoned Gamelin to say that there had been 'a rather serious upset [pépin]' at Sedan.

## 13 May: The Germans Cross the Meuse

Sedan, already notorious as the site of a German victory in 1870, was a small city of about 12,000 inhabitants, lying mostly on the Ardennes side of the Meuse. It had been decided in advance to abandon the city and destroy the bridges if an attack occurred. The French would defend the other side of the Meuse, exploiting the natural obstacles offered by the river and the high ground of the left bank. From the forested hill of La Marfée, the French defenders had a superb view over the Germans on the other side. Thus, Huntziger considered Sedan to be the least vulnerable sector of his line. His main worry was that the Germans might attack further to the south-east in the vicinity of Mouzon with a view to taking the Maginot Line from the rear. To counter this eventuality Huntziger had stationed his

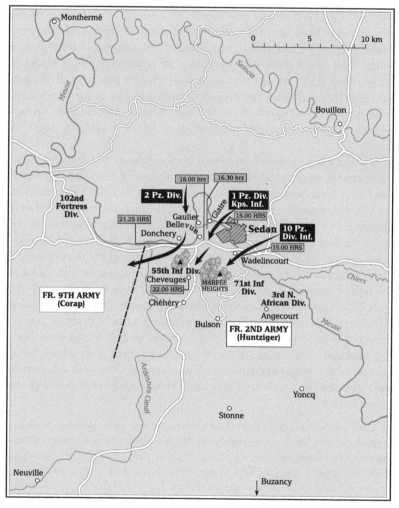

**Map VI** The Sedan sector in detail: 13 May 1940

best units on his right flank. The 17 km of the Sedan sector, on his left flank, was defended by the B-Series reservists of the 55DI. Quite apart from their deficiencies as soldiers, they were extremely short of anti-aircraft weapons—there was only one anti-aircraft battery in the whole area—and when the German planes attacked many men had only machine-guns and rifles to use against them.

On the night of 12–13 May, French artillery was effective in hampering German movements to the north of the Meuse where the steady arrival of German troops and armour provided an easy target. Then at 7 a.m. on the morning of 13 May, German planes started to attack the French positions. The Kleist group had about 1,000 planes at its disposal, mostly around Sedan. This was a massive concentration of airpower for such a narrow sector of the front. For the next eight hours, wave upon wave of German Stuka bombers pounded the French in what was one of the heaviest air assaults so far in military history. Although these attacks did little damage to French bunkers and gun positions, they had a devastating effect on morale.

At about 3 p.m., after this prolonged bombardment, the Germans started their attempt to cross the Meuse. Guderian planned to use his three divisions for a three-pronged attack. The 10th Panzer Division was to cross on the left, and, once across the river, to secure the high ground of the Marfée heights above the village of Wadelincourt. The crossing was difficult. To reach the edge of the river and launch their rubber dinghies, the German troops had to wade through waterlogged meadows, all the time offering a prime target to the French troops defending the Marfée heights. Most of the boats were shot to pieces before they could even be thrown into the river. If the Germans did succeed in obtaining a foothold on the other bank, this success was due above all to the initiative of a few individuals. Among these was Staff Sergeant Rubarth and his squad of assault engineers. Having managed to cross the river, their dinghy only precariously afloat because of the weight of equipment it was carrying, they were able to rush the French bunkers with surprising ease. As Rubarth himself described the events later:

In a violent Stuka attack, the enemy's defensive line is bombarded. With the dropping of the last bomb at 1500 hours, we move forward and attack with the infantry. We immediately sustain strong machine gun fire. There are casualties. With my section I reach the bank of the Meuse in a rush through a woodline. . . . Enemy machine guns fire from the right flank across the Meuse. . . . The rubber boat moves across the water. . . . During the crossing, constant firing from our machine guns batters the enemy, and thus not one casualty occurs. I land with my rubber boat near a strong, small bunker, and together with Lance Corporal Podszus put it out of action. . . . We seize the next bunker from the rear. I fire an explosive charge. In a moment the force of the detonation tears off the rear part of the bunker. We use the opportunity and attack the occupants with hand grenades. After a short fight, a white flag appears. . . . Encouraged by this, we fling ourselves against two additional small bunkers, which we know are around 100 metres to our half left. In doing so we move through a swampy area, so that we must temporarily stand in the water up to our hips.[23]

In the end Rubarth and his men were able to destroy seven bunkers. There was no sign of the French 'interval' troops who ought to have been guarding the flanks of the bunkers but had possibly taken cover from the German bombers. By the evening Rubarth, having suffered six casualties out of his original eleven men, had reached the ground above Wadelincourt. For this achievement he was later awarded the Knights cross of the Iron Cross.

The most vital sector of the Sedan crossing point was assigned to the 1st Panzer Division, which was to cross at the village of Glaire just west of Sedan, at the base of a small peninsula formed by a loop in the river. As the troops hurled hundreds of rubber boats into the river and jumped after them, many were killed by French gunfire, but enough reached the other side to rush the French defences. Particularly spectacular results were achieved by troops of the 1st German Infantry Regiment commanded by Lieutenant Colonel Hermann Balck. A tough veteran of the Great War, in which he had been wounded five times, Balck was an exceptionally inspiring commander who was to end the war as an army group general. Having succeeded in crossing the river, Balck and his men found four French bunkers in their path. They bypassed one; two others succumbed relatively easily (and indeed may have been abandoned by their defenders); and the fourth held out for about three hours. By 7 p.m. Balck's men had covered the 2.5 km from the Meuse to the Château of Bellevue; three hours later they had reached the village of Cheveuges, about 3 km further south. Already by 5.30 p.m. the German foothold on the left bank was sufficient for engineers to begin building a bridge; meanwhile rafts ferried over equipment; by 11 p.m. a bridge capable of bearing a weight of 16 tons was ready, and the first tanks started to cross.

Of the three German divisions at Sedan, it was the 2nd, taking the right-hand prong of the attack at the village of Donchery, which had the hardest task crossing. The Germans came under intensive French artillery fire from the opposite bank. Most of the boats were destroyed, and only one officer and one man managed to get across. They both promptly swam back. Only when the 1st Division had established a foothold on the other side was it possible for elements of the 2nd Division to cross at about 10 p.m. It was not possible to start constructing a bridge until 9 a.m. on the morning of 14 May, and continued French artillery fire meant that it took 20 hours to complete. Once fully across the river, however, the 2nd Panzer Division was to assume a major strategic significance, since it found itself directly attacking the hinge between the French Ninth and Second Armies.

By the end of the day (13 May) the Germans had succeeded in crossing at Sedan in three places. Despite pockets of fierce resistance, the French defence overall, weakened by the aerial bombardment, was unimpressive. During the afternoon, some soldiers of the 55DI had begun to flee their positions. In the evening this developed into a full-scale panic. As well as crossing at Sedan, the Germans had breached the Meuse at two other localities. In fact the first German troops to cross the river on 13 May did so not at Sedan but at the little village of Houx, about 4 km north of Dinant. Troops from Rommel's 7th Panzer Division had crossed by stealth at night along an old weir that connected an island to the two banks of the river. This sluice had not been destroyed by the French for fear that it might excessively lower the level of the river. Thus, some of Rommel's soldiers were on the other side of the Meuse by the early hours of 13 May.

The main attack by Rommel's troops occurred later that morning. They were helped by the fact that two of Corap's divisions, the 18DI and the 22DI, were still not fully in position. Neither of them was motorized. The 22DI had to cover 85 km on foot to reach the Meuse and only arrived there on 13 May after three consecutive night marches. As for the 18DI, which had slightly further to go, French planning had only required it to be fully in place by the morning of 14 May. Those troops in position by 13 May were tired from their march, and four battalions had yet to arrive. Furthermore, the Houx crossing point happened to be at the junction of these two divisions. Despite all these weaknesses, the French defenders fought hard, and the Germans might not have succeeded in crossing had it not been for Rommel's inspiring leadership and resourcefulness. Rommel ordered houses upstream of the crossing point to be set alight in order to provide a smoke-screen. When German engineers seemed momentarily unnerved by machine-gun fire coming from the French side of the river, Rommel called up tanks to provide covering fire. In responding, the French were handicapped by their shortage of anti-tank weapons. At one point Rommel himself took direct command of a battalion and crossed the Meuse on one of the first boats, joining the men who had been there since the early morning.

The most difficult of the three German crossings on 13 May was that undertaken by Reinhardt's XLI Panzer Corps at Monthermé (about 32 km north of Sedan). Here the Meuse flows faster than at Sedan and cliffs plunge down to the river. On the west side, where Monthermé lies in a small isthmus, the ground rises up steeply again. This provides a superb defensive position. At the end of 13 May, the Germans had crossed the river but only succeeded in establishing a tiny bridgehead. The French defenders, who were regular troops, fought hard, and the Germans were not yet able to bring tanks across the river.

By the end of the day, then, three German bridgeheads had been established—one of about 5 km at Sedan, one of less than 3 km at Houx, and one of barely 1.5 km at Monthermé. At last the French realized the gravity of the situation. Arriving at 3 a.m. on 14 May, with Doumenc, at Georges's headquarters, General Beaufre witnessed the despair of the French High Command:

The room was barely half-lit. Major Navereau was repeating in a low voice the information coming in. Everyone else was silent. General Roton, the Chief of Staff, was stretched out in the armchair. The atmosphere was that of a family in which there has been a death. Georges got up quickly and came to Doumenc. He was terribly pale. 'Our front has been broken at Sedan! There has been a collapse . . .' He flung himself into a chair and burst into tears.

He was the first man I had seen weep in this campaign. Alas, there were to be others. It made a terrible impression on me.[24]

### 14–15 May: The Counter-attack Fails: The Tragic Fate of the Three DCRs

Despite Georges's tears, the bridgeheads need not in themselves have been catastrophic. The real failure on the French side was not so much allowing the crossing to occur as being unable to mount an effective counter-attack. The French doctrine of 'methodical battle' proved quite inadequate to respond to the speed of warfare as the Germans were practising it.

At Sedan a counter-attack, which should have taken place on the evening of 13 May, when the German bridgehead was still extremely vulnerable, was fatally delayed until the next morning. At 7 p.m. on 13 May two infantry regiments and two battalions of light tanks had been made available to General Lafontaine of the 55DI to mount a counter-attack. Only nine hours later did he issue the order for the counter-attack to go ahead. Lafontaine, schooled in the doctrine of *colmatage* and the careful preparation of combined infantry and artillery response, was reluctant to send his forces in too fast. His ability to do so was compromised by faulty communications and by the difficulties of moving troops forward along roads clogged with retreating soldiers. His tanks were only able to crawl forward. The delay was disastrous. All this time the Germans were feverishly transporting tanks over the river and then moving them ahead immediately.

When the French tank finally attacked at dawn, they were initially successful until German tanks began to arrive in sufficient quantity to overwhelm them. Most of the light French tanks were destroyed. After this, the 55DI, which had already been badly mauled and demoralized on the previous day, ceased to function as a fighting force. The collapse of the 55DI had a terrible effect on the morale of its neighbouring division, the 71DI, also made up of B-Series reservists. The divisional commander of the 71DI, General Baudet, had moved his command post back and lost contact with his troops. Lacking any clear orders and demoralized by rumours about the collapse of the 55DI, many of the troops fled. By the end of 14 May the 71DI had more or less disintegrated without ever seeing action.

One remarkable feature of the battle had been the almost complete absence of the Allies in the air (apart from two bombing raids around Houx). This was due partly, of course, to their inferiority in the air, but also to the fact that they had concentrated their limited air resources in the wrong place—in central and northern Belgium. On 13 May, Air Chief Marshal Barratt, in charge of the British air force in France, had felt it necessary to rest his forces for a day after the heavy losses they had incurred in Holland and Belgium. Once the Allies had realized their mistake, they did send planes to Sedan at dawn on 14 May to attack the German bridges over the river. About 152 bombers and 250 fighters concentrated over Sedan, suffering 11 per cent losses. The small size of the target made their task difficult, and the effectiveness of the operation was reduced by sending in the planes in small groups of 10 to 20. Of 71 British bombers only 41 returned. According to the official RAF history, '[N]o higher rate of loss in an operation has ever been experienced by the Royal Air Force.'[25] In the afternoon, for lack of any other bombers, the French were reduced to sending in obsolete Amiot 43 bombers, which were entirely unsuitable for operations of this type and also suffered heavy casualties.

On 14 May there was nothing the air force could do to retrieve the situation: all would depend on the armoured reserves. As we have seen, on 11 May Georges had begun sending forces to reinforce the Second Army, among them the 3rd DIM and 3rd DCR. Grouped together into the XXI Corps, under the command of General Flavigny, one of France's most experienced leaders of mechanized operations, these units were dispatched on the evening of 13 May towards the left flank of the Second Army to prepare a counterattack. To the south of Sedan lies a ridge on which is

6. By dawn on 14 May Rommel's men had built an 18-ton bridge across the Meuse at Bouvignes, north of Dinant. An armoured vehicle is already crossing. Since Rommel was extremely publicity-conscious, his campaign is well documented. He made good use of the Leica camera given him by Goebbels

situated the Mont-Dieu wood and the village of Stonne. This position was important because it controlled the route south into the centre of France. In fact, although the French did not know this, Guderian, instead of pushing forward to secure this ridge, had decided immediately to pivot two of his Panzer divisions to the west and drive them deep into French territory, leaving only the 10th Panzer Division to consolidate the position. His superior, Kleist, had initially opposed this strategy as too risky, because it exposed his flank to a counterattack from the south. Guderian's plan offered a real opportunity for the DCR to cause the Germans difficulty.

The deployment of the 3rd DCR proved, however, very disappointing. Formed only on 20 March 1940, it had had little time to train, was short of key equipment (tracked fuel tankers, anti-tank batteries, radios) and had never yet manoeuvred as a division. Having only just arrived from Châlons, where the division had been stationed in reserve, the tanks needed to refuel. For all these reasons, the commander of the DCR, General Brocard, did not consider that he would be ready to attack before 15 May, while Flavigny wanted him to move in on the morning of 14 May. Finally they settled on the afternoon of 14 May, but further delays intervened. Flavigny was now rapidly losing confidence in Brocard's ability to mount a rapid attack, and he decided against launching the operation on that day. Instead he ordered Brocard to disperse his tanks in 'pockets' along a 12-mile front west of the River Bar to Stonne. Thus, the French squandered the best chance of checking Guderian before he broke out of his bridgehead.

On the next morning (15 May), there was fierce fighting at Stonne between a company of B1 tanks from the 3rd DCR and tanks from the 10th Panzer Division. But before the French could launch a concerted counterattack, to reassemble the tanks that had been dispersed on the previous evening and refuel those that had participated in the fighting during the morning. Eventually the long-awaited counterattack fizzled out as a raid by a tank battalion in the evening while many tanks were still idling uselessly, away from the action. Further fighting took place at Stonne on 16 May and subsequent days. The French tanks performed well, and the village changed hands several times. Unfortunately, this battle had become irrelevant, since Guderian was already pushing north-westwards into France. The caution and hesitation of Flavigny and Brocard, and the impetuosity and boldness of Guderian perfectly encapsulated the difference between the French and the Germans in 1940.

Another chance was missed by the 1st DCR further north on 14 May, while Rommel's bridgehead was still vulnerable as he waited for the bulk of his forces to cross the river. A counter-attack was launched on that day by

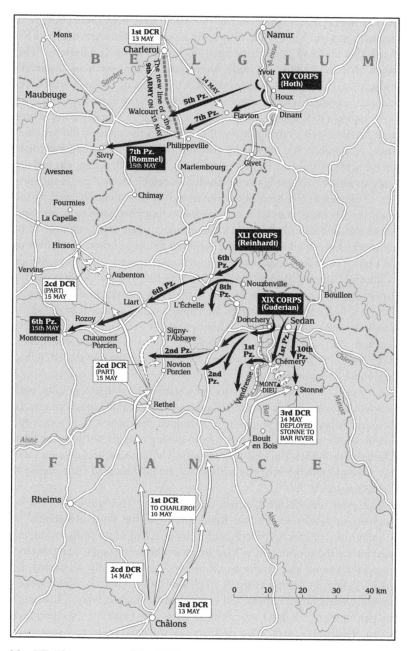

**Map VII** The movements of the 3 DCRs: 13–16 May

the 4th North African Division, but this would have been more effective in conjunction with the 1st DCR. Originally assigned to the reserve of the First Army, this unit had been dispatched on 10 May towards Charleroi. This meant that on 13 May its tanks were only 40 km north of Rommel's bridgehead, but Billotte, still unsure where the main German attack was coming, hesitated to order them south. Not until the early morning of 14 May was the DCR instructed to head for the rear of Corap's army. There were delays in transmitting this order, and when the division did set off at 1 p.m., its progress was slowed by columns of refugees clogging the roads. On the next morning the DCR's commander, General Bruneau, was still not ready to attack because his tanks needed to refuel. He had made the mistake of placing his fuel tankers at the rear of his columns. Delayed by the chaos on the roads, they took several hours to arrive. Moving south-west out of the bridgehead, Rommel's troops came upon two battalions of B1 tanks, which were refuelling. Some confused fighting ensued. If the bulk of the French tanks had been ready, they could have posed a serious challenge to Rommel. Instead he was able to continue his progress, leaving the 7th Panzer Division to deal with the rest of the French tanks. In the afternoon, there was fierce fighting between the Panzers and the French tanks whose refuelling was now complete. Although about 100 German tanks were knocked out, the French also suffered heavy losses because their tanks had been thrown in piecemeal. By the end of the day the DCR had been more or less wiped out.

By now Corap's Ninth Army was in a state of total disintegration, with Rommel threatening his northern flank and Guderian his southern one. In the early hours of 15 May, Corap was granted his request to abandon the line of the Meuse and fall back on a line running roughly north–south from Charleroi to Rethel. But this was a position with no natural defences and the chaos of implementing the withdrawal merely hastened the collapse of Corap's troops.[26]

The most remarkable German advance on 15 May was made not by Rommel or Guderian, but by Reinhardt from the third bridgehead at Monthermé. For two days the French defenders had successfully contained him, but on the morning of 15 May he finally broke through. The penetrations by Rommel and Guderian on either side had fatally weakened the French centre. In Alistair Horne's vivid description, Huntziger had opened up one sluice gate on 14 May and Corap another the next day: '[T]hrough the pair of them the flood was about to burst into France.'[27] Nothing now lay in Reinhardt's path. The problem, as we have seen, was that once Georges had identified a threat to the Ardennes, he had initially thought

7. This photograph, taken by the Germans, shows four B1bis tanks from the 1st DCR in Beaumont on 16 May. Having no petrol left (an all too frequent fate of these huge tanks), and being almost encircled, their crews decided to sabotage their vehicles

that the danger lay on Huntziger's right flank, and moved his reserves to deal with this eventuality. This caused him to neglect the possibility of a danger to Huntziger's left flank, that is of a breach opening up between the Second and Ninth Armies. When he became belatedly aware of this possibility, he had decided to assemble a force (soon dubbed the Sixth Army) under General Touchon to plug (*colmater*) the gap and attack the flanks of the German advance.

It proved difficult to assemble Touchon's troops fast enough. One of the units assigned to him was the 2nd DCR. Early on 14 May, it had been ordered to move from Châlons, where it was stationed in reserve, to Charleroi in order to join the counterattack against Rommel. Before the tanks had set off, this order was countermanded once it was clear that they would not be able to reach Charleroi fast enough. This mission was given to the 1st DCR, while the 2nd DCR was ordered to head for the Signy-l'Abbaye area for a counterattack against the central German bridgehead. Unfortunately, its accompanying wheeled vehicles had already set off for Charleroi and had to be redirected in mid-morning. They were slowed down by troops fleeing from the east. Meanwhile the tanks were being loaded on trains for transportation to Hirson, which was a time-consuming operation. The result was that on 15 May the units of the 2nd DCR were widely dispersed around the region lying between the Oise and Aisne rivers. Some tanks were being unloaded; others were still on the trains; the wheeled vehicles were still on the move. As Reinhardt's Panzers moved west, they passed unwittingly through the centre of the area in which the tanks were being unloaded from the trains. The 2nd DCR ended the day scattered uselessly on both flanks of Reinhardt's thrust—the tanks mainly to the north and most of the wheeled vehicles and supporting artillery to the south. Of the abortive counterattacks by the three DCRs, this unit's effort had proved most futile.

By 4.00 p.m. on 15 May Reinhardt, reaching Montcornet, had covered about 60 km, meeting little opposition. By the end of that day Touchon recognized that there was nothing he could do to plug the gap, since Reinhardt's troops were already west of the point where he had intended to position his forces. He therefore ordered his army to fall south below the River Aisne. Nothing now lay between the Germans and the Channel.

On the next day (16 May), it was Rommel's turn to take the lead. In one of the most daring exploits of the campaign, he surged forward with two tank battalions ahead of the bulk of his forces. Moving through the day and the night, and circumventing larger agglomerations in order not to slow himself down, he stopped only when reaching Le Cateau at 6 a.m. on

17 May. He had covered about 110 km. Pushing so exposed a force so far ahead of the infantry and artillery was both unconventional and dangerous, but its very audacity only served to demoralize the French and further disorganize their lines. Rommel's advance was less a battle than a mopping-up operation as French troops moving forward to reinforce the line were stunned to find themselves encountering German forces so far west. By 16 May the three German bridgeheads across the Meuse formed one compact mass, which measured about 95 km at its widest point. This was the situation when Churchill arrived in Paris on 16 May for his crisis meeting with Reynaud.

## 17–18 May: The Tortoise Head

During 17 May the panic in Paris somewhat subsided when it appeared that the Germans were not heading immediately for the capital, but probably for the coast. This at least offered a breathing space. Reynaud reshuffled his government, bringing in the legendary First World War hero Marshal Philippe Pétain to boost morale. Meanwhile many German commanders,

8. After the rupture of the front, the Germans at times found themselves moving west along almost deserted roads; at others they found themselves driving past columns of refugees or even troops marching in the opposite direction

themselves taken aback by the speed of their success, remembered how close they had come to Paris in 1914. Although troops were being hurried forward as fast as possible to 'line' the walls of the German bulge, its flanks appeared dangerously exposed. Kleist, who had twice already tried to slow Guderian down, now ordered him to halt. In fury, Guderian offered his resignation, and on the next day the advance resumed.

The vulnerability that worried Kleist was no less obvious to the Allies. As Churchill put it in a characteristically striking image on 18 May: '[T]he tortoise has protruded its head dangerously far from its shell.' The problem was that the French were not yet in a position to do anything about this. On the morning of 15 May Georges had sacked Corap and replaced him with Giraud, but by the time Giraud was ready to take over in the afternoon the situation of the Ninth Army was catastrophic, although no one knew how bad because of the chaotic state of communications. From 16 May, the armies in Belgium had begun to fall back to avoid being cut off by the German armies advancing to the coast. Meanwhile efforts were being made to build a new Seventh Army (under General Frère) to the south of the German corridor, out of divisions transferred mainly from Alsace-Lorraine and from behind the Maginot Line. Once again this took time, and the High Command had hesitated as to how many divisions it could release for this purpose because it was worried by rumours emanating from the Swiss intelligence services that the Germans were about to mount an invasion through Switzerland. This fear subsided after 15 May, but even then the deployment of units for Frère's army was complicated by uncertainty as to whether the Germans might be intending to turn southwards to Paris once they had reached the coast: should Frère's forces be concentrated for a single thrust or spread out along the corridor to protect the route to Paris?

For the moment therefore the French were in no position to launch any concerted action against the German corridor, although several local counterattacks did take place, some of them enjoying tactical success. On 17 May there was an attack on Guderian at Montcornet by the 4th DCR under the command of Colonel (as he still was) de Gaulle. This unit, assigned to Touchon's army, had been hastily assembled only days earlier out of a battalion of infantry support tanks, a battalion of B1 tanks, and a few other medium tanks, making about 95 tanks in total. They had never trained together before, and they lacked radios, anti-tank guns, and air support. The attack took the Germans off guard, but they were able to fend it off easily enough. It was no discredit to de Gaulle that his ramshackle unit, hastily cobbled together, had been unable to achieve greater results. To the north of the German corridor, on 17 and 18 May, the Germans were

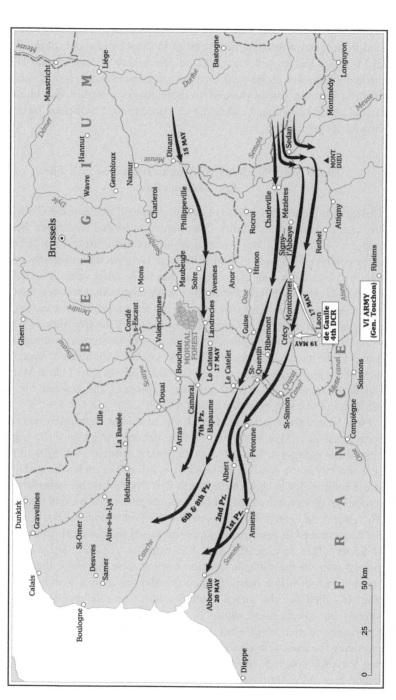

**Map VIII** The German advance to the Channel

engaged in fierce fighting at the Forest of Mormal by elements of the First DLM, which had arrived from Holland. On 19 May de Gaulle's 4th DCR carried out another attack near Laon, which enjoyed more tactical success than the first one. But in the end all these attacks were like flies buzzing around the tortoise head, while never concentrating sufficient force to threaten its jugular.

## 19–20 May: 'Without Wishing to Intervene . . .': The End of Gamelin

Throughout these dramatic days Gamelin retained, on the surface at least, his legendary imperturbability. He frequently visited Georges's head-quarters—twice on 14 May—but studiously avoided intervening directly in the conduct of 'Georges's battle', although Georges was manifestly over-whelmed by events. Gamelin claimed that these visits were intended to reinforce Georges's morale. Given the uneasy relationship between the two men, Gamelin's unnervingly silent presence was probably more unsettling than it was encouraging. At Gamelin's headquarters the atmosphere, in the words of one of Gamelin's aides, was sombre, with 'mysterious comings and goings in the antechambers and corridors' and Gamelin himself 'serene on the surface, but visibly prey to a creeping and insidious fear'.[28] On 18 May, at Daladier's request, he drafted a report explaining the reasons for the débâcle, and blaming everyone except himself.

Now Gamelin was persuaded by Doumenc that he must take control of events, and on 19 May he drafted his first and only order since the begin-ning of the fighting. It opened with the words: 'without wishing to inter-vene directly in the conduct of the battle which comes under the authority of the commander in chief of the North East front'. Was this formulation a scrupulous observance of proprieties or an elegant way of passing the buck? The essence of Gamelin's order was that the French armies should attack the flanks of the German corridor from the north and the south 'in a matter of hours'. This was clearly what the situation required, but Gamelin glossed over all the difficult realities, starting with the claim that it was necessary to act within hours. Gamelin's order was more a wish list than a plan. It called for the attack from the north to use 'specially mobile forces'—but where were these? It stressed the need to 'maintain' air superiority in the north—but had this ever existed? It recommended extending the front along the south flank of the German advance to ensure that Paris was covered—but did this not require stretching the forces out rather than concentrating them for a counter-attack?

When he drafted this document Gamelin knew that his days were numbered. On 17 May, Reynaud had summoned General Weygand, who was in command of the French forces in the Levant, to come to Paris immediately. Weygand arrived on the next day, and Gamelin can have had little doubt what this signified. Gamelin's order was therefore conceived primarily with an eye for posterity. This probably explains the rather casual manner in which Gamelin delivered his instructions to Georges. Arriving at Georges's headquarters in the early morning of 19 May, he shut himself away to draft his order. Then, without comment, he handed it over to Georges in an envelope. Although remaining for lunch, Gamelin avoided any discussion of the document's contents. The occasion, as described (with doubtless a certain poetic licence) by one of those present, seems surreal:

Then, with Gamelin still calm and apparently indifferent, we sat down to lunch. This meal left me with a horrible memory. The cook, like all of us in despair at the defeat, had put all his frustrated talent into the preparation of a veritable wedding breakfast. With Georges pale and beaten and his senior officers practically dead with fatigue and worry, the lunch had more the atmosphere of funeral baked meats. But, sitting in the centre, Gamelin, who knew even then that he had lost the confidence of the government . . . felt it necessary to put on an act, to talk of this, that and the other and make jokes; it all sounded terribly false. Then came the sweet: an enormous confection covered with spun sugar. I felt like weeping or hoping that the ceiling would fall on us. It was grotesque and pathetic. Gamelin ate heartily, drank his coffee and left, as imperturbable as ever; the guard turned out on the steps of the chateau and regimental trumpets sounded. I was never to see him again.[29]

Returning to his headquarters at Vincennes, Gamelin was informed at 9 p.m. that he was to be replaced by Weygand. On the next morning (20 May), Weygand arrived to take over. Few words were exchanged between the two men. According to Gamelin, Weygand accompanied him to the door and, tapping a folder he was carrying, remarked: 'I have the secrets of Foch.' 'I could have retorted that *I* had those of Joffre and that they had not sufficed for me. But Marshal Joffre had no secrets.'[30] On that evening the first Panzers reached the Channel at the mouth of the River Somme: the armies in Belgium were now completely encircled.

# 2

# UNEASY ALLIES

## 21 May 1940: Weygand in Ypres

As soon as he assumed command, Weygand could see, like Gamelin, that the Allies' only hope lay in attacking the German corridor simultaneously from north and south at its narrowest point, which lay between Arras (near the British sector) and the Somme (where Frère's new army was being assembled[1]). To assess the prospects of implementing such a plan, Weygand decided to visit the northern armies, which had now almost fully retreated from Belgium to the French border.

Weygand's journey north on 21 May was bedevilled by problems, which enabled him to witness the prevailing chaos at first hand. Arriving at Le Bourget airport near Paris at 7 a.m., Weygand had to wait two hours before a plane and escort could be found for him. Once he had reached the airbase at Béthune in the north-west, he expected to be met by General Billotte, who was in overall command of all the northern armies. Instead Weygand and his aide found the place deserted:

After wandering past empty hangars in which everything indicated a precipitate departure, at last we met a small soldier, very dirty but with an attractive face, who told us what had happened and asked me what he was to do with 20,000 litres of petrol about which he was greatly concerned, having received no orders. A telephone would have been of much more use to me, but there was none left. So the General who had just been invested with the command of all the theatres of operations . . . found himself, through the incredible negligence with which his journey had been organised, alone in the countryside with his ADC, without the means of getting in touch with any of those whom he had come to meet in Flanders and to whom his visit had been announced.[2]

They discovered a lorry, and the 'dirty' soldier drove them in search of a telephone. Eventually they discovered a village whose post office had one. Weygand now discovered that Billotte had thought their meeting was to have taken place in Calais where he had been vainly searching for him all morning. Since then Billotte had disappeared and no one knew where he was. Having not eaten since the morning, Weygand managed to grab an omelette in a country inn. On the wall was a picture of the signing of the Armistice at Rethondes in 1918 with Weygand himself accompanying Foch. Weygand then flew on to Calais, where he landed with difficulty because the runway had been damaged by bombing. Billotte was still not to be found, but there was a message that King Leopold III, Commander-in-Chief of the Belgian army, was waiting for both Weygand and Billotte at Ypres town hall. Weygand thereupon drove off to Ypres along roads clogged with refugees. He finally arrived at 3 p.m. Leopold was himself still on the way, and Weygand took the opportunity to talk to three ministers from the Belgian government while waiting for the King to arrive.

Three confused meetings occurred at Ypres that afternoon. The first was between Weygand and King Leopold, assisted by his military adviser General van Overstraeten. Weygand wanted the Belgian forces to retreat yet further west to the River Yser. The purpose of this manoeuvre was to shorten the Allied line so that the French and British could attack southwards. Leopold was not enthusiastic. He felt that his troops were so demoralized and disorganized by the retreat that anything more would finish them off as a fighting force, especially since the proposed manoeuvre involved giving up almost all but a tiny portion of Belgian soil. On the surface the discussions between the French and Belgians were cordial, but in reality each side was suspicious of the other. Ever since Leopold had declared Belgian neutrality in 1936, the French suspected him of harbouring pro-German tendencies, and van Overstraeten was seen as the evil genius encouraging him down this path. Against this background Weygand was all too ready to conclude that Leopold had lost faith in the Allies, felt little obligation to them, and was already thinking of leaving the war. This was indeed more or less what he had been told by Leopold's ministers, who had as little trust in their sovereign as the French did.

Leopold claimed that before reaching a decision it was necessary to hear the opinion of the British commander, Lord Gort, who had not received notice of the Ypres meeting. Since Gort was visiting his troops somewhere, it was impossible to track him down. Meanwhile Billotte arrived, and a second meeting now took place between him, Weygand, and the Belgians. Billotte, who struck Weygand as heavily marked by the 'fatigues and anxieties of the past two weeks', was pessimistic about the fighting capacity of the French armies, which had been thrown into chaos by their retreat. He felt, however, that the British Expeditionary Force (BEF), which had hardly been involved in fighting so far, still possessed the potential to launch an attack. Billotte confirmed that the assistance of the Belgians was necessary to shorten the line. Weygand now modified his request to the Belgians, asking if they would at least be ready to extend the length of their line so as to release British troops for an offensive southwards. This was more palatable to Leopold, but it remained crucial to ascertain Gort's view. Van Overstraeten set off by car to find him.

In the end, Weygand, having considered staying the night so that he could see Gort, decided he had to return to Paris. German bombing of airfields had now made it impossible to fly back, but there was the possibility of taking a torpedo boat from Dunkirk to Cherbourg. At 7 p.m. Weygand therefore left Ypres for Dunkirk, from where he departed in the middle of an air raid. An hour after Weygand's departure from Ypres, Gort finally arrived, and a third meeting occurred, this time without Weygand. Gort was less sanguine about the BEF's ability to attack than Billotte had been on his behalf earlier, but he did not refuse outright to undertake an attack. Overall the results of the conference were inconclusive. No one was happy about the role they had been allotted, but no one was ready to say so openly. As van Overstraeten put it: 'The conference closed towards 9.30 on the affirmation of the French generals that a British counterattack could still have a decisive impact; neither Gort nor Pownall [Gort's Chief of Staff] seem persuaded of this ... Gort says to the King on leaving: "It's a bad job".'[3]

As for Weygand, he finally reached Paris at 10 a.m. the next day. He had left Ypres convinced that Gort's failure to turn up was at the very least a slight. Later he came to believe it proved that Britain was already planning to betray the French, although his own misadventures on that day should have been enough to demonstrate that no sinister reason was necessary to explain Gort's absence. The fact that Weygand and Gort did not meet allowed Weygand to leave Ypres with an entirely false impression of what the British were able (or willing) to offer. But probably even if they had met, Weygand would have heard what he wanted, or needed, to hear rather than what Gort wanted to tell him.

## Looking for Allies: 1920–1938

This catalogue of misunderstandings, abortive meetings, and suspicions reminds us that the Fall of France was not only France's defeat but also an *Allied* one: France was defeated partly because it failed to coordinate its operations sufficiently with its allies, and partly because there was so little in 1939–40 that its allies could offer. That France should end up going to war in 1939 with only Britain as an ally was itself a sign of the failure of France's diplomatic efforts in the inter-war years to construct an effective alliance system: the battle was in part lost through a lack of allies. Pétain's lapidary comment on 1940 was: 'too few children, too few arms, too few allies'. The first and second terms of this proposition are debatable, the third is indisputable. In 1914 France and Britain had been allied with Russia, and in 1915 they had been joined by Italy and Rumania. It is at least arguable that the Germans lost the Battle of the Marne in September 1914 because von Moltke felt it necessary to move two divisions to the eastern front. Thus before proceeding further with the inadequacies of the Franco-British alliance, we must examine why it was that France went to war in 1939 with only one ally.

French strategy against Germany required an eastern counterweight in order to be able to impose a two-front war. Before 1914 this role had been played by Russia. After the Russian Revolution, French leaders looked for an alternative by signing a series of treaties with newly created eastern states: Poland (1921, 1925), Czechoslovakia (1924, 1925), Rumania (1926), and Yugoslavia (1927). In addition France signed a military alliance with Belgium in 1920. By no stretch of the imagination did this patchwork of treaties constitute an alliance 'system', even if Czechoslovakia, Rumania, and Yugoslavia were grouped together into a loose alliance known as the Petite Entente. All that France's allies had in common was a stake in defending the Versailles settlement. This did not stop them from having strong disagreements with each other. The worst of these was between Poland and Czechoslovakia who were at loggerheads over the border region of Teschen, which had a large Polish population. When in 1938 France was faced with the dilemma whether to go to war to protect the territorial integrity of Czechoslovakia against Germany, the Polish government made it clear they would do nothing to help; and indeed they took advantage of Czech weakness in October 1938 to seize Teschen.

France's alliances started to unravel in the 1930s. In January 1934 Germany signed a non-aggression declaration with Poland. This did not invalidate the alliance with France, but it signified that the Poles, in the face of a more assertive Germany, felt that they had to look to their own interests. In March 1936, as we have seen, Belgium cancelled its military treaty with France, and then in October of that year declared its neutrality. One reason for this was to avoid being drawn into war as a result of France's Central European commitments. Furthermore the alliance had never been popular with Flemish speakers, who distrusted French influence on

Belgian affairs. France's prestige with all its other allies was dealt a blow when Germany reoccupied the Rhineland in March 1936. This event reduced France's ability to intervene effectively on behalf of its allies and cast doubts on whether it would even try to do so: if France would not stand up for its own interests, would it really do so for anyone else's? While French prestige was on the decline, Germany was simultaneously trying to increase its influence in Central and Eastern Europe. In June 1937, Hitler's Foreign Minister von Neurath made a tour of the region.

French governments tried intermittently to shore up their diplomatic position. In December 1937, the French Foreign Minister Yvon Delbos went on his own grand tour of Eastern Europe, visiting Warsaw, Bucharest, Belgrade, and Prague, but this public relations exercise did not cost the French more than words. When it came to offering material assistance to its allies, France's main effort was directed towards Poland. In order to counter the pro-German proclivities of the Foreign Minister Jozef Beck, the moving spirit behind the non-aggression pact with Germany, France tried to cultivate the leading military figure in Poland, Marshal Eduard Rydz-Smigly. In September 1936, following a visit by Gamelin to Warsaw, Rydz-Smigly was given red-carpet treatment in Paris and signed an agreement whereby the French government opened a 2-billion-franc military credit for Poland.

In general, however, France lacked the economic resources to underpin its alliances with material help of this kind. It was also debatable how much it wanted to. As from the mid-1930s Germany grew more threatening, some French politicians began to wonder whether their allies were not more of a liability than a source of strength. Among these doubters was Georges Bonnet, who became Foreign Minister in April 1938. Bonnet was convinced that France, being too weak to act as the policeman of Europe, should extricate itself from its treaty obligations and allow the Germans a free hand in the east. But most politicians were not ready to go so far. The truth was, in the words of the historian Robert Young, that they wanted 'allies who would fight for France but not make France fight for them'.[4] This gave French policy an air of incoherence, irresolution, and duplicity. For example, when in the summer of 1936 the Rumanian leader, Titulescu, proposed a new pact reinforcing the mutual obligations of the Petite Entente, the French government was non-committal and allowed the discussions to peter out. Yet in the summer of 1937, the Rumanian and Yugoslav Chiefs of Staff were treated with the greatest of ceremony when they attended French military manoeuvres, and Gamelin reciprocated by attending Yugoslav and Rumanian manoeuvres in the autumn.

One problem in France's relations with its allies was that, not being geographically placed to offer direct military assistance to them, its attraction to them was a diminishing asset. A possible solution to this lay in an alliance with Italy, which offered a geographical bridge to Central Europe and the Balkans. Using the Italian railways, the French could transport substantial numbers of French troops to the Danube in weeks. An Italian alliance offered other benefits: Italian naval power in the Mediterranean would protect France's contact with its North African possessions, and if France was released from the need to guard the Franco-Italian border, fifteen divisions would be liberated for the north-east.

Italy's potential importance was demonstrated in 1934 when Mussolini moved troops to the Brenner Pass to warn Hitler off any attempt to seize Austria. In January 1935 the French premier Pierre Laval visited Rome. This was followed in April by a meeting at Stresa where Britain, France, and Italy affirmed their common commitment to the independence of Austria. Two months later Gamelin and his Italian opposite number, Marshal Badoglio, held talks about military cooperation in a war against Germany. But this burgeoning Franco-Italian relationship was jeopardized in October 1935 when Mussolini invaded Abyssinia, outraging public opinion in France and Britain. Whether or not Mussolini was right to believe that Laval had offered him a free hand in Abyssinia—Laval had probably been ambiguous, hoping Mussolini would get what he wanted in Africa without war—Laval certainly did not consider Abyssinia important enough to compromise Franco-Italian relations. But he was unable to resist the pressure to impose sanctions on Italy. The 'Stresa front' had well and truly collapsed.

Franco-Italian relations deteriorated further in 1936 after the outbreak of the Spanish Civil War. Italy intervened on the side of Franco, while the French government followed a policy of non-intervention. By now Laval was out of power, and the French government was a left-wing administration with a strong ideological antipathy to Mussolini. Between November 1936 and October 1938 the French had no ambassador in Rome because the government would not acknowledge Mussolini's conquest of Abyssinia. Although Gamelin continued to place hopes in his personal relationship with Badoglio, from 1937 French military planners had to assume that Italy would be hostile in any future conflict. In March 1938, Mussolini accepted Hitler's annexation of Austria.

## Elusive Albion: Britain and France 1919–1939

France had reluctantly sacrificed Italian friendship on the altar of sanctions in respect of Abyssinia because these were backed strongly by Britain. When choosing between Italy and Britain, no French leader, even one as anti-British as Laval, could hesitate. France could not expect to fight and win a long war without the resources of the British Empire behind it. Similarly when the French had responded warily to the possibility of strengthening the Petite Entente in 1937, one of their reasons was the fear that this might complicate relations with the British, who were chary of French entanglements in Central Europe.

Ever since Clemenceau's decision in 1919 not to push France's claim to the Rhineland in order not to alienate Britain, the Franco-British relationship had been the anchor of French policy. Yet the galling fact was that for most of the inter-war years the British refused to offer France any binding military or diplomatic commitments. The French found themselves jeopardizing the substance of existing alliances for the shadow of a better, but as yet non-existent, one with Britain. This caused understandable frustration. The French resented their dependence on the British yet knew that they could ultimately not do without them; the British resented the fact that, although usually out of sympathy with French policy, they knew that they could ultimately not let France down.

Franco-British relations were shaped by a stock of assumptions, prejudices, myths, and memories that each country entertained about the other. Although they had fought the Great War together, this had left bad memories as well as good. There had been the moment in 1914 when the Commander of the British Expeditionary Force, General French, had come close to deciding that it was necessary to withdraw to the Channel ports. There had also been the tense days at the end of March 1918 when the Germans had broken through the Allied lines and a breach threatened to open up between the British and French armies. When the British General Haig asked Pétain to counterattack in order to prevent this, Pétain had replied that he could not do so because his orders were to cover Paris at all costs. This episode convinced Haig of the irreducible selfishness of the French; it convinced Pétain the British were always looking for an opportunity to scuttle off to the Channel ports.

The euphoria of victory did not entirely erase such memories. Haig commented in 1919: 'I have no intention of taking part in any triumphal ride with Foch, or with any pack of foreigners, through the streets of London.' In the 1920s, Britain could not understand France's paranoia about a resurgence of Germany, and thought that the French brought their troubles upon themselves. Lloyd George saw France as 'a poor winner', and Balfour commented that 'the French are intolerably foolish ... they are so dreadfully afraid of being swallowed up by the tiger, but they spend their time poking it'. Britain's *bête noire* in the 1920s was the conservative nationalist politician Raymond Poincaré. 'I can't bear that horrid little man. I can't bear him. I can't bear him', screamed Lord Curzon after one particularly trying encounter. On another occasion, after exchanging *au revoirs* with Poincaré at the Gare du Nord, he closed the window and muttered 'and you can go to hell'. The Labour Party was even more anti-French than the Conservatives. When the French sent troops, some of them black, into the Ruhr in 1923, Philip Snowden, denounced this 'horror on the Rhine'— these 'barbarians ... with tremendous sexual instincts' thrust into the heart of Europe.[5]

In the 1920s the British had seen the French as the bullies of Germany; in the 1930s they became the bullies of the French, treating them with ever less ceremony. On 18 June 1935—the anniversary of Waterloo!—the British independently signed a naval agreement with Germany. When Germany reoccupied the Rhineland in March 1936, the French government initially made belligerent noises, but once it became clear that Britain would not provide support, the French quietly acquiesced. When the Spanish Civil War broke out in July 1936, the initial response of the French government was to send help to the Republicans, but once it became clear that the British did not approve, the French agreed to a non-intervention pact. By 1938, British bullying of the French had become so much second nature that the Ambassador, Sir Eric Phipps, had no compunction about interfering in internal French politics. In April 1938 he let it be known that the British government was opposed to the appointment of Joseph Paul-Boncour as Foreign Minister because of his anti-appeasement views (he had notoriously once described Mussolini as a 'fairground Caesar'). Paul-Boncour was not appointed. Although France, not Britain, had the alliance with Czechoslovakia, it was the British government that made the running in trying to accommodate Germany's claim to the Sudetenland, the German-speaking region of Czechoslovakia. Chamberlain sent Lord Runciman as an independent negotiator to Germany without even telling the French in advance; and he went to see Hitler on 14 September without bringing the French premier, Daladier, along with him. At the Munich conference later that month, Daladier and Chamberlain hardly had any contact with each other, and afterwards Chamberlain had another private meeting with Hitler without consulting Daladier.

The French fretted at being treated in such a cavalier manner. Laval, Prime Minister in 1935, complained that Britain was treating France like Portugal. For Laval, and the head of the French fleet, Admiral Darlan, the signing of the naval agreement perfectly exemplified Britain's reputation as 'perfidious Albion' (the soubriquet was invented by Bishop Bossuet in the seventeenth century after England's conversion to Protestantism). The belief that Britain had a habit of making agreements with Germany at the expense of its allies was certainly in their minds in 1940 when they preferred to come to terms with Germany before the British beat them to it. 1935 was the low point of inter-war Franco-British relations. It was the year in which the journalist Henri Béraud produced his famous pamphlet *Should England be Reduced to Slavery?* Having run through every French grievance against Britain from Joan of Arc to Napoleon, he ended: 'I say that I hate this people . . . I say and I repeat that England must be reduced to slavery.'

Although the French maintained that the British were constantly letting them down, the truth was more complicated. For example, the Rhineland reoccupation, retrospectively seen as the last chance to stop Hitler, was not viewed in this way at the time. French military planners were more worried in 1936 by the estrangement of Italy than by the reoccupation of the Rhineland, which they had long expected. When the Foreign Minister, Pierre-Étienne Flandin, announced in London on 11 March 1936 that the French were ready to fight to keep German troops out of the Rhineland if the British were ready to help, he would have been most disconcerted to receive a positive response. The British provided an alibi for the French to do nothing, and let them off an awkward hook when they were neither militarily nor psychologically prepared for war. The same was also partly true at Munich: it was easier on the conscience to abandon the Czechs if the British could be blamed.

If the French constantly harped on how they had been let down by Britain, it was in the hope of squeezing out compensation in the form of a British commitment for the future. For this reason the Rhineland reoccupation was in reality viewed by the French government less as a crisis than as an opportunity. But the British held back from any Continental commitment, and what they offered was consistently less than what the French sought. The British did agree to staff talks after the Rhineland reoccupation but confined these to a low-level exchange of information by military attachés. It was not until after Munich in February 1939 that the British finally agreed to high-level staff talks with France. In that sense, the sacrifice of the Czechs finally achieved what the French had been trying to obtain for 20 years. This radical shift in policy occurred because at the start of 1939 the British government became alarmed by (false) intelligence that Germany's next move would be to the west not the east. At the same time the British began to worry, in the words of a memorandum by the British Chiefs of Staff in January 1939, that the French were becoming tempted to 'give up the unequal task' of containing further German expansion. Britain took a step further towards France on 30 March 1939 by agreeing to guarantee Poland's security after Hitler breached his promises at Munich and marched into Prague. In April, the British government introduced conscription. Little remained of France's eastern alliances, but Britain was at last at its side.

Efforts were now undertaken to build up friendship between the two countries. Already in July 1938, King George VI and Queen Elizabeth had paid a four-day visit to France. This event was accompanied by enormous publicity. Almost every window in central Paris was decorated with the Union Jack, while buses were decked out with French and British flags. An actress from the Comédie-Française read an 'Ode to England' on the radio; a stamp was produced depicting two hands clasped across the Channel with the Houses of Parliament and the Arc de Triomphe between them. In March 1939, President Lebrun of France paid a state visit to London. He was invited to a reception in Westminster Hall as a guest of the two Houses of Parliament. This was followed by an entertainment laid on by performers like the French actor Sacha Guitry and the British actress Cicely Courtneidge. The atmosphere was genuinely cordial, apart from the dyspeptic comments of irreducible Francophobes like the Conservative MP 'Chips' Channon who dismissed the whole affair as 'Frog week' laid on for the sake of 'pro-Frog boys' like Eden and Churchill. But even Neville Chamberlain, certainly no 'pro-Frog boy', was impressed by Lebrun's speech. At the entertainment afterwards, he laughed so much that he got hiccups. In April 1939, the French propaganda film *Entente cordiale* (Marcel L'Herbier) opened in Paris in the presence of Bonnet and Phipps.

Two decades of mutual suspicion could not be overcome in a few weeks. The British had become used to treating the French with a certain condescension and clung to stereotypes about them. They regarded French politics as Byzantine, French politicians as frivolous, and the country as decadent. Phipps commented: '[V]eracity is not, I regret to say, the strongest point of the average politician, but there is a rather better chance of extracting the truth from him when he is not in the presence of another French politician.' This tone of mandarin hauteur affected even a Francophile like Harold Nicolson, who described Daladier on a visit to London in

April 1937 as like 'the Iberian merchant visiting the Roman Senate ... compared to our own ministers who were resplendent in stars and ribbons'. Few British politicians could speak French, and many of them knew little of France beyond resorts like Aix-les-Bains or Nice. At the first Anglo-French staff talks, there were no interpreters present. Gamelin spoke so fast that General Gort, the then CIGS, understood very little, and would from time to time optimistically mutter 'd'accord'.[6]

French politicians were even more ignorant of Britain (and the English language) than the British of them. The image of 'Perfidious Albion' ran deep. When Chamberlain visited Rome in January 1939, Daladier confided his opinion to the American Ambassador, William Bullitt, who passed it on to Roosevelt:

He [Daladier] fully expected to be betrayed by the British and added that this was the customary fate of allies of the British. Daladier went on to say that he considered Neville Chamberlain a desiccated stick; the King a moron; and the Queen an excessively ambitious woman who would be ready to sacrifice every other country in the world in order that she might remain Queen of England. He added that he considered Eden a young idiot and did not know a single Englishman for whose intellectual equipment and character he had respect. He felt that England had become so feeble and senile.[7]

Daladier often poured out his heart to Bullitt in this way, and formed an extremely close relationship with him. But he never got on as well with the British diplomatic representatives in Paris. Phipps had discredited himself by becoming excessively associated with the pro-appeasement faction in France; his successor, Sir Ronald Campbell, who took over in October 1939, was an unknown quantity whose rather frigid manner corresponded to French notions of British phlegm and reserve.

Once France had secured the elusive British commitment, French policy-makers became more assertive towards Britain. This was most visible in the two countries' policies towards Italy. French efforts to woo Mussolini had never entirely ceased, and one obstacle to better relations was removed when the French finally recognized the Italian conquest of Abyssinia in October 1938, and sent an Ambassador to Rome. But almost immediately French hopes were dashed when the Italian press embarked on an obviously orchestrated campaign for Italy to be given some of France's colonial possessions, or even bits of French territory. On 30 November 1938, France's new Ambassador was invited to witness a noisy demonstration in the Italian Parliament at which the assembled members rose to their feet clamouring 'Nice, Corsica, Tunis'. This seemed to scotch any prospect of detaching

Mussolini from Hitler. The British, however, still had hopes of doing so—that was why Chamberlain visited Rome in January 1939—and they were not in the target zone of Italian imperial ambitions. But when the British leaned on Daladier to be more conciliatory towards Mussolini, they were brushed off. There were French politicians who still believed that Italy could be won over, but from March 1939 this was no longer the official view of the government. 'They can have a pier but no more' as one minister put it contemptuously.[8] Daladier told Phipps that the Italians were 'gangsters'. Although the British came back to the matter in July, Daladier would not be moved. The British Foreign Secretary, Lord Halifax, worried that Daladier was turning into a 'new Poincaré'—which as far as the British was concerned was no compliment. It was a long time since the French had stood up to Britain in this way.

## The Alliance That Never Was

After Munich, the French government set about trying to salvage something of its position in Central and south-eastern Europe, hoping either to deter Hitler from war, or, if not, to create a second front against him when war broke out. A high-level economic delegation headed by the civil servant Hervé Alphand was sent to Rumania, Bulgaria, and Yugoslavia in November 1938. But little came of its efforts to reassert French influence. The French lacked the financial or economic resources to back up their diplomacy. One piece of practical help that they might have afforded Rumania would have been to buy more of its grain, but this was vetoed by the French Minister of Agriculture.

The Balkans were in the front line again after Mussolini invaded Albania on 7 April. Fearing this was the signal for Hitler to move against Rumania's substantial oil reserves, the French, pulling the British behind them, now offered guarantees to both Rumania and Greece, as they had to Poland in the previous month. The key to security in the Balkans lay in acquiring the support of Turkey. Negotiations between France and Britain, on the one hand, and Turkey, on the other, started in April 1939, and an Anglo-Turkish Declaration was signed on 12 May. Negotiations with France, however, were complicated by a long-standing dispute over the Sanjak of Alexandretta, a Turkish-speaking enclave in the French mandate of Syria. Not until the French agreed to cede the Sanjak was a tripartite pact signed on 19 October. The agreement was strictly limited, committing the Allies to more than it committed the Turks.

Turkey, it was hoped, might become the anchor of French security in south-eastern Europe (the Balkans), but what about Central and Eastern Europe? More specifically, what could be done for Poland? Here the only country able to offer direct help was the Soviet Union. In 1939, therefore, the British and French embarked on an attempt to build an alliance with the Soviet Union. In fact France had already had talks with the Soviets earlier in the decade, and this unhappy precedent partially explains the suspicion with which Stalin viewed the negotiations in 1939.

In the early 1930s relations with the Soviet Union, almost non-existent since 1917, had started to thaw. France had an Ambassador in Moscow from 1932, and under the growing threat from Germany, the two countries had signed a mutual assistance pact in May 1935. The Soviet government immediately started to press for this to be turned into a full military alliance. But most French army leaders were sceptical of Soviet military capacities. Dissenters from this position were sidelined. This was the fate of General Loizeau, who was reprimanded for producing a positive assessment of the Red Army after attending its manoeuvres in September 1935. More representative of French military opinion was General Schweisguth, who observed manoeuvres in 1936 and produced an entirely negative account of what he had seen. Such allegedly technical judgements were certainly coloured by anti-Communism. Schweisguth speculated that the Soviets intended to push France into a war with Germany and pick up the pieces afterwards. Few politicians felt strongly enough about the desirability of a Soviet alliance to challenge the judgements of the military.

On the other hand, although the French had no desire for a military alliance, they were worried about any possible Soviet-German rapprochement, on the lines of the Rapallo Treaty of 1922. The French had no faith in the Soviets as an ally, but feared them as an enemy. Thus, French policy was to allow exploratory talks while avoiding firm commitments. 'Drag things out', Gamelin advised his negotiators in January 1937. In March he instructed: 'gain time without proceeding to staff talks'. Stalin's purges of the Red Army in the summer of 1937 brought the talks to an end, and gave further ammunition to those asserting that the Red Army could be of no military use.

This was the inauspicious background to the attempt by the French and British to create an Anglo-French-Soviet alliance against Hitler in 1939. This time Stalin held the cards. He knew that the western powers needed him to give teeth to their guarantee to Poland, and from the start of 1939 he was also the recipient of advances from the Germans through their Ambassador in Moscow. The negotiations with France and Britain started in April. The British sent the diplomat William Strang to Moscow in June. In the first stages the British were more reticent than the French. Chamberlain, who felt he had been bounced into talks by his cabinet, remained lukewarm throughout. In July he wrote to his sister: 'I am so sceptical of the value of Russian help that I should not feel our position was greatly worsened if we had to do without them.'[9] During the weeks of diplomatic preliminaries, the Soviets set their terms: an extension of the Polish and Rumanian guarantees to the Baltic States, and a full military convention before any political agreement.

Having conceded this last point in July, the Allies set about appointing military negotiators. The British took ten days longer than the French to do this. The joint military delegation finally set off by slow boat from London on 5 August. It was symbolic that Strang left Moscow by plane, the fastest method, while the military negotiators arrived by the slowest. The French were represented by General Doumenc, the British by Admiral Sir Reginald Plunkett-Ernle-Erle-Drax. Neither had received clear instructions from his governments. On the eve of his departure Doumenc was told by Daladier to bring back an agreement 'at any price', but he had been given no guidelines on the thorniest issue: the problem of Poland. Since Russia had no common border with Germany, any military assistance to France meant crossing Poland. But the Poles, even more suspicious of Russia than of Germany, were unlikely to agree to this. Having acquired Russian territory in the Russo-Polish War of 1919–20, they feared that the Soviet Union would try to take it back. As a Polish official told Bonnet in 1939: '[M]y government will never permit the Russians to occupy the territories we took from them in 1921. Would you allow the Germans into Alsace-Lorraine?'[10] The incompatibility between a Soviet alliance and a Polish one was another reason why the French military had been reluctant about a Soviet alliance earlier in the decade.

On their four-day boat journey, the British and French delegations drafted reassuringly vague proposals to put to the Soviets. They arrived on 10 August and the talks started two days later. On 14 August these reached an almost complete impasse when the Soviet negotiator Marshal Voroshilov, who delighted in tormenting the two negotiators at every opportunity, cut straight to the quick: 'Do the French and British General Staffs think that the Soviet land forces will be admitted to Polish territory in order to make a direct contact with the enemy if Poland is attacked?' Having no answer to this enquiry, Doumenc and Drax tried to stonewall, but Voroshilov was implacable: 'I want a clear answer to my very clear question.' The French now tried to exert pressure on Poland, and a member of the French delegation, Captain Beaufre, was hurriedly sent to Warsaw. But the Poles would not be moved. In desperation, on 21 August, Daladier authorized Doumenc to guarantee that Soviet troops would be allowed to cross Poland, although Paris had received no such assurances. Voroshilov made it clear on the next day that he required a formal expression of consent from the parties involved. The French would certainly not have been able to persuade the Poles to provide this, but it was anyway too late. On 23 August 1939, the German and Soviet governments concluded a non-aggression pact.

Critics of the whole idea of a Soviet alliance were confirmed in their view that Stalin could not be trusted, and to this day no one knows whether in 1939 he was still ready to sign an alliance with the western powers. There had always been some within the Soviet leadership who mistrusted a western alliance, and given how many rebuffs this policy had received in the west, it is remarkable how persistently it was pursued by the Soviets from 1935 to 1938. If an alliance was still possible in 1939—which is unlikely since Germany could offer so much more—the western powers would have needed to demonstrate more conviction and urgency. It was symbolic that Hitler sent Ribbentrop to Moscow, while the British sent Admiral Drax. The problem was that while Germany was hostile to Russia, the western powers were too complacent; and once they were no longer so, they were too late. 'We were never told that the Germans and the Russians had started negotiations with one another,' remarked one British diplomat querulously in September.[11]

## Gamelin's Disappointments: Poland, Belgium, Britain

The announcement of the Nazi-Soviet Pact was a terrible shock to the west, but if the French military had really been forced to choose between the Soviet Union and Poland, they would probably even at this stage have chosen the latter. The leading British authority on Gamelin tells us that until Poland's defeat he remained convinced 'that Poland was a better bet than the Soviet Union as an anti-German bulwark'.[12] Although this seems remarkable in retrospect, one must not underestimate the extent to which Stalin's purges had undermined western confidence in the fighting qualities of the Red Army. The Polish army, on the other hand, was the fourth largest in Europe after the German, French, and Russian, and the Polish military had been granted substantial credits by France in 1936 to modernize its equipment. But French governments had done nothing to monitor this process, and their own experience could have told them that spending money was not enough to guarantee success in rearmament.

Ultimately the French believed in Poland because there was nothing else to believe in. Poland was all that remained of France's twenty-year effort to build up a security system against Germany in Eastern Europe. At Franco-Polish staff talks in May 1939, the two sides discussed what each would do in the event of an attack on the other. Gamelin promised that France would begin a limited offensive to relieve pressure on Poland within three days of mobilization, and that after sixteen days, once mobilization was complete, major French forces would carry out relief offensives. Vuillemin offered ambitious assessments about the help to be expected from the air force. All these assurances were absolutely cynical, since there were no French plans for action on this scale. The French and British knew that there was nothing they could do for Poland. There was never any intention of saving Poland, at least in the short term. Poland's role was to allow the western powers the chance to save themselves by providing them a breathing space. Gamelin told Gort in July 1939: '[W]e have every interest in the conflict beginning in the east and only generalising little by little. That way we shall enjoy the time we need to mobilise the totality of the Franco-British forces.'[13]

Poland proved a terrible disappointment. Gamelin had expected it to hold out between four and six months, but within a week of the German invasion this was revealed as a wildly optimistic prediction. On 7 September, French forces advanced beyond the Maginot Line into the Saar. They halted on 12 September, having moved about 8 km along a line of about 12 km, and 'taken' a handful of abandoned German villages. This 'Saar offensive', which involved only ten divisions, represented the full extent of western assistance to Poland. On 4 October, after Poland's defeat, the French fell back behind the Maginot Line.

The defeat of Poland meant that Gamelin was faced earlier than he had expected by the prospect of an attack in the west. During the autumn there were frequent alerts about an imminent German invasion. In October 1939, Hitler had indeed ordered his military commanders to prepare an attack on France immediately. So Gamelin's fears were well founded, and sharpened his exasperation at the way that Belgian neutrality complicated his plans. This was Gamelin's second great disappointment. Even after Belgium had repudiated its alliance with France in 1936, Gamelin had retained informal and ultra-secret contacts with General van den Bergen, his Belgian opposite number. These led him to hope that once war was declared the Belgians would after all invite the Allies in as French military planning ideally required. But Gamelin was guilty of wishful thinking which took no account of Belgium's reasonable desire to try to avoid becoming the battlefield of the next war. Britain's Minister in Paris, Oliver Harvey, wrote in his diary:

Poor Leopold is in a desperate dilemma. If he commits himself to a military agreement, the Germans will say he has violated his neutrality and so justify a German invasion. If he doesn't get agreement with us and France we cannot afford him proper help if he is attacked—a vicious circle. Moreover, it can be represented as an allied interest that Germany should not invade Belgium and therefore that Belgium should not provoke Germany. The answer is, I suppose, that Germany will invade Belgium if it suits, whatever Belgium does.[14]

Although Gamelin maintained his contacts in Belgium during the Phoney War—as did the British, through Sir Roger Keyes, a friend of the Belgian royal family—and although van Overstraeten did allow some intelligence to be communicated to France, none of this was a substitute for proper joint military planning. The Belgians did try, without success, to get the Allies to agree that, if invited into Belgium, they would advance to the Albert Canal despite the fact that this was the line furthest away from the French frontier, and required more advance warning than any other position.

From time to time during the Phoney War, the British and French thought that Belgium was about to invite them in. One such occasion occurred after the Mechelen incident, which seemed to confirm that Germany intended to invade Belgium. Gamelin assembled units along the frontier on 14 January, but then had to withdraw them when Belgium reiterated that there was no intention of deviating from neutrality. Van den Bergen was dismissed as Chief of Staff for taking too pro-Allied a stance. After the Germans invaded Norway, the Allies again asked permission to enter Belgium (on 11 April), and were again refused. What the Allies did decide, however, at a joint meeting on 23 April, was that if Germany invaded Holland and not Belgium, they would enter Belgium irrespective of the Belgian government's attitude. But for the moment at least Britain and France were on their own.

The Belgian attitude created enormous resentment. The normally equable Gamelin wrote in October:

The Belgians ... are unthinking, short-sighted mediocrities ... in large part to blame for Poland's obliteration; they have considerably handicapped Franco-British action when they could have helped in numerous ways. ... Belgium must bear a heavy responsibility—and she will pay for it by serving as the powers' battlefield.[15]

The diaries of General Henry Pownall, Gort's Chief of Staff, are stuffed with contemptuous comments on the selfishness of the Belgians during the Phoney War. These resentments were to resurface later.

Gamelin was also disappointed by how little the British could offer him. What he had most wanted from the British were two armoured divisions to supplement French deficiencies, but this was exactly what Britain did not have. The first British armoured division was ready for action in France only in May 1940 after the Germans had attacked and the BEF was already stranded in Belgium. Instead of armour, the British were proposing to send men. In the spring of 1939, the British War Minister Leslie Hore-Belisha announced that Britain was preparing to raise a force of thirty-two divisions, but it rapidly emerged that this was too optimistic. Pownall wrote in his diary in April 1939: '[I]t will take at least 18 months more . . . before this paper army is an Army in the flesh.'[16] In November 1939 General Edmund Ironside, recently appointed CIGS, thought that it would take until September 1940 before the British could provide fifteen divisions.

Five regular British divisions had arrived in France by the end of 1939. This was a considerable achievement given that when planning started the War Office did not even possess up-to-date maps of France. During the spring, eight more Territorial units were sent over, but these were woefully under-equipped and most of them had never done more than guard duties. Seeing one of these divisions in April, Gort wrote that he had never 'believed it possible to see such a sight in the British army. The men had no knives and forks and mugs.'[17]

There were even more serious deficiencies from the French point of view. Because the RAF was strongly committed to a strategic bombing policy, the BEF was given little air support. The ten-squadron strong Advanced Air Striking Force (AASF) that the RAF deployed in France took its orders directly from Bomber Command and was not designed to cooperate with the land force. It was intended for bombing raids into Germany. The BEF's own dedicated Air Component was considered by both British and French commanders to be totally inadequate. Pownall presciently observed: 'The struggle as to what air forces should be maintained in this country and what in France is going to be one of our major and perpetual difficulties all through the war.'[18]

By May 1940 the BEF had ten divisions ready for action.[19] British commanders were acutely conscious of the paucity of their contribution, and for that reason they deferred to the French in most planning decisions. In November 1939, when Gamelin proposed his plan to advance to the Dyle, the British accepted the role ascribed to them without demurring. General Gort, commanding the BEF, was answerable to the French

Commander-in-Chief of the north-east theatre, General Georges. Thus, the Anglo-French forces were under unified command. In the previous conflict this had not been achieved until April 1918, almost four years into the fighting. But the situation in 1940 was somewhat ambiguous. It was agreed that Gort could appeal over Georges's head if he felt he had received orders that might imperil his force. But when Ironside asked Hore-Belisha to whom Gort would be expected to appeal—'the Cabinet, the Prime Minister, the War Office or what?'—there was no clear response.[20]

Gort was a straightforward soldier of total integrity, a 'jovial battalion commander', as he has sometimes been dubbed. His biographer describes him as 'the kind of Englishman who, while accepting foreigners as a regrettable necessity, finds foreign touches and tendencies in a compatriot wholly repellent'. Nonetheless the relations between the BEF commanders and the French military were not bad. The British commanders spent much time liaising with French officers. This involved lots of eating—'a high test of the entente cordiale' commented General Alan Brooke after a large plate of oysters—but Pownall thought the effort worthwhile: '[A] bit more of that sort of thing on the part of GHQ last war would have smoothed over some of the difficulties which cropped up.' Gort, he felt, was better at making contact than Generals Haig and French in 1914 'who were pretty bad' at it.[21]

Gort's major defect, in the eyes of his corps commanders, was his failure to see the big picture and his excessive concern with trivialities. One of the first questions he concerned himself with on arrival in France was whether a tin hat, when not being worn, should be carried on the left or right shoulder. Gort spent much time visiting his troops and his staff often did not know his whereabouts, as was the case on 21 May at Ypres. This was more of a virtue for a division commander than a commander-in-chief. Gort's relations with Ironside, who had himself hoped to be appointed to Gort's position, were cool, but both men were united in their detestation of Hore-Belisha, whom they saw as a vulgar publicist (as a Jew he had those 'foreign touches' Gort did not appreciate). This source of tension was removed once Hore-Belisha was forced to resign in January 1940 after having been unfairly judged to have made public criticism of the BEF.

On the whole the British military seem to have had confidence in the French army once one discounts the kind of cultural prejudices that informed many of their judgements about anything French. Pownall felt the French could be training harder, but otherwise he was not too unhappy with what he saw of them. Ironside was impressed by the fact that all the officers he saw were, unlike in 1914, 'shaven in and out of the trenches . . . all better looking in the way of fitness and cleanliness'. The main British dissenter from these positive opinions was General Brooke, who had little confidence in the French—'French slovenliness, dirtiness and inefficiency worse than ever' he noted in September—but he was generally considered by his colleagues to have a 'very defeatist frame of mind' at this time. Gamelin, who was trying to instil greater urgency in the British about increasing their military build-up, would probably have preferred the British to be less confident in France, but this was not something he could say directly.[22]

## Britain and France in the Phoney War

At the political level, Anglo-French relations started the war harmoniously, but quickly deteriorated. To coordinate strategy, the Allies immediately set up a Supreme War Council (SWC), meeting alternately in Britain and France. In the previous war it had taken three years (until November 1917) to create a similar entity. November 1939 saw the creation of a joint Anglo-French Purchasing Committee and an Anglo-French Coordinating Committee, chaired by Jean Monnet, to coordinate joint economic planning. In December 1939, saw the conclusion of an Anglo-French financial agreement allocating the respective financial contributions that the two governments would make to the war (to be fixed on the basis of their respective national wealth—40 per cent for France, 60 per cent for Britain). Trading agreements (16 February 1940) and industrial agreements (7 March 1940) were also signed.

Officials spent much time discussing schemes to make the British and French populations view each other more favourably. These ideas ranged from the sublime to the ridiculous. It was suggested that the Marseillaise might be played in cinemas after 'God Save the Queen', and that English could be made compulsory in French schools and vice versa. The President of the Board of Education proposed getting British children to 'learn something about French food, and I believe there are a number of unemployed French chefs in London whom we might get to go round the schools and cook French meals'. More grandiose ideas also circulated about creating, in the words of one Foreign Office official, 'a permanent system of Anglo-French unity' to allow the two countries to operate as a 'single unit' on the international scene after the war. Only if the French were offered guarantees of this kind did the British feel that they could be deflected from the desire to impose punitive peace terms on Germany after victory. A committee chaired by Lord Hankey was set up to examine the possibilities.[23]

First, however, it was necessary to win the war. The two governments were agreed on the fundamental strategy: to avoid any precipitate action and build up their war economies. The plan was to prepare for a long war, but there were disagreements over what to do in the meantime. More or less whatever the French suggested the British rejected, and vice versa. In general, the French tended to be more impatient for some kind of action than the British because with 2.7 million Frenchmen under arms they feared that total inactivity would demoralize the population. Increasingly desperate to do *something*, by the end of the Phoney War the French seemed close to abandoning the long-war strategy, even if they had not openly admitted this fact.

The first SWC meeting took place at Abbeville on 12 September. Afterwards Chamberlain told his sister that it was 'the most satisfactory conference I have ever attended'. This was probably because it had decided not to do anything. Daladier was less upbeat. He told Bullitt that Chamberlain had 'aged terribly since last he had seen him ... [and] passed from middle age into decrepitude'. He was, in Daladier's view, 'as typical an Englishman as anyone in the pages of Dickens'.[24]

At the next three SWC meetings (22 September, 17 November, 19 December), the French promoted the idea of opening up a 'Balkan front' by sending Allied troops, presently stationed in the Levant, to either Salonika or Istanbul. This was supposed to pre-empt any possible German move south-east and bring the Balkan States, whose combined military forces were optimistically estimated at a hundred divisions, into the Allied orbit. The British, however, feared that this might provoke Italy, and were unconvinced by French confidence that Italy could be persuaded not to object. Sir Alexander Cadogan, Permanent Undersecretary at the Foreign Office, saw the scheme as 'moonshine'.[25]

The disagreement over the Balkan States partly derived from each country's different experience in the First World War. Britain was haunted by the memory of the disastrous Gallipoli expedition, while the French had had a happier experience with their expedition to Salonika. In this instance, the British view prevailed, and the Allies shelved the idea of a Balkan operation. On the other hand, the French vetoed a British proposal that if Germany entered Belgium, the RAF would bomb industrial targets in the Ruhr. The French view was that this would do nothing to hinder German operations in Belgium but would invite reprisals against France and Britain. The French, in other words, were keen to do 'something' but not in their own backyard. Despite these differences, the mood of the early SWC meetings was generally cordial. Ironside noted after one of them: '[A]ll went well, but then there is no adversity to make the French more feminine than usual.'[26]

By the end of 1939, Scandinavia had replaced the Balkans as the site of possible operations. On 30 November 1939, the Soviet Union had invaded Finland. Public opinion displayed widespread sympathy for the 'plucky little Finns' whose initial military successes aroused admiration. This conflict had no bearing on the wider war, since Finland was not at war with Germany, and the Allies were not at war with Russia. In France, where anti-Communist feeling was strong, many people convinced themselves that hitting at Russia by helping the Finns also represented an oblique way of weakening Germany. The Northern Department of the Foreign Office, which was quite anti-Soviet, shared this view on the grounds that Germany was receiving considerable economic aid from Russia. Generally, however, in Britain, where anti-Communism was less intense than in France, such arguments had less appeal, and the idea of intervening on behalf of the Finns would have gone no further had it not also offered the prospect of undermining Germany's war economy by cutting off its imports of iron ore from Sweden. In the winter months, when the Baltic froze, most of these exports went via the Norwegian port of Narvik. From the start of the war, the First Lord of the Admiralty, Winston Churchill, had wanted to lay mines in the waters off Narvik. This proposal had been rejected by the British War Cabinet, but it was now overtaken by an even more ambitious proposal, namely to send an expedition to Scandinavia. Its pretext would be to assist the Finns, but the real objective would be to seize the Swedish iron ore fields en route.

At an SWC meeting on 5 February, the British rejected what Cadogan described as France's 'silly scheme' for an expedition to the Finnish port of Petsamo, on the grounds that it would bring the Allies into direct conflict with the Soviet Union, but they did accept an alternative French plan for an expedition to Narvik, having first requested the approval of neutral Norway and Sweden. The meeting was harmonious. Ironside wrote: 'everyone purring with pleasure. Wondered if we should all be in the same state if we had a little adversity to touch us up.' This was a prescient observation. Not surprisingly Norway and Sweden, desperate to preserve their neutrality, refused their consent. The British assumed that this meant the operation could not proceed. The French claimed it had been agreed to go ahead regardless. Daladier became increasingly incensed at British procrastination. His 'hysterical' behaviour did not impress Cadogan: 'I think we must face up to the French. This is 1920–24 all over again—they take the bit between their teeth. We should jab them in the mouth.' Ironside echoed these sentiments: '[T]he French who are not responsible for the military execution of the plan, put forward the most extravagant ideas. They are absolutely unscrupulous in everything.' On 13 March, before any resolution of this impasse, the Finns signed an armistice with the Soviet Union.[27]

The defeat of Finland removed the pretext for intervention in Scandinavia. In both Britain and France there were domestic political repercussions. Chamberlain was forced to reshuffle his cabinet, a move that did not entirely appease his increasingly vociferous critics. In France, criticisms of the government led Daladier to resign on 20 March. He was succeeded as premier by Paul Reynaud. This might have been expected to improve Franco-British relations, since Reynaud was a known Anglophile, spoke English, and enjoyed good relations with Churchill. Perhaps it was this latter fact that made official circles in London unhappy about the change of government. Chamberlain, despite their disagreements, appreciated Daladier's down-to-earth solidity (he might have been less appreciative if he had known what Daladier said about him in private) and thought that Reynaud had a 'sly manner'; he told his sister that Reynaud would more appropriately be called 'Renard' [fox]. Reynaud was seen as impulsive, and the British Ambassador, Campbell, felt that his qualities were 'seriously undermined by his insatiable ambition'.

In fact, although his style was more assertive than Daladier's, Reynaud's policies were not new. He continued to urge a Scandinavian operation to strike at German iron imports, if necessary without the consent of Norway and Sweden. He also produced another proposal (which had been prepared under Daladier) for yet another military operation away from France's borders—to bomb the Soviet oilfields at Baku in the Caucasus. The objective was to deprive Germany of Russian oil supplies even at the cost of risking war with the Soviets. On first hearing of this idea, Chamberlain, in Ironside's words, 'went through the ceiling'. He felt that Reynaud was acting like 'a man who was rattled and who wished to make a splash to justify his position'. Meanwhile the British produced a scheme of their own, originally conceived by Churchill, to drop fluvial mines in the Rhine as a way of disrupting communications inside Germany.[28]

At the first SWC meeting that Reynaud attended as Prime Minister, on 28 March 1940, the British firmly rejected any idea of bombing the Caucasus, but accepted a plan to mine the waters off Narvik. In return, Reynaud agreed to the mining of the Rhine. Almost immediately the entire agreement was jeopardized when other members of Reynaud's government blocked the mining of the Rhine for fear that it might invite direct retaliation against France. The British responded by refusing to go ahead with

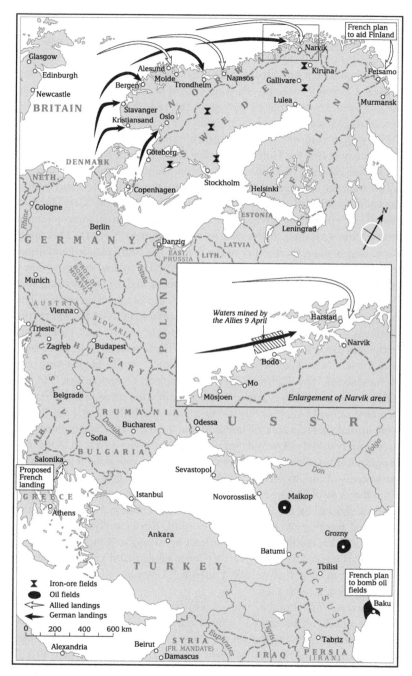

**Map IX** The Phoney War plans of the Allies: Salonika, Caucasus, Norway

the Narvik operation: 'No mines, no Narvik' in Cadogan's words. The French, he said 'talk about "vigorous prosecution of the war" which means that *we* should do it provided that we remove the war as far as possible from France'. Churchill rushed to Paris on 5 April to lobby for the British plan, but the French would not be moved. In the end, the British caved in and agreed to go ahead with the Norwegian operation regardless. The mining of Norwegian waters was set for 8 April, but the Allies had been too slow. At dawn the next day, the Germans invaded Denmark and Norway.

Despite the fact that months had been spent discussing Norway, the Allies were so unprepared for this German action that Reynaud had to summon an atlas in order to locate the ports where the Germans had landed. An emergency SWC meeting was convened in an atmosphere of feverish improvisation. It decided to send troops to Norway. This operation, largely the responsibility of the British, was badly planned and disastrously executed. Some of the troops sent to Norway had no snow shoes; others were so weighed down with equipment and winter clothing that they could hardly move; most had no experience of mountain terrain. The Allies dithered about whether to counterattack in Narvik, where the Germans seemed least well entrenched, or further south near Trondheim. In the end they tried both. The men sent to Trondheim were supplied only with maps of Narvik; those who had maps of the Trondheim area were sent to Aandalsnes. The Germans enjoyed complete air superiority, and the British soon decided to evacuate Trondheim in order to avoid total disaster. Reynaud refused to accept this was necessary and believed that the British were revealing their lack of commitment to the war. Having somewhat prematurely told the Assembly on 12 April that the German road to the iron supplies had been 'permanently cut', Reynaud had staked his reputation on the success of the operation. When he was formally told on 26 April that Trondheim would have to be evacuated, Reynaud was incensed. Chamberlain was shocked by the 'sharp' letter Reynaud sent him. At another hastily convened meeting of the SWC on 27 April, Reynaud obtained the false impression that the British would at least be willing to postpone an evacuation. This misunderstanding further inflamed Reynaud's rancour. He told a colleague that the British lacked energy: '[T]hey are all old men who do not know how to take a risk.'[29]

Returning from London with a cold which turned into flu, Reynaud became utterly disheartened. A final letter on 1 May appealing to the British to reconsider only inflamed Cadogan further: '[T]he French . . . have done absolutely *nil*. . . . It is *our* ships and *our* aircraft that are shot down.' Campbell told Halifax that Reynaud was behaving like a 'pocket Napoleon'.

The French fell back on stereotypes of perfidious Albion, and the British on stereotypes of temperamental foreigners. At a meeting of the French cabinet on 4 May, Daladier declared: '[W]e should ask the British what they want to do: they pushed for this war, and they wriggle out as soon as it is a matter of taking measures which could directly affect them.'[30]

On the eve of the German attack, then, the entente was anything but cordial. None of this predestined the alliance to unravel, and mutual suspicion might easily have dissipated in the wake of military success. But in the wake of military failure, the tensions of the Phoney War had not provided a firm foundation for fruitful cooperation. Resentments were already deeply entrenched on both sides of the Channel.

## 10–22 May: 'Allied to so Temperamental a Race'

On 10 May 1940 the Belgian government invited the Allied armies into Belgium. The BEF advanced to its position on the Dyle and held its line without being involved in much fighting. To its left were Belgian forces that had fallen back to the Dyle from the Albert Canal. One of the first matters to resolve was how to coordinate operations with Belgium which, having so far been neutral, had no place in the Allied chain of command. When hostilities broke out, Gamelin informed King Leopold that he was giving Georges authority to coordinate relations with the Belgians, as he already had with the British. But Georges, who had not been told of this in advance, felt he was too far from the Belgian theatre to perform this task effectively. At a meeting near Mons on 12 May between all the parties involved, it was agreed that the role of coordinator would be delegated—along with Georges's authority over Gort—to General Billotte. Given that in the Great War it took until March 1918 to appoint a coordinator of Allied forces, this certainly represented a considerable achievement. But the decision had been hastily improvised and although Billotte, as Commander of the First Army Group, was a logical choice, he lacked the staff suddenly to liaise at short notice between five armies. Furthermore, the fact that he was only an Army Group Commander put him in a potentially difficult position should it become necessary to impose his authority on the British or Belgian commanders. Perhaps Billotte had some presentiment of this. He was startled to receive such a sudden increase in his powers, and burst into tears when Georges informed him of it.

Problems started to arise almost immediately. On 15 May, Billotte ordered Blanchard's First Army to begin falling back towards the French frontier, but said nothing about the other forces in Belgium. The sector held by the British and Belgians was not in imminent danger, but clearly the German advance westwards would soon threaten the entire Allied position. In the early hours of 16 May, having heard nothing from Billotte, King Leopold and General Gort, quite independently of each other, took the initiative of sending an envoy to sound out his intentions. At 10.00 a.m. on 16 May, Billotte finally gave the order for the entire Allied forces in Belgium as a whole to fall back. For the Belgians this was a terrible blow, since it meant abandoning both Brussels and Antwerp, but Leopold did not question its necessity. What did worry both him and Gort was not the nature of the orders received, but the fact that it had been necessary to solicit them.

At the first test Billotte had proved himself an ineffectual 'coordinator'. In fact morale at Billotte's headquarters in Douai was at rock bottom. On 15 May, Major Archdale, the British liaison officer attached to Billotte, saw several officers in tears. For the next two days, to their growing frustration, neither the British nor the Belgians received a word from Billotte. Archdale, alarmed at the 'malignant inaction' he observed around Billotte, arranged for him to visit Gort's headquarters on 18 May. This meeting achieved nothing except to reveal to the British the depths of Billotte's despair and the fact that he had no plan of any kind. On the drive back to his headquarters, he told Archdale: 'I'm shattered and I can't do anything against these Panzers.' 'My God, how awful to be allied to so temperamental a race', commented Pownall.[31]

So alarmed were the BEF commanders by Billotte's state that the next morning Pownall rang the War Office in London to warn that the BEF might eventually have to consider withdrawing from the Continent. Pownall's call aroused such concern in London that it was decided to send Ironside over to see what was going on. Arriving at Gort's headquarters on 20 May, Ironside communicated the government's hostility to any idea of withdrawal. He suggested that Gort break out of his encirclement by heading south-west towards Arras. Gort's view was that this risked opening a dangerous gap between himself and the Belgians, but he agreed to attempt a limited operation on these lines using two divisions. Ironside and Pownall now set off to see Billotte. According to Ironside:

I then found Billotte and Blanchard at Lens (1st Army) all in a state of complete depression. No plan, no thought of a plan. Ready to be slaughtered. Defeated at the head without casualties. *Très fatigués* and nothing doing. I lost my temper and shook Billotte by the button of his tunic. The man is completely beaten. I got him to agree [to a plan] and Blanchard accepted to take Cambrai. There is absolutely nothing in front of them. They remain quivering behind the water-line north of

Cambrai while the fate of France is in the balance. Gort told me when I got back that they would never attack.

As Pownall tells it:

Blanchard and Billotte were in a proper dither, even Blanchard who is not *nerveux*. But the two of them and Alombert were all three *shouting* at one moment—Billotte shouted loudest, trembling, that he had no means to deal with tanks ... Tiny [Ironside] was quite good in speaking to them firmly ... and I too had a straight talk with all three of them singly.[32]

Under this onslaught from 'Tiny' Ironside—in fact a huge man—Billotte and Blanchard agreed to attack east of Arras towards Cambrai with two divisions, making the proposed Arras operation by the British part of a concerted Allied counter-attack. In effect, Ironside had assumed the coordinating role that seemed beyond Billotte.

Gort was ready to go along with the plan, although sceptical about it. His doubts seemed vindicated when Blanchard announced that the French were not ready to participate in any counter-attack on the next day. General René Altmayer, who was to lead the operation on the French side, said

9. General Gamelin with General ('Tiny') Ironside after a meeting of the Supreme War Council. One can see how alarming it must have been for Billotte to have this colossus 'shake him by the button of the tunic'

that he would not be ready to attack for two days. Major Vautrin, the officer whom Blanchard had sent to liaise with Altmayer, reported:

General Altmayer, who seemed tired out and thoroughly disheartened, wept slightly ... he told me that one should see things as they are, that the troops had buggered off, that he was ready to accept all the consequences of his refusal and go and get himself killed at the head of a battalion, but he would no longer continue to sacrifice the army corps of which he had already lost nearly half.[33]

For the moment, the French could offer no more than a few detachments of the 3rd DLM of General Prioux, one of the rare French commanders whose morale remained intact. Nonetheless, the British attack on Arras went ahead on 21 May. It achieved a success out of all proportion to its limited scale. Two British battalions, covered by a few squadrons of light French armour, considerably rattled Rommel, who lost more tanks that day than in any previous operation. This suggests that a concerted attack towards the south-west on 21 May by the French, British, and Belgians might have stood some chance of success against the still vulnerable 'German tortoise head'.

It was while the Arras attack was in progress that Weygand arrived in Ypres. Not only did Weygand fail to meet Gort on this occasion, but he was never to hear from Billotte what had been decided with Gort—to the extent anything had been—because Billotte was mortally injured in a car crash after returning from Ypres to his own headquarters. Two days later he was dead. Pownall commented: '[W]ith all respect he's no loss to us in this emergency.' For the next two days there was no Allied coordinator of any kind until Billotte was replaced by Blanchard, who seemed even more overwhelmed by events than Billotte had been. 'Pretty wet' was Pownall's verdict.

By now direct communications between Paris and the northern armies had completely collapsed. Equally the British government had little idea what was happening to Gort. Given the total confusion and lack of direction, Gort sounded out Leopold on his possible willingness to act as the Allied coordinator. On 24 May, Gort was even approached by the French General de la Laurencie about taking over the role himself!

## 22–25 May: The 'Weygand Plan'

On his return from Ypres, Weygand attended a meeting in Paris with Churchill and Reynaud on 22 May. This was Churchill's first visit since 16 May. Although the military circumstances had not improved, Weygand, despite his seventy-three years, exuded a confidence and energy that impressed everyone. One British observer wrote: '[H]e was darting around like a minnow, as fresh as a daisy, showing no signs of fatigue.'[34] Weygand communicated his plan to breach the German corridor: the British and French in the north would attack southwards while the new army of General Frère assembling to the south of the Somme would move simultaneously northwards. Weygand claimed that Frère's army comprised between eighteen and twenty divisions, but this was a wild exaggeration. Frère's strength at this time was nearer to six divisions, still moving into position, and stretched thinly over about 105 km. Not knowing this, Churchill enthusiastically endorsed Weygand's plan. Once back in London, he sent Gort a telegram instructing him to play his part. When Pownall received this order he was incandescent:

He [Churchill] can have no conception of our situation. . . . Where are the Belgian cavalry corps? How is an attack like this to be staged involving three nationalities at an hour's notice? The man's mad. I suppose these figments of the imagination are telegraphed without consulting his military advisers.[35]

Pownall would have been even more enraged if he had realized that the French attack from the south was largely a figment of Weygand's imagination.

In fact, despite the 'scandalous (i.e. Winstonian) plan' which, to Pownall's fury, Gort was being asked to carry out, it was realized in London that Gort's position was growing increasingly vulnerable. On 23 May, Churchill rang Paris to express his concern. He was somewhat reassured when Weygand told him at the end of the day that General Frère's army had taken Amiens. Although this excellent news—in fact completely untrue— did nothing to alleviate Gort's plight, it did make the attack southwards a risk worth taking. The 'Weygand Plan' was the only hope, if a slim one. But everyone expected someone else to assume the main burden of the attack: Weygand believed it must be Gort or Blanchard; Gort that it must be Frère; Blanchard that it must be Frère and Gort.

On the night of 23–24 May, Gort decided to withdraw from Arras where he found himself occupying an increasingly exposed salient. This did not mean that Gort had abandoned the Weygand Plan, but that is how the event was interpreted in Paris. Reynaud's military adviser, Colonel de Villelume, darkly observed to the British Ambassador that Gort's behaviour reminded him of General French in 1914. When Weygand heard the news, he telegraphed Blanchard, at 4.30 p.m. on 24 May, that he was free to decide for himself whether the southward attack was still possible; and Frère was told a few hours later that an offensive across the Somme would after all

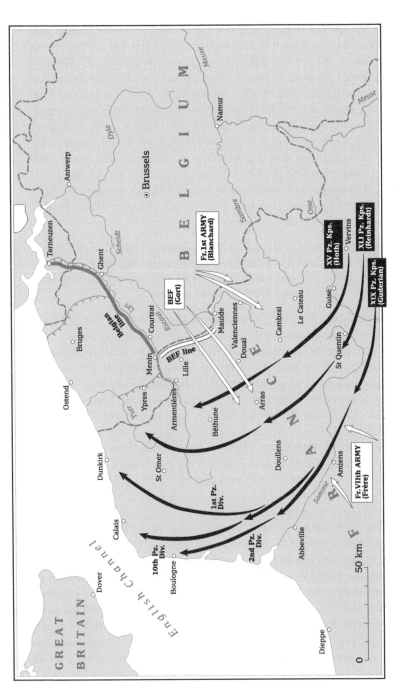

**Map X** The Weygand Plan

not be possible for the moment. Reynaud sent a sharp telegram to Churchill that evening complaining that 'the British withdrawal had obliged General Weygand to modify his whole plan'. Churchill could only reply, in good faith, that he knew nothing of any withdrawal and remained committed to the Weygand Plan. But once the French had decided that Perfidious Albion was reverting to type—Gort's withdrawal by 25 km in a northeastern direction (parallel to the coast) was being talked about as a 40-km retreat 'towards the ports'—nothing could appease them. When Churchill in his reply to Reynaud recalled the importance of Frère's participation, Villelume commented: '[H]e is trying to shift responsibilities in feigning to believe that the main effort should fall to this army whose front, stretched far to the east, is no more than an onion skin.'[36] This was a bit rich given how much had been claimed for Frère only the day before. If anyone was trying to shift responsibility, it was surely Weygand. The alacrity with which he dumped his own plan suggests that Gort had offered him the alibi he needed.

Weygand genuinely believed that the British government was deceiving him and that Churchill was not saying the same to him as he was to Gort. He remarked after a telephone conversation with Ironside that it was 'impossible to command an army which remains dependent on London in the matter of military operations' and that he would have liked to have 'boxed Ironside's ears'—causing one British witness to observe that to do this Weygand would have had to climb on to a chair. If anything, Churchill was, at this stage at least, too ready to trust Weygand's assurances. The major difference of perception lay less between Churchill and Weygand than between London and Gort—but Weygand refused to believe this.

To smooth the growing tensions in the Franco-British relationship Churchill decided to send over his friend General Louis Spears as a personal envoy to Reynaud. Spears was a bilingual Conservative MP, half French by birth, who had served as a liaison officer between the French and British military in the First World War. He was extremely well connected in French military and political circles. But Spears's role in the previous war had also won him many enemies in France. Marshal Foch had never liked him, and in 1918 the French Ambassador in London had described him as a 'most dangerous person ... a very able and intriguing Jew who insinuates himself everywhere'.[37] Spears arrived in Paris on 24 May.

It was ironic that although Gort's evacuation of Arras was being taken by Weygand as an excuse to abandon his plan, on 24 May Gort and Blanchard were still discussing the details of their offensive southwards,

10. A tract dropped by the Germans on the British and French troops encircled in the north at the end of May

Camarades!

Telle est la situation!
En tout cas, la guerre est finie pour vous!
Vos chefs vont s'enfuir par avion.
A bas les armes!

British Soldiers!

Look at this map: it gives your true situation!
Your troops are entirely surrounded —
stop fighting!
Put down your arms!

now projected for 26 May. Neither of them had any faith in it, but they were conforming to orders they still believed to be operative. Blanchard had not yet received Weygand's telegram effectively cancelling the operation.

At 6.00 p.m. on Monday, 25 May, Gort, without consulting either the British government or his nominal French commander, decided to call off his participation in the offensive. The Germans had broken through the Belgian line on the Lys near Courtrai, and Gort felt that he had to move north to plug this gap in order to keep open the route to the Channel at Dunkirk. Although Gort had taken this momentous decision on his own, his action was approved by the British War Cabinet on the next day. All evidence received by the British government on 25 May confirmed that Gort's position had become untenable. Gort's decision was probably a great relief to Blanchard, who called off his part in the joint operation on the evening of 25 May and issued his own orders to withdraw north and form a bridgehead around Dunkirk. Weygand approved this order on the next day. The Weygand Plan was dead and buried.

## The Belgian Capitulation

French and British woes were further compounded two days later when the King of the Belgians decided to ask the Germans for a ceasefire. Early on the morning of 28 May he declared Belgium's surrender. Although the French and British had some cause for complaint at not having been consulted in advance, they had hardly behaved better towards the Belgians who were usually the last to be informed of any major military decisions. Gort did not inform the Belgian military that he had decided to withdraw to the coast, and twenty-four hours later London had still not officially apprised the Belgian government of the fact.

The Belgians felt, with some justice, that the British might have been able to offer more military assistance to them in the previous days. The German attack towards Courtrai on 23/24 May had moved *across* the British front, and those British divisions not earmarked for the operation to the south might have been able to assist the Belgians by attacking the German flank. Whether or not this would have been possible, the British now so despised the Belgians that there was no chance of their taking any risks for them—although in fact the Belgians were protecting them. When the head of the British military mission to the Belgian headquarters enquired on 23 May whether some Belgian troops might be evacuated with the BEF, Pownall replied: '[W]e don't care a bugger what happens to the Belgians.' Two days later he wrote: 'What we have to fear is a Belgian break which would let the enemy across the Ypres canal.... They are rotten to the core and in the end we shall have to look after ourselves.' Once Gort had decided to retreat to the sea, the only role allotted to the Belgians, in Churchill's own words, was 'to sacrifice themselves for us'.[38]

Franco-British attitudes towards the Belgians were fuelled by bitterness over the Belgian attitude during the Phoney War and by the rapidity of the Belgian collapse on the Albert Canal. It was believed that Leopold had been lukewarm about the Allied cause from the start, although after the Ypres meeting he had in fact done more or less what was asked of him—extending his right wing as far as Menin to aid the British counterattack. On hearing the news of Leopold's capitulation, Reynaud was 'white with rage'. He told the French people in a radio broadcast that 'there has never been such a betrayal in history'. 'Ce roi! Quel cochon! Quel abominable cochon!' exploded Weygand when he heard the news. Lloyd George in a newspaper article on 2 June wrote: '[Y]ou can rummage in vain through the black annals of the most reprobate Kings of the earth to find a blacker and more squalid sample of perfidy and poltroonery than that perpetrated by the King of the Belgians.' The violence of the British and French reaction to an event that can hardly have come as a surprise—although its exact timing could not have been predicted—suggests that the Belgians were being set up as scapegoats. This was the last occasion when the two Allies could find themselves in agreement: once Belgian 'betrayal' had been exhausted as an excuse they could only blame one another.[39]

## 26 May–4 June: Operation Dynamo

At 6.45 on 26 May the Admiralty had issued the order to begin the evacuation of troops from Dunkirk: 'Operation Dynamo is to commence.' The execution of this operation was further to fuel the flames of Franco-British animosity. When Blanchard and Gort had met on the morning of 26 May to discuss the consequences of Gort's move north, Pownall noted: '[W]e didn't say a word about moving to the sea though I strongly suspect that it was in the mind of the French as it was certainly in ours.' Blanchard's own order to fall back on the bridgehead and defend it without 'thought of retreating' ('sans esprit de recul') was not what the British were intending.

This potential misunderstanding could have been ironed out later that day when Reynaud paid a trip to London. Churchill, anxious to avoid the impression that Gort's withdrawal was an abandonment of France, wanted to associate the French with any decision. He informed Reynaud of the British intention to withdraw. Reynaud thereupon telephoned Weygand from London to instruct him to 'order a withdrawal to the ports'. Even though this did not mention embarkation specifically, it must have been clear enough that this was the point. Nonetheless Weygand gave no orders to the French to prepare for evacuation, and held on to the idea of defending the Dunkirk bridgehead. It seems impossible that Reynaud in London had not understood what the British were intending, and it can only be that either he failed to make this clear to Weygand or that Weygand took no notice. This was perplexing for Gort, who had been told by London that the French were informed of the plan. Yet despite Gort's urging, Blanchard refused to order French troops to fall further back. Not until 29 May did Weygand authorize the evacuation of French troops.

Even after this had been done, the situation remained confused. Churchill telegraphed Reynaud on 29 May that he had issued instructions for French troops to be included in the evacuation, but did not say how many. Gort's own instructions from the War Office sounded a different note. He was told that his primary consideration should be the safety of the British troops, and he interpreted this to mean, as he told the CIGS, that 'every

Frenchman embarked is at the cost of one Englishman'. Thus by the end of 30 May, while 120,000 troops had been evacuated, only 6,000 of these were French. At an SWC meeting in Paris on 31 May, Reynaud complained about this discrepancy. Churchill, while pleading for greater mutual understanding—'we are companions in misfortune there is nothing to be gained from recriminations'—pointed out that the French partly had themselves to blame. Nonetheless he promised them that the evacuation would now proceed on equal terms and even that three British divisions would form a rearguard defending Dunkirk to allow more French troops to escape.

Gort was instructed to leave Dunkirk on 31 May. Before doing so, he informed Admiral Abrial, the French commander of the Dunkirk bridge-head, that the three remaining British divisions would be put under French orders. It fell to General Alexander, the senior British commander left in charge, to give substance to Churchill's effusions and Gort's orders. The War Office in London, however, wanted the evacuation brought to an end as quickly as possible and all British troops to be pulled out of France. Receiving these somewhat contradictory signals, Alexander therefore refused when Abrial asked for the three British divisions he had been promised. Alexander said that he had had no orders to this effect. Despite being told by Abrial that 'Your decision dishonours Britain', Alexander held firm, and the British did not form the final rearguard in the evacuation. The bitterness that this caused on the French side was partially alleviated by the fact that, even after the final British troops were evacuated on 2 June, British air and naval support continued to be made available. This allowed another 53,000 French troops to leave over the next two days, before Dunkirk fell on 4 June.

Until the last moment, the evacuation was dogged by chaos and disorganization. Several British ships sailed half empty on the night of 2 June because not enough French troops had arrived. Alexander toured the beaches looking for more men to take but could not find any. In the end 338,226 soldiers were evacuated—198,315 British and 139,911 Allied (mostly French). The British had contributed over 700 vessels of all kinds and the French about 160. Between 30,000 and 40,000 French troops remained to be taken prisoner. The last ships left the shattered and burning port of Dunkirk in the early hours of 4 June. When the Germans arrived later that morning, the quays were jammed with French soldiers who had been unable to get away and the dunes strewn with the detritus left by the armies who had marched so confidently into Belgium three weeks earlier.

The Dunkirk operation, carried out under constant German air bombardment, was a remarkable achievement. It was made possible partly by

11. The beach at Dunkirk after the evacuation

the fact that, after Pownall's call to London on 19 May, the government had as a precautionary measure begun to assemble a small fleet for evacuation. But the key factor was the breathing space afforded to the Allies by an order from Hitler on 24 May for the German troops to stop their advance along the Channel coast (the *Haltbefehl*). At this moment Boulogne had already fallen, the siege of Calais was about to begin, and the Germans were some 24 km south of Dunkirk.

There has been much debate as to why Hitler issued this order. Hitler subsequently claimed that it had been a gesture of goodwill to encourage the British to enter negotiations with him, but this seems highly implausible. The likeliest explanation is that Hitler and his senior generals were still nervous that the advance was going too fast and that its southern flank was still vulnerable. Possibly also Hitler was misled by Goering's assertion that the Luftwaffe could finish off the job. The *Haltbefehl* may also have been conceived as a modification of the final stage of the original Manstein Plan. Instead of Army Group B in the north acting as the anvil against which the hammer of Army Group A, moving up along the coast, would crush the Allied armies, now the role of hammer would fall to Army Group B. This would allow Army Group A to start preparing for the final assault south-wards once the encircled Allied armies in Flanders and Belgium had been finished off. Hitler's order remained in effect until 27 May—three days lost for the Germans and gained for the Allies. Curiously, although the British did intercept the order, neither they nor the French fully picked up its significance. It is remarkable that one of the most important acts of the campaign passed almost unnoticed at the time, possibly because, as Pownall observed, it seemed 'too good to hope for'.

## After Dunkirk: 'In Mourning For Us'

At Dunkirk the Allies had legitimate grievances against each other. The British were justified in feeling that the French had delayed too long in preparing their troops for evacuation; the French in feeling that Churchill's promises had not all been fulfilled by the British on the ground (or even in London). But even without these problems, it would have been impossible for the two countries to view the event in the same light. What was for the British a sort of victory snatched from the jaws of defeat, was for the French only another step on the road to catastrophe.

After Dunkirk there was hardly any further British army presence on the Continent, apart from one British division, under General Fortune (General Misfortune, Weygand dubbed him), which had not accompanied the rest of the BEF into Belgium. To avoid accusations that the British had deserted their ally, Churchill agreed to send two divisions back to France as soon as they could be organized. Despite the Foreign Office view that this was 'so much down the drain', they started to arrive on 13 June. But almost as soon as they had disembarked, it became necessary to start sending them back before it was too late.

Most French recriminations against Britain in the wake of Dunkirk concentrated on the issue of air support. Weygand and Reynaud repeatedly pressed the British to send more squadrons to France. But Churchill felt constrained to accept Dowding's view that this would compromise the defence of the British Isles. This made Weygand so furious that at the French War Committee of 6 June he ended up 'screaming . . . yelling in a high-pitched voice' at Spears. For good measure he once again brought up Gort's 'betrayal' at Arras.

Since Dunkirk the two allies' confidence in each other had completely drained away. All that remained on the French side were memories of past betrayals and forebodings of future ones. 'The British lion seems to grow wings when it's a matter of getting back to the sea' was the view of one dyspeptic French observer during the Dunkirk affair. Weygand commented: '[E]very people has its virtues and defects. Apart from his distinguished qualities the Englishman is motivated by almost instinctive selfishness.' As he said on 3 June, the British could not 'resist the appeal of the ports . . . even in March 1918 they wished to embark'. Memories of British perfidy went even further back. In a break during one meeting Villelume recalled that Spears, whom he found 'more and more antipathetic', showed him a piece of a gauntlet given to one of his Irish ancestors: 'In return I recounted one of my own family memories: the destruction of Villelume almost 600 years ago by the British.'[40]

The British, especially those who witnessed the French collapse at close quarters, were increasingly filled with contempt for their erstwhile allies. On his return to Britain Gort gave the cabinet a scathing account of what he had witnessed in France. He described Blanchard as 'the professorial type', Billotte as 'completely flabby', Van Overstraeten as 'a courtier', and the French soldier as on the whole 'apt to retire' when the Germans attacked. Having heard Gort's exposé, Chamberlain wrote to his sister: '[T]here hardly seems to be any mistake the French did not make. . . . Their generals were beneath contempt.'[41]

Reynaud's adviser, Paul Baudouin, commented during the Dunkirk evacuation: 'England has already put on mourning for us.'[42] This was not entirely untrue. On his return from Paris on 16 May, Churchill had set up a committee to examine the consequences for Britain of a French defeat. On 19 May it produced a draft report on what was euphemistically described as 'a certain eventuality'. After Dunkirk, the 'eventuality' was a probability. But the truth was that many French leaders had also begun to 'put on mourning' for themselves without being willing to admit it to the British openly. Thus, they were in effect asking Churchill to commit everything to a lost cause on the assumption that once France had fallen Britain would not be able to fight on. It therefore had nothing to lose in sacrificing the RAF in the Battle of France. For the British, however, the Battle of France was not the war. This differing perspective was strikingly encapsulated in a confrontation between Weygand and Churchill on 11 June at the penulti-mate Supreme War Council meeting. When Weygand yet again demanded air support with the words 'Here is the decisive point . . . this is the decisive moment', Churchill replied: 'This is not the decisive point, this is not the decisive moment.'

Weygand, who had a notoriously short fuse, and was bitter at being asked to shoulder responsibility for a defeat that was probably already consum-mated before he had taken over, was the most vociferous in these argu-ments with the British. But even the Anglophile Reynaud was subject to periodic bouts of anti-British irritation, fuelled by his own recent disap-pointments with the British during the Phoney War. In the immediate firing line of French displeasure was General Spears, but he was probably not the most suitable person to be in such a position. Although viewed in Britain as a Francophile—he was known in Parliament as the 'right hon-ourable member for Paris'—Spears was touchy about any assumption of French superiority, especially in military matters: 'why is it' he asked Rey-naud on 27 May 'that all Frenchmen think English soldiers are fools whereas theirs are one and all incipient Napoleons?' It was characteristic of Spears, whose temper was as short as Weygand's, that he should not only think such thoughts but also voice them. Churchill said of Spears that he 'could say things to the high French personnel with an ease and a force which I have never seen equalled'. This was not necessarily a desirable quality. Weygand several times had to ask Spears to be 'more reserved' in remarks about Vuillemin. On one occasion Spears told Pétain: '[I]f I hear any more of Weygand's sneers about our people, I shall tell him what I think of him to his face and then return to England.' He said of Weygand: '[H]is own hostility to me was as perceptible as is sulphuric acid, and I, on my side, was as loath to be near him as to someone suffering from a virulent disease.'

Even if Spears had been more emollient, his task would have been

12. Spears with General Catroux in 1941 in a characteristically hectoring posture. On 27 May Spears described to Churchill a recent meeting with Reynaud: 'at one time during this rather unusual interview I shook the little man, in quite a friendly way of course. Somehow it all worked.'

impossible. The British were not blameless, but the French needed scape-goats. As they convinced themselves that they had been let down by their allies, so too they started to feel released from any moral obligation to continue fighting for the sake of the alliance. The Franco-British relation-ship could hardly sink lower than it had done after Dunkirk, but in the final stages of the Fall of France it was to become caught up in internal French political disputes—between those who wanted an armistice and those who did not. What had started as a French military débâcle, and developed into a Franco-British dispute, was to end as a French political psycho-drama.

# 3

# THE POLITICS OF DEFEAT

## 12 June 1940: Paul Reynaud at Cangé (Loire)

DURING the first days of June, while the German troops closed in on Dunkirk, the Panzers were reorganized in preparation for the final battle, which would be fought on the line that Weygand had set up on the rivers Somme and Aisne. On 5 June, after the fall of Dunkirk, the Germans attacked. The French were now greatly outnumbered. About forty French infantry divisions and the badly mauled remnants of three armoured divisions faced fifty German infantry divisions and the remains of ten Panzer divisions. On 6 June, the Somme line was breached west of Amiens, and four days later the Aisne line gave way. On 9 June the Germans were in Rouen. Western and southern France lay open, and it would only be a matter of days before they reached Paris.

On 3 June Paris was bombed for the first time; five days later the sound of distant gunfire could be heard in the capital. Yet in the hot and cloudless days of this perfect summer, the city was, in the words of the British journalist Alexander Werth, 'strangely calm and beautiful'. In the warm night air there was a 'faint sweet smell of resin and burning trees'. Was this, wondered Werth, woods burning somewhere near the front or was it some 'tremendously pleasant smelling gas which in a few hours would burn the guts out of you?'[1]

On 10 June 1940 it was announced that the government had decided to leave the capital. Long-standing plans existed to evacuate the administration to the Loire region in the event of German bombing of Paris. But no one had expected the need for such a precipitate departure in the face of an enemy advance deep into French territory. In any circumstances, dispersing the government around various Loire châteaux would have been complicated, but in the conditions of 1940 it could only be chaotic. The journey south from Paris was painfully slow because the roads were choked with

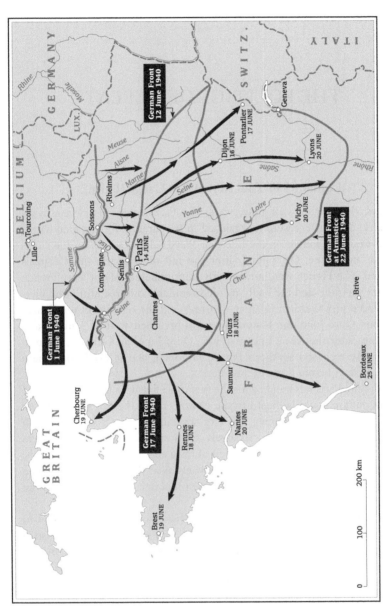

**Map XI** The German advance to mid-June

refugees fleeing towards the Loire in the hope of crossing the river before the Germans arrived. Jean Chauvel, of the Foreign Ministry, left Paris at 8 p.m. and only reached his destination, the Château de Langeais, at 5 a.m. the next morning. But Langeais was 25 km from the main body of his ministry, housed at the Château de Villandry. Covering even this distance was problematic because, in Spears's words, cars were as 'rare as horses on the battlefield of Bosworth', so Chauvel kicked his heels aimlessly while wandering around the glorious gardens of Villandry.

Telephones were as scarce as cars. The only link between Langeais and Villandry was a rather primitive field telephone on which it was difficult to hear anything. The Château de Champchevrier, where the British Embassy was billeted, contained no functioning telephone, and the Ambassador had to find one in the nearest village. The telephone in the Château du Muguet, where General Weygand lodged, was an old-fashioned contraption attached to the wall of the butler's pantry and blocking the entrance to the lavatory; it worked only, as Churchill remembered, 'with long delays and endless shouted repetitions'. On one occasion Spears amused himself by prolonging a telephone conversation in order to incommode Weygand who was bursting to use the lavatory. This was the tragi-comic level to which Franco-British relations had sunk in June 1940.

Reynaud was installed in the Château de Chissay, perched above the River Cher. This building was accessible only by a narrow road along which an endless stream of cars coming and going ran the constant risk of collision. Arriving at the Château, Spears saw Reynaud's mistress, Madame de Portes, clad in a red dressing gown over red pyjamas, directing the traffic and ordering drivers where to park. The whole place had the air of a madhouse in which the ancient owner of the property wandered about, rather bemused, in search of a spot of peace.

About 32 km north of Chissay, the President of the Republic was housed at the Château de Cangé. It was here that the members of the government gathered at 7 p.m. on 12 June for their first meeting since leaving Paris. Some ministers arrived late because they had confused Cangé with the Château of Candé, which was famous because the Duke of Windsor had got married there in 1937. At Cangé, Weygand informed the assembled ministers that in his opinion the war was lost and France must seek an armistice. Weygand's announcement caused consternation. While aware that the situation was grave, his listeners had not realized it was hopeless. Paris, after all, had been evacuated before, in 1914. Most ministers were too shocked to express a view, and most of those who did so opposed the idea of an armistice. Reynaud warned Weygand: '[Y]ou are taking Hitler for

Wilhelm I, the old gentleman who took Alsace-Lorraine from us, and that was that. But Hitler is Genghis Khan.'[2]

Weygand's advocacy of an armistice was perfectly understandable in the circumstances, but it was not the only option available. An armistice was an act engaging the responsibility of the government to end hostilities in all French territories. It made sense if it was assumed that the war was over and that the British would soon give up. Another option might have been for the government to go abroad—either to North Africa or to Britain—in order to continue the struggle from there. The assumption behind this option was that France's defeat was not the end of the war and that Britain would go on fighting. In such a case it made sense to send abroad whatever military forces could be salvaged while ordering the armies in the field to surrender. This had occurred in Holland, whose monarch and government escaped to London after the capitulation of the army.

The armistice option was inspired by the calculation that Britain would not be able to hold out after a French defeat. But this military judgement cloaked political *arrière-pensées*. An armistice would shift the responsibility for the defeat to the politicians—as Ludendorff had successfully done in Germany in 1918—and keep the army intact to ensure that defeat did not lead to revolution as it had in the Paris Commune of 1871. In the longer term, by allowing the army to salvage its honour from the débâcle, the armistice might one day allow it to become the instrument of France's spiritual recovery. When Weygand formally requested an armistice at Cangé he did not make these political considerations explicit, and they may not have been obvious to all his listeners, but they had been in his mind for several days. As early as 24 May, he had been heard to say that it was 'necessary to get France out of the ordeal which she is undergoing so as to allow her, even if defeated in the field, to rise again'.[3] Over the next few days this became an obsession with him, and many others.

After a confused discussion at Cangé, no decision was taken except to invite Churchill to attend a cabinet meeting on the following day. Since France and Britain had formally agreed that neither would sign a peace without the agreement of the other, Churchill's attitude was crucial. On the next morning (13 June) Churchill flew to Tours, landing safely despite the fact that the airfield had been badly bombed. Finding no one to meet them, the British party eventually found their way to the city Prefecture (temporary home of the Ministry of the Interior) where Reynaud was waiting for them. Reynaud told Churchill that many members of the government were inclining towards an armistice, and asked for Churchill's reaction. Churchill replied that he understood France's dilemma and would not indulge in recriminations. But, he said, Britain was not ready to release France from its pledge not to make a separate agreement with Germany. It was finally agreed to defer any decision until Reynaud had received an answer to a telegram he had sent to Roosevelt appealing for help. This was clearly only a delaying tactic. Churchill flew back to London. He was not to set foot in France again for another four years.

Later that afternoon, the government met again at Cangé. Reynaud reported on his conversation with Churchill. There was some irritation that Churchill was not himself present, but Reynaud had seemingly not passed on to him the invitation to attend. This turned the mood against Reynaud. Weygand tried to panic the government by announcing that the Communists had seized power in Paris, that their leader Maurice Thorez was installed at the Élysée and that telephone communications with Paris were cut off. The Interior Minister, Georges Mandel, thereupon rang the Prefect of Paris, to whom he had been speaking shortly beforehand, and had him tell Weygand that all was calm in the capital (Thorez had in fact been in Moscow since 7 October 1939!). Unabashed, Weygand berated the government for its cowardice in deserting the capital rather than waiting in their seats like the Senators of Rome when the barbarians arrived. He declared that if the government decided to 'take cover' abroad he would refuse to leave even if he were put in chains. Then, claiming that Mandel had smirked at him, he stormed out of the meeting, screaming abuse at politicians with 'their backsides in their armchairs'.[4]

More effective than Weygand's tantrums was the calculated intervention of Marshal Pétain. Although he had been expressing pessimistic views in private for several days, and had supported Weygand's proposal the previous day, Pétain now read out a formal statement of his own:

The government's duty is, whatever happens, to stay in the country or lose its right to be recognised as a government. To deprive France of her natural defenders in a period of disarray is to deliver her to the enemy.... I am therefore of the opinion that I will not abandon the soil of France and will accept the suffering which will be imposed on the fatherland and its children. The French renaissance will be the fruit of this suffering.... I declare that, as far as I am concerned, I will refuse to leave metropolitan soil.... The armistice is in my eyes the necessary condition of the durability of eternal France.[5]

The solemnity of this declaration, which bluntly served notice that, like Weygand, Pétain would not leave France even if ordered to do so by the government, was a sensational event. It represented a direct challenge to France's government by its most senior military figure. The crisis opened by Weygand's demand for an armistice had led to a complete breakdown of military–civil relations.

## The French Civil War

The military débâcle of 1940, then, confirmed the prejudices of conservatives like Weygand and Pétain regarding the decadence of France's democratic Republic and heightened their fears of social revolution. These two considerations explain why they were so quick, one might almost say eager, to end the fighting. What were the origins of these political prejudices and these social fears?

It is a commonplace that France's history since the Revolution has been characterized by deep political conflicts—between monarchists and republicans, Catholics and anti-clericals, socialists and conservatives. By 1914, however, a certain stability seemed to have been achieved. The Third republic had been in place since 1875 and this made it the longest-surviving regime since 1789. Superficially, the political system of the Third Republic was extremely unstable, and in the eyes of many foreign observers it was a miracle that the country was governed at all. The Head of State was a President who was elected by Parliament for seven years. He was a largely ceremonial figure with little power. This came about because the memory of Bonapartism had made Republicans suspicious of 'strong men' in politics. As Georges Clemenceau once advised before the election of a new President, 'vote for the stupidest'. In 1940 the President was Albert Lebrun, an honourable nonentity. Real power in the Third Republic lay with Parliament, but the highly fragmented party system meant that the average life of a government was only about nine months. In fact this statistic is slightly misleading, since many ministers of one government simply went on to serve in the next one. Thus, in reality, power was held by a small group of politicians who formed quite a tightly knit political elite.

Although many French people viewed their politicians with feelings ranging between suspicion and contempt, by the end of the nineteenth century the institutions, rituals, and symbols of the Republic had gained a considerable degree of acceptance. The creation of this Republican consensus owed much to the institution in the 1880s of a system of compulsory primary education. The primary schoolteachers (*instituteurs*) were supposed to inculcate Republican values in their pupils. In 1880 the Marseillaise, the Tricolour flag, and the Bastille Day holiday (14 July) were all still loaded with partisan associations; by 1914 probably most people saw them as forming the landscape of their national identity.

There was, though, still a sizeable minority who refused to accept this Republican consensus. These diehards included the virulently anti-Republican movement Action Française, whose leader, Charles Maurras, enjoyed an influence among conservative intellectuals; a significant number of conservative Catholics who were still lukewarm about the Republic; army officers who could not forgive the Republic for having, as they saw it, humiliated the army during the Dreyfus Affair at the end of the nineteenth century; and, finally, a hard core of nostalgic monarchists. Many of these dissenters were, however, brought into the Republican consensus after France's victory in the Great War.

During the war different political factions had buried their differences in the national cause in an élan of unity that was christened the 'sacred union'. In November 1918, the Republic was at the summit of its glory. Action Française continued to agitate for a monarchy, but even Maurras ended the war as an admirer of President Poincaré. The war had also healed much of the suspicion between the army and the Republic. France's premier from 1917, the ferociously anti-clerical Republican Georges Clemenceau, and France's chief military leader, Marshal Foch, a convinced Catholic and monarchist conservative, had proved, in working successfully together, that patriotism could triumph over ideology. During the war the ashes of Rouget de Lisle, author of the Marseillaise, had been solemnly transferred to the Invalides, a building strongly associated with France's monarchist and military past; on 14 July 1919, Bastille Day, there was a victory parade down the Champs Élysées with Marshals Joffre and Foch at its head.

This does not mean that all the old conflicts had disappeared. Conservatives were scandalized in 1919 when it was proposed to bury the Unknown Soldier in the Pantheon, which was the burial-place of France's Republican heroes. What, they asked, if the soldier had been a Catholic or a monarchist? In the end, the body was buried instead under the Arc de Triomphe. This was ultimately a somewhat artificial controversy. More significant for the future, perhaps, were the worries of conservatives about the Russian Revolution of 1917 and the foundation of the French Communist Party (PCF) in 1920. But the Communists were not a significant political force in the 1920s, and during most of that decade there was no serious reason to question the stability of the Republic.

In the 1930s, however, French politics entered stormy waters after the onset of the economic depression, which hit France in 1931. Although not as severe as in Germany or America, the Depression lasted longer in France. French governments, worried about inflation, refused to devalue the franc, even after both the British and Americans had devalued their currencies. French exports were priced out of already shrinking world markets. Politicians were at a loss how to react. Political instability reached alarming proportions even by the standards of the Third Republic—there were six governments between June 1932 and February 1934—and stoked anti-parliamentary sentiment among the population. This growing disaffection expressed itself in the emergence of anti-parliamentary right-wing organizations calling themselves 'Leagues'. Inspired partly by a tradition going back to Bonapartism and Boulangism, and partly by the contemporary example of Mussolini, the Leagues, which affected a paramilitary style, denounced what they claimed was the impotence and corruption of Parliament. At the beginning of 1934 the Leagues' hostility to Parliament was fuelled by a major financial scandal involving a flamboyant swindler named Alexandre Stavisky. The Leagues' street agitation became increasingly menacing, and culminated on 6 February 1934 in a demonstration at the Place de la Concorde, just across the river from Parliament. This 'Stavisky riot', as it became known, also involved war veterans and long-standing anti-Republican organizations such as Action Française. The riot turned violent, and the police opened fire, killing fourteen demonstrators. This was the worst day of violence in Paris since the Commune of 1871.

The centre-left government of Édouard Daladier resigned and was replaced by a right-wing government of 'national unity' under Gaston Doumergue. This substitution occurred because the centrist Radical Party (Daladier's own party), which usually formed the axis of any majority, panicked and shifted its support from the left (the Socialists) to the right. For the next two years, France was governed by right-wing coalitions supported by the Radicals. Meanwhile the Leagues grew in size and their rhetoric remained inflammatory. The most successful was the Croix de Feu of Colonel de la Rocque, who denounced what he called the 'gangrene' of democracy and spoke menacingly of 'H Hour', when his men would be ready to take power.

Politics became increasingly bitter and divided. The left viewed the riots of 6 February 1934 as an abortive Fascist coup, and believed the Leagues would try again to seize power. Such fears were understandable given the international context. In Germany Hitler had come to power in the previous year. To prevent something similar occurring in France, the Socialists and Communists signed a unity pact in July 1934. This represented a dramatic shift in attitude by the Communists, who had previously refused to cooperate with any other party or to accept any policy short of revolution. Only the year before they had described the Socialists as 'social democratic vomit'. Now the Communists declared themselves ready to defend Republican democracy against Fascism. They abandoned internationalism and the pursuit of revolution and took up patriotism and the defence of French democratic institutions. They started to sing the Marseillaise instead of the Internationale. This policy change was dictated by Moscow. Stalin, alarmed by Hitler's arrival in power, sought an alliance with the western powers. It was therefore not in his interest to destabilize France. He wanted the Communists to support French democracy and push for a military alliance between France and the Soviet Union.

By 1935, the Communists, adopting ever more moderate positions, were trying to extend their alliance with the Socialists to include the centrist Radical Party. Their name for the broad coalition they sought was the 'Popular Front'. Although there were Radical ministers in the Doumergue government, the party's rank and file were alarmed by the activities of the Leagues, and Daladier, who was not in the government, wanted revenge for 6 February. By the beginning of 1936, the Radicals had officially joined the Popular Front and left the conservative government. The Popular Front was also attracting voters who were suffering from the economic effects of the Depression. At the elections of May 1936, the left, united in the Popular Front, won a historic victory. The Socialists obtained the largest number of seats—though not an overall majority—and their leader, Léon Blum, became France's first ever Socialist premier. The Communists, previously little more than a sect, increased their parliamentary representation from 10 to 72. The election victory was almost immediately followed in June by a massive wave of strikes. There were over 12,000 strikes involving almost two million strikers in June 1936 alone. Even more dramatic was the fact that three-quarters of these strikes took the form of factory occupations. Nothing like this had ever been seen in France before. The strikes only ended once the employers granted substantial wage increases and agreed to accord full recognition to trade unions. The government legislated to reduce the working week to 40 hours and introduced compulsory two-week paid holidays.

Already traumatized by the election defeat, many conservatives were convinced that France was on the verge of a revolution fomented by the Communist Party. Was France going to go down the same road as Spain, where Civil War had broken out in July 1936 when the army tried to seize power from the left-wing Popular Front government that had won the elections five months earlier? In October 1936, the Bishop of Marseilles prepared to evacuate nuns in case of bloodshed. The conservative politician François de Wendel received a telegram from the Employers'

Federation telling him that a Communist plan to seize power had been thwarted by the Ministry of Defence. Historians have subsequently argued that France's situation was not revolutionary in 1936, that the mood of the strikers was festive not violent, and that the last thing the Communists wanted in 1936 was revolution (they played a decidedly moderating role in the strikes). But it was not surprising that conservatives were alarmed by the huge Popular Front demonstrations and unprecedented factory occupations.

Although the worst of the strikes was over by the start of July 1936, industrial relations over the next two years remained tense and stoppages were frequent. The membership of the main trade union, the CGT, had increased from about 750,000 in 1935 to around 4 million at the start of 1937. France may not have been on the verge of revolution, but there had been a significant shift in social and political power to the working class. To protect their interests many conservatives turned to extreme solutions. Although the Popular Front had dissolved the Leagues, the most important of these, the Croix de Feu, simply reconstituted itself as a political party. Its membership swelled to over a million, making it the largest political party in France. The former Communist Jacques Doriot formed a French-style Fascist Party, the Parti Populaire Français, which claimed 100,000 members by the autumn of 1936. Some right-wingers even turned to terrorism by becoming involved in a group of clandestine organizations that became known popularly as the Cagoule. In September 1936 they dynamited the headquarters of the Employers' Federation in order to try to discredit the PCF.

By the summer of 1937 the Popular Front was running out of steam. Its economic inheritance had been disastrous, and the government had to find the money both for its social programmes and rearmament. This was complicated by the hostility of the financial markets. There was an outflow of capital, which the Left believed to be inspired by political hostility. Blum's government was brought down by a financial crisis in June 1937, only one year after taking office. It was succeeded by what was technically another Popular Front coalition, in the sense that it was supported by the same three parties—the Communists, Socialists, and Radicals—but the axis of the majority had shifted to the right. The new premier was the Radical Camille Chautemps who, if he had any convictions at all, stood on the right of his party. Many Radicals who had joined the Popular Front out of alarm about the Leagues were now alarmed by the social upheavals of 1936. It was only a matter of time before the Radicals would again ditch their alliance with the left (as in 1934) and ally with the more moderate conservatives.

13. The most alarming aspect of the Popular Front for the middle classes was the factory occupations. Here is a group of strikers outside an occupied factory. One of them is holding up a copy of the Communist newspaper *L'Humanité*; the placard depicts the boss of the factory being hanged

Even if its days were numbered, the Popular Front had left a legacy of hatred and fear that long outlived it. Conservatives were not easily ready to forgive or forget what they had lived through in 1936–7. Their fear focused on the Communist Party, their hatred on Blum. As a dandy, Jew, Socialist, and bourgeois class traitor, Blum attracted the most extraordinary degree of hatred. 'A man to shoot in the back', wrote Maurras in April 1935. Robert Brasillach, a young Fascist journalist, wrote in March 1939: '[T]he morning when Blum is led out to be shot will be a day of rejoicing in French families, and we will drink champagne.' These attacks on Blum were not just verbal. During the election campaign of 1936, he was set upon in the street and so badly beaten as to need hospitalization. Politics in France in the 1930s had reached a pitch of violence that had something of the atmosphere of a civil war.

## 'Rather Hitler than Blum?'

France's political polarization spilled over into foreign policy. Traditionally, political alignments on foreign policy were fairly simple. The left was internationalist: it was committed to reconciliation with Germany, disarmament, and collective security through the League of Nations. The right was nationalistic: it was suspicious of Germany and preferred a policy of 'realism' based on military strength and alliances over the 'idealism' of the League. Thus, between 1932 and 1934, centre-left governments had cut defence spending and participated in the disarmament conference at Geneva; and soon after the right returned to power in 1934 the new Foreign Minister, Louis Barthou, announcing on 17 April that instead of pursuing disarmament talks France would henceforth 'guarantee her own security by her own methods', started to make overtures for an alliance towards Italy and Russia. Although Barthou was assassinated in October 1934, while accompanying King Alexander of Yugoslavia was making a visit to France, his successor, Pierre Laval, ostensibly continued down the same path. Laval was much warmer about an alliance with Italy than about one with the Soviet Union, but this did not stop him from signing the mutual assistance treaty with the Soviet Union in May 1935.

The interesting fact is that when the Soviet treaty came up for ratification in Parliament in January 1936 most conservative deputies voted against it because their growing fear of Communism in France was starting to dilute their hereditary suspicion of Germany. This was the beginning of a dramatic change in the right's attitude to foreign policy. Many on the left were simultaneously starting to question whether their traditional pacifism was appropriate in the face of Nazism. Already in 1935 the Communists had embraced patriotic values, and in 1936 it was Léon Blum's government that implemented the first large-scale rearmament programme, despite the fact that previously the Socialists had opposed military spending. It would be too simple, however, to say that after 1936 the right abandoned its hostility towards Germany and started to oppose war, while the left moved in the opposite direction. The truth was that both sides were now divided, although the left was more so.

On the left, only the Communists had no doubt that Germany must be resisted at all costs, including war. Many Socialists continued to feel that pacifism was a principle that could not be compromised even if the enemy was Nazi Germany; other Socialists felt that this position was no longer tenable. During 1938 this debate came near to dividing the party down the middle: its leader, Léon Blum, took the latter view, and his deputy, the Party General-Secretary Paul Faure, the former. The trade union movement (CGT) was also deeply split: its leader Léon Jouhaux was opposed to appeasement, his deputy, René Belin, was opposed to war. In the Radical Party, the majority probably lay with those, like Georges Bonnet, who, while not being unconditional pacifists, shared the right's worries about the true motivation of the Communists, but there were some Radicals on the other side, like Pierre Cot, who saw Germany as the principal enemy.

On the right, there was an increasingly broad consensus in favour of appeasement. The extreme right groups contained a few fervent admirers of Nazi Germany, but there were never many of these. More significant was the attitude of the moderate centre right. Nothing better illustrates its evolution than the case of Pierre Étienne Flandin, a leading centre-right politician of notably moderate views. Flandin, who dressed in Saville Row suits and had many contacts in London business and financial circles, had been Prime Minister briefly in 1935. At the moment when Germany reoccupied the Rhineland, he was Foreign Minister, and it was he who had visited London to lobby British support for a strong reaction. He also supported the Franco-Soviet Pact at that time. Two years later Flandin was one of the most vociferous advocates of French disengagement from Eastern Europe; he wanted to allow Germany a free hand in the region. In September 1938, just before Munich, when it seemed France might go to war for Czechoslovakia, Flandin had anti-war posters stuck up all over Paris: 'People of France, you are being deceived! A cunning trap has been set ... by occult elements [code for Jews and Communists] to make war inevitable.' After the Munich conference Flandin sent a message of congratulation to Hitler (and the other signatories).

MOBILISATION GÉNÉRALE
MOBILISATION GÉNÉRALE
MOBILISATION GÉNÉRAL

A.R.CHARLET

**LES COLLEURS D'AFFICHES**

14. Cartoon in the right-wing *Gringoire* (30 September 1938). Mobilization posters are being pasted up by the Socialist Vincent Auriol seated on the shoulders of the Communist leader Thorez, the Communist Jacques Duclos seated on those of the Communist Marcel Cachin, and Léon Blum. The message is that leftist politicians are war-mongers

Flandin would have justified his stance on grounds of 'realism', arguing that France did not have the resources to act as the policeman of Europe. But the pessimism that informed his realism was underpinned by social panic. Conservatives like him believed that the French social fabric had been too much weakened by the First World War, the Depression, and the Popular Front to withstand the strains of another conflict. War would sound the death-knell of the bourgeoisie and smooth the road to Communist revolution. Their suspicions were further aroused by the fact that the Communists seemed so keen to push France into a war: had not Lenin demonstrated that war was the mother of revolution? It was this blend of anxieties that led one journalist to characterize the attitude of the French right in 1938 in the phrase 'Rather Hitler than Blum'. These conservative 'realists' had not entirely despaired of France's future as a great power, but they now increasingly envisaged for it a Mediterranean rather than a Continental role. They showed increasing interest in the Empire and, somewhat contradictorily, also looked to a rapprochement between France and Italy.

No one was more convinced of the limitations of French power than Bonnet. He told a journalist around the time of Munich:

Let's stop playing the hero; we are no longer capable of it. The British will not come in with us. It's all very well to play at being the gendarmes of Europe, but if we are going to do so we need more than toy guns, papier mâché handcuffs, and cardboard prisons.... France cannot permit herself another bloodbath like 1914. Our demography is declining every day. The Popular Front has put the country in such a state that it can only prepare for a careful convalescence, any imprudence would be fatal.[6]

Not all conservatives had been won over to these positions. A minority still believed that it was possible and necessary to resist Germany, and refused to let anti-Communism blind them to the necessity for a Soviet alliance. Among conservative politicians, this was the view of Paul Reynaud, one of the leaders of the centre-right Alliance Démocratique, whose leader was in fact Flandin; Georges Mandel, who although not formally enrolled in any party had a considerable reputation because he had been the right-hand man of Clemenceau in 1917; and Henri de Kérillis, not a politician of front rank, but quite a widely read journalist. As the latter wrote in 1938: '[T]he regime of the Soviet Union is as repugnant to me as to all of you. But I do not allow the bourgeois to speak louder than the patriot.'[7]

By 1938, then, left–right polarization, so dramatically accentuated by the Popular Front, had gradually given way to a new division defined by external policy. A curious rapprochement developed between, on the one hand, left-wingers who were becoming anti-Communist because they were pacifist, and right-wingers who were becoming pacifist because they were anti-Communist; and, on the other hand, between conservative nationalists and left-wing anti-Nazis. By early 1938, Blum himself had come to believe that the Popular Front, founded to deal with one situation (Fascism and the Depression), was no longer appropriate for another (the rise of Germany and the need to rearm). When the Popular Front government led by Chautemps fell in March 1938, Blum therefore proposed a government of National Unity to stand up to Germany, stretching from the Communists on the left to the conservative Louis Marin on the right. He was even ready to offer the Ministry of Finance to a conservative. But the plan received little support on the right, except from a few isolated figures like Reynaud. Flandin spoke for the majority of conservatives when he opposed it. Blum therefore formed a new Popular Front government, supported by the left, although he had no illusions that this would last, or indeed that it was desirable for it to do so. This second Blum government fell after only a month, and the next government was formed on 10 April by Daladier.

## April 1938–September 1939: The Daladier Government

Where did Daladier's government stand? Was it pro- or anti-appeasement? Was it pro- or anti-Popular Front? Did all those opposed to appeasement necessarily share the same view about the Popular Front? The ambiguity of Daladier's position was clear from the fact that on its first appearance before Parliament, his government received an almost unanimous vote of confidence from every group. Far from signifying that Daladier had succeeded, where Blum had failed, in forming a National Unity government, this merely indicated that no one knew where the government stood. Everyone hoped to pull it in their direction. This was the first government since 1936 to contain anti-Popular Front conservatives like Reynaud and Mandel, but it also contained left-wing Radicals like Jean Zay, who had been in Blum's 1936 government. It contained ardent appeasers like Bonnet and ardent anti-appeasers like Mandel.

One test of where the government stood was its attitude to the 40-hour week, which had become the shibboleth of the Popular Front. Daladier was convinced that this measure was hampering industrial production and slowing down rearmament. But the truth was more complicated than this. Some union leaders were in fact ready to agree to exceptions to the 40-hour week if this was necessary for rearmament, providing that the principle of 40 hours as the basic working week was maintained, and that the extra hours were paid at overtime rates. The employers' leaders, on the other hand, hoping to exploit the urgency of rearmament to subvert the social policies of the Popular Front, wanted the extra hours to be paid at normal rates. In other words, the issue was as much about profits as hours. Daladier at first hoped to resolve the matter by encouraging negotiations between employers and unions, but when these seemed to get nowhere he announced in a speech on 21 August that he would if necessary be ready to sacrifice the 40-hour week. Although this led to the resignation from the government of two left-of-centre ministers, Daladier still hoped to achieve his ends by compromise.

Daladier was equally unwilling to make a clear choice about appeasement. Here the moment of truth was reached in September 1938 when the Czech crisis reached a climax. At one point the French government declared a general mobilization, but at the last moment Daladier backed down and accepted Hitler's proposals at Munich rather than risk a war. Reynaud and Mandel considered resigning from the government, but concluded that they could do more for their cause by staying to fight another day rather than leaving the field open to Bonnet. In Parliament, the Munich agreement was unanimously supported, except by the 75 Communists, one solitary Socialist, and de Kérillis. This unanimity was up to a point misleading, since many of those who voted for the agreement had profound reservations about it.

Munich was as significant in domestic terms as in international ones. It ended the political ambiguity that had existed since Daladier's arrival in power. The Communists, by voting against the government, had placed themselves in open opposition and killed off the Popular Front. There was no more reason for Daladier to tread carefully regarding the 40-hour week. Reynaud, newly appointed Minister of Finance, issued a series of decrees that effectively abolished it. The trade unions declared a one-day general strike on 30 November, but the government and employers responded firmly. Factories were evacuated by force, and thousands of union activists sacked. By the end of the year membership of the CGT had fallen by about 25 per cent from the peak it had reached in 1937. Organized labour had been well and truly crushed. Although presenting his decrees as a means of removing constraints on production, Reynaud was quite explicit that they were also intended to increase profits and restore business confidence. In this they were remarkably successful, and over the next four months there was a massive repatriation of capital.

This new financial climate immensely lightened the government's task of raising money in the markets for rearmament. The Popular Front was dead, and the right was getting rearmament on its own terms. Reynaud's laissez-faire and anti-labour policies were not the only possible solution to the problem of rearmament. After Munich, the Radical Paul Marchandeau, who was usually very much a conservative on economic matters, had proposed financing rearmament by a capital levy and exchange controls. Daladier hesitated before opting for Reynaud's policy, which was, whatever the economic considerations, the logical corollary of the new anti-Communist political configuration.

As far as foreign policy was concerned, those who hoped that Munich might lead to a durable Franco-German reconciliation were soon disabused by Hitler's occupation of Prague in March 1939. This was a blatant breach of the Munich agreement. In Parliament on 17 March 1939 almost every speaker urged the government to be firm. Bonnet's influence was now on the wane, and Daladier moved towards an unambiguously anti-German stance. For various reasons, such a policy was now acceptable to conservatives in a way that it would not have been eight months earlier. One reason was that Hitler had shown he could no longer be trusted. Another reason was the new atmosphere of patriotic fervour that had been stirred up by the Italian demands for French colonies. In response, Daladier made a much publicized visit to Corsica and North Africa in January 1939. He made it clear that France would not give up any of its colonial possessions. Although this had technically nothing to do with Germany, it helped boost national self-confidence (and it undermined the position of conservatives who argued both for a recourse to the Empire and a pro-Italian policy). The main reason, however, why Daladier was able to rally conservative support for his renunciation of appeasement was that the crushing of the labour movement in November 1938 had lowered the anti-Communist temperature. Even Action Française felt able to write on 27 June 1939: 'If in the discussion of the Moscow–Berlin alternatives we lose sight of the fact that Berlin is the most threatening, then, it must be said, everything is lost.' Those who might once have been tempted by Hitler over Blum were reassured: who needed Hitler when there was Daladier? The paradox was that once the Communist Party had been defeated at home, Daladier's government could pursue abroad the policy that the Communists had been advocating since 1936. This contradiction was resolved by the signing of the Nazi–Soviet Pact: after that it was possible to be anti-Communist both at home and abroad.

Although Daladier's government was by the spring of 1939 clearly identified with a policy of resistance to further German expansion, it was not the kind of national unity government that Blum had wanted a year earlier. The decisions taken in the autumn of 1938 had ensured that it was unmistakably a government of the right. This considerably compromised Daladier's freedom of manoeuvre when the war finally broke out in September 1939. But would a government of national unity have been possible so soon after the end of the Popular Front? To some extent, Daladier compensated for the strongly conservative identity of his government by his own enormous personal popularity in the country. Like Baldwin in Britain, Daladier embodied a certain image of provincial solidity. From his modest background as the son of a baker in Carpentras, Daladier had worked his way up as a scholarship boy through an education system that rewarded talent. He was in every sense a child of the Republic. Although a man of few words, which added to his air of dependability, he was an effective radio performer (also like Baldwin). He did not lecture or hector his listeners; he talked to them as if he were conducting a fireside chat.

Daladier was a politician with whom ordinary Frenchmen could easily identify.

Daladier was much admired for having prevented war in September 1938; but no less so for having stood up to Mussolini in November 1938. As one politician remarked of him after Munich, Daladier 'incarnated the hesitations of the French soul'. He was neither an unconditional appeaser like Bonnet nor a convinced *belliciste* like Reynaud. Thus, he was well placed to sell peace in 1938 and war in 1939. He told one of his ministers early in 1939 that he could not enter a café without people standing up and shouting 'Go on, we will follow you.'[8] Capitalizing on his popularity, Daladier was largely able to govern without Parliament. After Munich he had been voted successive sets of emergency decree powers to deal with the dangerous international situation: between October 1938 and September 1939 he ruled by decree for seven months. On 27 July 1939, he issued a decree proroguing Parliament and suspending by-elections until June 1942, a measure unprecedented in peacetime. Daladier after Munich was able to govern France more like a dictator than anyone since Clemenceau in wartime.

France, then, went to war in September 1939 with one of the most effective governments since 1918 and its most popular leader since Clemenceau. The economy was at last recovering; rearmament was accelerating; the political instability of the mid-1930s seemed to have come to an end. The change in just a few months was remarkable. A British diplomat who observed French affairs closely had written in November 1938: 'Daladier . . . has much deteriorated . . . France is in a bad way I'm afraid, and people are in a thoroughly non-cooperative mood.' Three months later he wrote: 'I found opinion in France far more optimistic and far less impressed by the German menace than we are. . . . Daladier is greatly respected . . . and the general impression I received was of greater confidence than a few months ago, less defeatism, less self-criticism, better economic outlook.'[9]

This dramatic reversal in the political mood in France needs to be stressed, since it is too often alleged, in the light of the defeat, that the French Republic in the 1930s was in a state of terminal decline. On the other hand, one should not go too far in the opposite direction. The divisions of the 1930s had not been forgotten. Hatreds bubbled close beneath the surface, and Daladier's public image of earthy solidity was a façade. In reality, he was racked with self-doubt, hesitant, and liable always to agree with the last person he had spoken to. Only days after the declaration of war, he was wondering if he had done the right thing. One of his advisers observed on 24 September: '[O]n the attitude to adopt toward eventual German proposals, [Daladier] is still hesitant. On Wednesday he was for peace,

Thursday for war; Friday, on his return from London he again wanted to stop the fighting.' On Monday, 16 October he was 'even more in favour of peace' than on Saturday; three days later he had become a '*dur*' again. The President of the Senate noted on 7 December: '[H]ow indecisive he is! How slow to act! Incapable of saying no.' Daladier's mood swings were violent. He told Bullitt only six days after the start of the war that he felt 'his political life and probably his personal life as well could not last more than 3 months'. His view was that once Poland was finished the Germans would attack France and 'the bombardments would be so terrible that the French people would blame him for the lack of French planes and would drive him from political life and indeed would probably kill him'.[10]

Daladier knew that his public persona was hollow, and his inability to live up to it made him privately moody; he was also prone to drink quite heavily. To one British observer in 1939 he seemed like 'a drunken peasant ... his face blurred by the puffiness of drink'.[11] Governing largely without Parliament, Daladier, never a convivial person, took little trouble to culti-vate other politicians, and became increasingly isolated from them. This did not matter at the start of the war when he was so popular in the country, but once his popularity started to decline, Daladier found that he had accumulated enemies waiting for him to make a wrong move.

## Daladier at War

On 2 September 1939 Parliament was called into session to vote for war credits. A group of twenty-two anti-war MPs unsuccessfully tried to get Parliament called into secret session so that the case for war could be properly debated. It was later alleged by Laval and others that the declar-ation of war had been illegal because approving credits for mobilization was not equivalent to approving war. Although the argument was specious, since everyone knew the significance of the vote, Daladier certainly had been evasive when questioned directly on the issue. His speech to Parliament, despite consciously echoing René Viviani, the premier in 1914, mentioned peace eleven times and war three times; Viviani had mentioned peace six times and war sixteen.

On 13 September Daladier reshuffled his government. The most import-ant decision was appointing Raoul Dautry to the newly created Armaments Ministry. Daladier also offered two portfolios to the Socialists, but they refused them. Daladier himself took over the Quai d'Orsay as well as keeping the Ministry of War. This was too heavy a burden for one man, and merely gave Daladier more to be indecisive about. But the most serious problem for those wanting a vigorous prosecution of the war was that Daladier retained several figures who were distinctly lukewarm towards it, on the principle that they could do less harm in the government than outside it. These included the leading Radical politician Camille Chautemps, Bonnet (who was supposedly neutralized by being moved to the Ministry of Justice), and the Italophile centrist politician Anatole de Monzie, who had close contacts with the Italian Ambassador.

Although Parliament only rarely convened in full session during the Phoney War, this did not prevent plotting in the corridors. About fifteen anti-war deputies formed themselves into a 'parliamentary liaison group'. Other influential anti-war politicians, like Laval and Flandin, both former Prime Ministers, were not directly involved with the committee but active behind the scenes. Phipps, seeing Flandin in October 1939, found him 'more defeatist than I had supposed ... he fears Communism in France'.[12] The Chamber and Senate committees continued to meet, and offered a platform for anti-war politicians. The Chairmen of the powerful Foreign Affairs Committees of both the Senate—Henry Bérenger—and Chamber—Jean Mistler—were unenthusiastic about the war, anti-Communist, and pro-Italian. The number of anti-war MPs was limited, but there were some heavyweight figures among them.

The anti-war faction pinned its hopes on a much anticipated speech by Hitler on 6 October, which was trailed beforehand as a bid for peace after Poland's defeat. But Hitler offered too little for all except the most committed anti-*bellicistes*. This helped Daladier to silence the corridor plotters when he made effective appearances before the two Foreign Affairs Commissions (4 and 6 October). He announced that he was intensifying his clamp-down on the Communists. On 26 September 1939, the government had issued two decrees, one outlawing the PCF and the other allowing the suspension of Communist local councils. In October, thirty-four Communist deputies were arrested, and several Communist municipalities suspended. A decree issued in November facilitated the internment of people deemed dangerous to national security; in February 1940, the Communist leader Thorez was stripped of his nationality; in March, thirty-five Communist deputies were put on trial, and most received sentences of up to five years. By the spring some 300 Communist municipalities had been suspended, 3,400 Communist activists arrested, and over 3,000 Communist refugees interned as foreign undesirables.

This anti-Communist campaign had slightly preceded the Communist Party's formal adoption of an anti-war position. No one had been more startled by the Nazi–Soviet Pact than the French Communist leadership.

15. The trial of 27 Communist deputies in March 1940. They were accused of having reconstituted an illegal organization after the dissolution of the PCF. The Party leader, Maurice Thorez, was not among them since he had made his way to Moscow after deserting from the army in October 1939

Lacking guidance from Moscow, their first reaction was that the Pact did not affect their commitment to national defence. The Communists unanimously voted for war credits on 2 September, and declared their 'unshakeable will' to defend France on 19 September. This was the last such statement. By the end of the month, Comintern had declared the war to be an 'imperialist' conflict in which the French Communists could not choose sides. On 1 October, the Party's group in Parliament (which had renamed itself the Groupe Ouvrier et Paysan) signed a letter calling for peace and inviting the government to take a positive view of Hitler's forth-coming peace proposals. On 4 October, Thorez deserted from the army and escaped to Moscow.

Clearly the government could not have failed to act against the PCF, but had Daladier wanted to win the approval of the largest possible number of Communists, it would have made sense to wait until the party had unequivocally adopted an anti-war line. This might have played on the doubts that many Communists felt about the new policy rather than encouraging them into reflexes of solidarity with their persecuted comrades. The Communist Jean Renaud wrote to Daladier from jail that if it had not been for his imprisonment he would have opposed the Party's position; as it was he could not bring himself to abandon his party given the repression against it. In the end about 30 Communist deputies (out of 72) did renounce their party as did 12 out of 22 Communist mayors in the Seine district. But Daladier's main objective was not to rally the Communists who could be 'saved'. In return for backing a war that they had so recently opposed, conservatives were rewarded with a campaign against Communist 'traitors'. For the next three months the right-wing press gave itself up to an orgy of anti-Communism. When de Kérillis suggested in Parliament in January 1940 that the government should act with equal vigour against German sympathizers, he was accused of being a Communist agent.

Persecuting Communists could not act as a diversion indefinitely; nor could it disguise the fact that the war was not going anywhere. Political rumblings against Daladier began to revive at the end of November 1939. His critics had an opportunity when he called Parliament into session in order to renew the decree powers that were due to expire on 30 November. Although Daladier easily won the vote—318:175—the number of his enemies had swelled to include not only open or covert opponents of war, but also many from the opposing camp who felt he was prosecuting the war insufficiently energetically. This explains Daladier's enthusiasm for an expedition to help Finland, which became his main preoccupation over the next three months. Combining an end to the demoralizing military inactivity with a healthy dose of anti-Communism, the Finnish operation offered a means of appeasing both the factions that opposed him. Daladier's fate was now entirely bound up with Finland's.

### Reynaud v. Daladier

Waiting in the wings was the Finance Minister, Paul Reynaud, who had been grooming himself to replace Daladier since the start of the war. By the end of 1939 he was increasingly being spoken of as the Dauphin. Reynaud itched to prove that he could be a new Clemenceau. In the first months of the war, his obsession was to avoid the mistakes of 1914, when the conflict had been financed by printing money. Inevitably this had caused rapid price inflation. To mop up the massive purchasing power that rearmament expenditure fed into the economy, Reynaud introduced a raft of new taxes, including an exceptional 40 per cent tax on all overtime earnings above 40 hours. Since many workers were now doing a 60-hour week, Reynaud's tax promised to bring in substantial sums. Reynaud also promoted a vigorous campaign to encourage people to invest in rearmament bonds. These anti-inflation policies received the accolade of approval from John Maynard Keynes in Britain, who regretted that the British government was not doing the same. But for Reynaud the purpose of the measures was not just economic. He wanted also to inculcate a wartime spirit in the population. In a speech on 10 September he announced that the 'economic, financial and monetary front' was as vital as the military; in December, he declared that 'we will not this time, as in 1914, wage a war by reacting to events, but a war through the exercise of will'.[13]

By the start of 1940, Reynaud was arguing that these objectives required the introduction of rationing of essential commodities. This policy also met his concern that the purchase of planes in America was draining France of its gold reserves and compromising its financial independence. The only solution was to draw up a comprehensive list of all France's requirements in order to prioritize expenditure. In short, Reynaud was bidding to take over the overall direction of the French war economy in addition to the Ministry of Finance. He was ready to force a government crisis if he did not get his way. Reynaud's undisguised ambition caused a complete breakdown in his relations with Daladier, whose mood was not improved by a serious riding accident at the end of January. The two men were not on speaking terms for most of February and communicated only by written notes. Throughout February, Daladier was planning how to eliminate Reynaud from the government, but the crisis simmered without coming to a head.

Meanwhile Daladier's own position became more precarious as the situation of the Finns worsened. At the start of February, without consulting the British, Daladier recklessly and desperately promised Finland 100 planes and 50,000 men by the end of the month, without having any idea where they would come from. After the signature of the Soviet–Finnish armistice, Daladier was unable to avoid a parliamentary debate. His speech in Parliament on 13 March contained some remarks so wild that they were struck off the record; it was rumoured that he had been drinking. Effective anti-war speeches were made in the Senate by Pierre Laval and in the Chamber by Gaston Bergery, a leading light of the anti-war liaison committee. But Daladier was also criticized from the opposite standpoint by Blum for not prosecuting the war effectively enough. On 20 March, Daladier called a motion of confidence. Although he won by 239 votes to 1, there were 300 abstentions. These included members of both the pro- and anti-war factions. Daladier felt that he had no alternative but to resign. Reynaud's moment had arrived.

## Reynaud at War

Paul Reynaud (1878–1966) was one of the outstanding conservative politicians of his generation. Born into a comfortable bourgeois family that had made its fortune in Mexico, he was first elected to Parliament in 1919. Immediately viewed as a rising star, he first held ministerial office in 1930. During most of the 1930s, however, he had in effect excluded himself from power by adopting a number of controversial positions, which led one British observer to describe him as 'something of a French Winston'. He had advocated devaluation when most of the political class saw this as more or less tantamount to treason; he had been one the few politicians to take up de Gaulle's ideas on the modernization of the army; he had, unlike most other politicians of the right, opposed appeasement. He resigned from his own party, the Alliance Démocratique, when Flandin sent his notorious telegram to Hitler after Munich. As one of the leading conservative anti-Munichois, Reynaud was loathed by the extreme right.

Politically, then, Reynaud was something of a maverick and loner. But socially he was entirely at home in those Third Republic salons where politicians mixed with aristocrats, diplomats, and writers. This is worth noting because it helps explain the curious lack of resolution that Reynaud was ultimately to reveal: he was less of an outsider than he, or others, had believed him to be. At his best, Reynaud was a brilliant parliamentary performer, with a gift for the telling phrase or snappy formula, but much less effective when it came to playing on the emotions of his listeners. He tended to dazzle rather than persuade, and certainly lacked Daladier's popular touch. Oliver Harvey noted the difference between the two men a few days before Reynaud assumed the premiership: 'Paul Reynaud has undoubtedly intrigued against Daladier—egged on by his own entourage and by his own vanity—while Daladier undoubtedly distrusts Paul Reynaud as a peasant distrusts a bourgeois.'[14]

Supremely intelligent, Reynaud had a tendency to self-congratulation. Even although he was often proved right by events, he would have been better advised to spend less time reminding everyone of this fact. André François-Poncet, French Ambassador in Rome, rather disloyally told Ciano: '[H]e has all the faults of men under five feet three.'[15] Certainly Reynaud had a complex about his small stature (he reminds the readers of his memoirs that Daladier was hardly taller!) and perhaps compensated for this by an obsession with physical fitness. He was most unusual among French politicians of this period in regularly exercising in a gym. During the Phoney War, it was his gym instructor who told him what people were saying about him in the metro.

Reynaud quickly disappointed those who expected him to form a tightly knit government focused on winning the war. The satirical magazine *Le Canard enchaîné* commented that the government was so large that only the Vél d'Hiver sports stadium would be able to accommodate it. Reynaud broadened the government to the left by bringing in two pro-war Socialists (not Léon Blum, who would have been unacceptable to the right), but he did not sack the Italophile de Monzie. Daladier was too powerful to be removed and remained as Minister of Defence, although Reynaud took over the Foreign Ministry from him. One unexpected decision was the appointment of the conservative banker Paul Baudouin as Secretary of the War Cabinet. Baudouin's lack of enthusiasm about the war was notorious. Although Reynaud had been a supporter of de Gaulle in the 1930s, and continued to take his advice, as his chief military adviser he appointed Paul de Villelume, an army officer who acted as liaison with the Quai d'Orsay and had never disguised his scepticism about France's chances of winning the war. On 24 March de Villelume listened to de Gaulle give a 'long exposé' on the possibility of winning the war militarily: 'I was stupefied. I thought him more intelligent ... I did not bother to interrupt his long and absurd monologue.'[16]

These curiously inconsistent appointments suggest that Reynaud was less sure of himself than he seemed. Some of them have been explained by the influence of his mistress, Helène, Comtesse de Portes, who had many connections in anti-war and defeatist circles. Baudouin was one of her protégés. Since de Portes died in a car accident at the end of June 1940, her side of the story is lost to history, and she forever remains Reynaud's evil genius, responsible for all his errors of judgement. It is difficult to know how much political influence she exercised at this stage. Reynaud himself never mentioned her in his memoirs, but his recently published wartime notebooks confirm how besotted he was with her and suggest a certain guilty conscience on his part about the role she had played. He wrote: '[S]he was led astray by her desire to be in with the young ... and to distance herself from Jews and the old politicians. But she thought she was helping me.'[17]

Whatever the influence of Madame de Portes, a more prosaic explanation for many of Reynaud's stranger appointments was that, lacking a solid political base, he was obliged to form as broadly based a government as possible. This did not prevent the parliamentary confirmation debate for his government degenerating into an unedifying and partisan occasion, far removed from the ideal of the patriotic 'sacred union'. Reynaud scraped through by one vote: 268 in favour, 156 against, and 111 abstentions. Over half his support came from the Socialist Party. If those who voted against both Daladier and Reynaud (29 votes) and those who abstained in the vote on Daladier but voted against Reynaud (62 votes) are taken to represent the true extent of anti-war feeling, they totalled almost 100 deputies. The true figure was even higher, since many Socialists who had voted for Reynaud out of party discipline were in truth opposed to the war. Thus, Reynaud's government was in parliamentary terms weaker than the one it succeeded.

In his first weeks in power Reynaud was a whirlwind of activity. He was a naturally energetic person, but he was also under pressure to produce results as quickly as possible. Gamelin commented: '[A]fter Daladier who couldn't make a decision at all, here we are with Reynaud who makes one every five minutes.'[18] This began to poison his relationship with the British, and it propelled him to advocate dangerously risky policies like the bombing of the Caucasus. Even after this had been vetoed by the British, it remained very much on the agenda in France (and among some circles in Britain). Whether Reynaud would ever have gone ahead without British approval cannot be known, but the fact that he embraced the idea at all, despite previously being immune to the wilder anti-Communist obsessions of other French conservatives in the late 1930s, reveals his political desperation.

It may also have reflected a growing doubt among some of Reynaud's advisers as to the viability of the entire Allied strategy of sitting tight in preparation for a long war. As one Foreign Ministry official put it at the end of March: '[T]o believe that time is at present working for us is, today, an error.' Such pessimism was encouraged by the problems of the war economy and the shortfalls in armament production. The debate over the war economy continued to rumble on in the government. On 26 April ministers discussed whether to impose widespread rationing. Henri Queuille, the Minister of Agriculture, put the case against, with the support of Chautemps: '[S]hould we make the country suffer and so to speak punish it so that the French acquire a war mentality, or should we maintain normal life as long as possible in order to allow us to put up with the war for longer?'[19] For the moment it was decided to stick to petrol rationing only. Whatever Reynaud's own preferences in this regard, he was restrained from more radical policies by the more cautious members of his government.

Nor was Reynaud helped by the attitude of Daladier. By any standards Daladier behaved with extraordinary pettiness after his replacement by

Reynaud. Refusing to accompany Reynaud to London for his first Supreme War Council meeting, Daladier then tried to sabotage the decisions that had been taken.[20] Harvey commented in April that Daladier was 'behaving disgracefully, crabbing and cramping everything out of jealousy'; he was 'sulking and evidently determined to get Reynaud's blood'. He was even rumoured to be plotting with Laval to bring Reynaud down.[21] Given Laval's opposition to the war, this would have been a dangerous game to play.

The rivalry between Reynaud and Daladier spilled over into hostility between Reynaud and Gamelin. Reynaud had genuine doubts about Gamelin's abilities, but he also resented Gamelin's closeness to Daladier. In fact relations between Gamelin and Daladier, previously quite cordial, had deteriorated markedly since the declaration of war. Within three weeks of the outbreak of war Gamelin was complaining that Daladier was a 'weathervane, immeasurably lightweight'.[22] For his part Daladier found Gamelin insufficiently energetic. In January he likened him to Tartuffe, declaring, 'I should have got rid of him before the war'. But Daladier shelved these doubts when it came to defending Gamelin against Reynaud. When the Norwegian operation started to go wrong, Reynaud saw his chance to get rid of Gamelin, whom he blamed for having been too half-hearted about the operation. He was right that Gamelin distrusted any expedition liable to siphon soldiers from the Western Front.

Reynaud launched his assault on Gamelin at a meeting of the War Cabinet on 12 April. As Baudouin wrote:

He stated his case in an icy silence under the frown of M. Daladier who sat there with his jaw set, and continually shrugging his shoulders. When the Prime Minister stopped, for a minute that seemed an hour, nobody spoke. Then in a deep and harsh voice M. Daladier ranged himself with General Gamelin, and said it was the last time he would attend a meeting of this nature.[23]

Reynaud therefore decided that it would be necessary to get rid of both men, and he spent the following weeks squaring political heavyweights so as to isolate Daladier. Gamelin also set about lobbying his own political contacts. His view on 16 April was that Reynaud was 'deranged . . . he must not be left where he is'. Gamelin felt, however, that if Daladier was forced to resign, he would go too: 'I cannot tolerate for a moment longer being treated as I have been by Reynaud.' Reynaud's bout of flu at the end of April caused a further delay, and it was not until 9 May that he was ready to call a cabinet meeting to discuss the issue. His voice still hoarse from his illness, Reynaud launched into a diatribe against Gamelin lasting over an hour. He paused only when someone tried to light a cigarette and Reynaud asked him to put it out because his throat was still sore from his illness. When Reynaud had finished, no one spoke except Daladier, whose only comment was 'I cannot agree'. In view of Daladier's opposition, Reynaud announced his resignation. His intention was to form a new government without Daladier the next day. Thus, on the morning of 10 May, when Germany attacked, France was technically without a government and was about to get a new commander-in-chief. In these circumstances, however, Reynaud suspended his decision. Hitler's offensive had afforded Gamelin a final reprieve—and the chance to prove that Reynaud was wrong about him.

## 25–28 May: Weygand's Proposal

During the next few days the politicians were forced to take a back seat and wait on the military events—although Daladier and Reynaud continued to feud when there was an opportunity. On 11 May, Reynaud informed Daladier that he intended to pay a visit on the next day to King Leopold to discuss the issue of coordination with the Belgian armies. Daladier advised him that it would be best to postpone such a visit for two or three days in order not to get in the way of the generals during the initial fighting. But the real reason for this reaction was that Daladier had decided to pay a visit to Leopold himself on the next day, and did not want to have to go with Reynaud. At the meeting with Leopold near Mons on 12 May,[24] Reynaud was not present. Instead the French government was represented by Daladier, decked out in a vaguely military-looking outfit inspired perhaps by Poincaré's dress in the previous war—not altogether a happy model, since many observers had thought it made Poincaré look more like a chauffeur than anything else.

On 17 May, once it was clear that a military disaster had occurred, Reynaud decided to take control. He himself took over the Ministry of Defence from Daladier, who was given the Foreign Ministry. Mandel was promoted to the Ministry of the Interior to act vigorously against fifth-column activity. But the two most important decisions were the appointment of Pétain to be vice-premier and Weygand to be commander-in-chief. Pétain, the most revered figure in France, was brought in as a figurehead to boost public confidence. Weygand was believed to possess the inspirational qualities that Gamelin seemed to have lacked. Both these appointments were to prove fateful to Reynaud, but initially most of the running was made by Weygand, while Pétain remained gloomily silent.

Maxime Weygand (1867–1965) had graduated from the Cavalry School at Saumur in 1887. His inter-war reputation derived primarily from his role as

16. Reynaud with his three nemeses—General Weygand, Paul Baudouin
and Marshal Pétain—all of whom had been appointed by him

staff officer to Foch during the previous war. The two men had formed
a close intellectual relationship. In 1920 Weygand was sent as an adviser to
the Polish army, and he acquired international celebrity as the man who
had helped the Poles successfully fight off Bolshevism in the Russo-Polish
War of 1920–1. Like Foch, Weygand was a man of pronouncedly tradition-
alist views. Clemenceau claimed in 1919 that Weygand was 'up to his neck in
priests'. Weygand's views were not untypical of the closely knit and socially
conservative world of many cavalry officers. But his exceptionally close
identification with the army and its values may also be linked to his
peculiar family circumstances. He was born in a room above a tavern in
Brussels, and his parentage was a mystery. Some people believed he was the
illegitimate son of Leopold II of Belgium. Early in life he was placed under
the wardship of a tutor in Marseilles. Whoever his father was, someone
provided for his education at the military academy of St Cyr and then at
Saumur. At the age of 21, he was recognized as a son by an accountant of the
name of Weygand who worked for his tutor. Thus, he acquired a new
name and French citizenship. Perhaps, then, the army offered Weygand an

identity, and a social milieu, which his mysterious origins had not provided for him. It was in a literal sense his family.

When he was appointed Chief of General Staff in 1930, Weygand had had to make a public declaration of his Republican loyalty, which was read out in Parliament. This was a unique event and must have been very humiliating to him. Weygand's relationship with the left-wing governments in power between 1932 and 1934 was extremely fraught. This was a period of severe cuts in military spending, and Weygand was convinced that the left was sacrificing the army for ideological motives. He was deeply embittered when he retired in 1935. Having said this, it would probably be wrong to see Weygand as a politically ambitious, factious, or plotting general. Certainly he despised politicians as a breed. Of Daladier he noted in his journal in 1933: '[W]e do not understand each other. The world of St Cyr and the Army and the world of the political café [Café de Commerce] and the Masonic lodge are not the same.' But he was also schooled in the traditions of obedience to the State. He told André Maginot in December 1931: '[T]he army does not get involved in politics; she obeys the government whatever it is, Louis XVI, Napoleon.'[25] Of course a lot had happened between then and 1940, but even so one should probably treat with a certain degree of scepticism Gamelin's claim that when he took over from him Weygand burst out: '[A]ll this politics; that's got to change. We have got to be done with all these politicians. Not one of them is worth any more than the others.' There is no reason to suppose that when he succeeded Gamelin, Weygand was motivated by anything other than a sense of patriotic duty, and a hope that he might still be able to reverse the military disaster. Once he lost faith in that possibility, Weygand's increasing resentment against the politicians may well have been motivated by a feeling that he had been given an impossible task and was now being asked to shoulder the blame.

It was at a meeting of the War Cabinet on 25 May that Weygand first raised the possibility of giving up the fight. He explained that he was setting up a new defensive line on the Somme and Aisne with orders to resist 'without thought of retreat'. But given that the French would be facing considerably larger German forces, he held out little hope that this represented more than a last-ditch defence to preserve honour. He also for the first time expressed the view that it was necessary to save the army from total destruction in order to prevent anarchy from breaking out in France.

Weygand's exposé was followed by a rambling discussion. In future years, no one was ready to admit having been the first to utter that fateful word 'armistice on this occasion'. But does it matter? The idea was not yet tainted by its later associations with Vichy. As Eleanor Gates correctly observes in her study of these events, on 25 May the word 'armistice' was only one of various possibilities being tossed around 'by a few puzzled and apprehensive people in something of a state of shock, mulling over possible solutions to a most unpromising situation, quite unconscious that their words would one day be enshrined in history—or used in briefs drawn up against them'.[26] The meeting also discussed whether Italy could be kept out of the war, and even whether Mussolini might be prevailed upon to mediate on France's behalf. All these debates were inconclusive, but in the light of a Franco-British agreement of 28 March that neither party would sign a separate peace without the other's consent, it was agreed that Reynaud must go to London to discover Britain's views on all the matters discussed. Weygand's hope was that the British would accept the necessity to come to terms with Germany while the Allies still held some cards in their hand (that is, before the entire destruction of the armies).

Arriving in London for a flying visit on 26 May, Reynaud did not disguise the seriousness of the French military situation, but nor did he explicitly ask Churchill what Britain would do if France was forced to give up. As for whether the British favoured making an overture towards Italy, Reynaud was told to expect an answer on the next day. This delay was because Reynaud's visit coincided with an attempt by Halifax to persuade the British cabinet to make an approach to Italy. The British could obviously not offer guidance to the French until they had worked out their own view on Halifax's proposal. Reynaud's visit had done nothing to clarify the situation for the French.

Weygand was annoyed that Reynaud had not tackled the British directly about the possibility of France's leaving the war, and it was from this moment that the relationship between the two men began to deteriorate. Weygand's frustration was understandable. There was nothing unreasonable about his request that the government should at least sound out the British. At the War Cabinet of 25 May this strategy had even been supported by César Campinchi, who was later to be one of the ministers most firmly opposed to an armistice. Nor is there any sign at this stage that Reynaud had thought of continuing the war from abroad once it was lost in France. Since Reynaud was offering no alternative to Weygand's Franco-centric view of the war, Weygand felt that he was evading an issue that did need to be discussed with Britain.

Reynaud at this stage seems to have been unsure what he wanted. On returning from London he told Baudouin (if Baudouin is to be believed) that: 'The only one who understands is Halifax, who is clearly worried

about the future, and realises that some European solution must be reached
... Churchill is always hectoring and Chamberlain undecided.'[27] This suggests that Reynaud was partly aware of the discussions going on within the
British government, and that his reluctance to consider Weygand's policy
stemmed less from real conviction that it could be avoided than from a
desire not to be the person responsible for having proposed it to the British. It
has to be said also that Weygand was not alone in his fear of political disorder.
Bullitt noted on 28 May that Reynaud and Mandel 'expect a Communist
uprising and butcheries in the city of Paris'. A few days later he reported:
'Everyone believes that once the government leaves Paris the Communists
of the industrial suburbs will seize the city, and will be permitted to
murder, loot and burn for several days before the Germans come in.'[28]

While the French awaited the British response regarding a possible
approach towards Italy, Daladier, now Foreign Minister, was seized by
panic at the prospect of Italy's entering the war. On 27 May, he drafted a
telegram offering extensive territorial concessions to Italy: in French Soma-
liland, on the frontier with Libya, and even possibly in Tunisia. But Reynaud insisted that nothing should be done without consulting the British.
On 28 May, after three days of discussions, the British cabinet finally came
down against Halifax. The British answer to Daladier was unambiguous:
offering territorial concessions to Mussolini would only whet his appetite,
would be disastrous for Allied public opinion, and must be avoided at all
costs. Daladier's telegram was never sent.

It is symptomatic of years of Anglo-French misunderstanding that they
should never have agreed on Italy: in 1935 it was the British who pressured
the French to accept sanctions against Italy after the invasion of Abyssinia;
in 1938 it was the French who resisted British urging to be more accom-
modating to Italy over its imperial demands; in 1939 it was Britain who
scotched France's Balkan projects, largely in order not to alienate Italy; in
1940 it was Britain who vetoed desperate French suggestions to buy off
Mussolini at almost any price. Attempting to bribe Italy at this stage would
certainly have got nowhere. As one French commentator put it: '[Y]ou can't
attempt a Munich after a Sedan.'[29] Italian policy was pragmatic. Ciano told
the French Ambassador on 2 June: '[H]ave some victories . . . and you will
have us with you.'[30] Italy finally entered the war on 10 June, but from the
end of May the possibility of an Italian solution to France's dilemma had
been ruled out. Reynaud, who had probably never really favoured this idea,
had to think of something else.

## 29 May–9 June: Reynaud's Alternative

At the War Committee of 25 May Reynaud had not questioned Weygand's order to hold the Somme/Aisne line 'without thought of retreat'. He did not immediately grasp that by offering no fall-back positions of any kind, this strategy closed off future political options. Weygand made this even more explicit in a memorandum that he submitted to Reynaud on 29 May. Now Reynaud realized his mistake in not having challenged Weygand's military decisions, and he replied with a memorandum of his own requesting Weygand to study the possibility of setting up a defensive bridgehead in the Brittany peninsula.

This idea of a 'Breton redoubt' was discussed on various occasions over the next ten days. Weygand was totally dismissive, and so was Villelume who ridiculed it as 'all very grand, very noble, very "Twilight of the Gods" ... but chimerical'.[31] De Gaulle and Spears were keen, and so, when he heard about it, was Churchill. But it was not taken seriously by the British military, who saw just another trap from which they would have to prepare yet another evacuation. Even Mandel, one of the members of Reynaud's government most firmly opposed to an armistice, considered the scheme to be impracticable. It does not seem that when Reynaud first broached the idea, he conceived of it as a possible stepping stone towards taking the conflict abroad. Rather he saw Brittany as the last stand of the Allied armies.

It was on 29 May that Reynaud also raised for the first time the prospect of sending two classes of conscripts to North Africa. Over the next few days Reynaud returned to this idea, and it gradually came to replace the Breton redoubt as his alternative to Weygand's proposal. But neither Weygand nor the naval leaders did anything to prepare the ground for such a plan and constantly emphasized its impracticability.

To strengthen his position, Reynaud reshuffled his government again on 5 June. Two 'defeatists', Lucien Lamoureux, the Finance Minister, and de Monzie, were sacked, along with Daladier (who went with very bad grace). All those who might still have favoured approaching Italy had now gone. Reynaud also brought in de Gaulle as Under-Secretary of State for National Defence to liaise with the British about transferring men and supplies to North Africa. But if Reynaud had really wanted to construct a government unanimously committed to resistance, he continued to display curiously bad judgement or weakness. He retained Chautemps, promoted Baudouin to be Under-Secretary of State for Foreign Affairs, and brought in as Finance Minister the competent civil servant Yves Bouthillier, whose pessimism about the war was no secret. The British Ambassador thought that the government was hardly more 'firm' than the one Reynaud had started with in March.[32] For the next few days political developments awaited the outcome of the fighting on the Somme and Aisne. But behind the scenes the atmosphere became more venomous. Pétain told Baudouin, who entirely agreed, that the Popular Front was responsible for France's troubles, and that the army must be saved to reconstruct the nation. On the day that battle opened on the Somme, Weygand commented: '[W]hat we are paying for is twenty years of blunders and neglect. It is out of the question to punish the generals and not the teachers who have refused to develop in the children a sense of patriotism and sacrifice.' As yet these were only private conversations, but three weeks later they would become an agenda for government. For conservatives who had been traumatized by the events of the 1930s, explanations for France's misfortunes offered themselves readily.[33]

By 10 June any hope of holding the Somme/Aisne line was dashed; the government embarked upon its ramshackle exodus from Paris. On the next day Churchill flew to France for a meeting at the Château du Muguet (Weygand's temporary residence) in Briare. There were two fractious meetings at Briare on the evening of 11 June and again the next morning. Relations were strained between the British and French, but even more so between Reynaud and Weygand. There were the usual French demands that the British throw all their planes into the struggle, even though Weygand made it abundantly clear that, in his eyes, the battle was over. Churchill's attempts to reinvigorate the French fell on deaf ears. When he conjured up a vivid picture of the French defending Paris street by street, 'the French perceptibly froze'.[34] He was told that Paris had been declared an open city. Nothing was decided at this meeting. There was talk of the Breton redoubt, none of North Africa. Although the word 'armistice' had not been uttered, it hung menacingly over the meeting. Churchill, however, left with an assurance that France would decide nothing irrevocable without consulting him.

## 12–16 June: Reynaud v. Weygand

It was later that evening at Cangé, after Churchill's departure, that Weygand formally proposed an armistice to the government. The debate was now in the open, and Reynaud's government entered its final stages. As we have already seen, on the next day Churchill paid his last visit to France for the meeting at Tours. Later that evening there was another meeting at Cangé in which Pétain too came out in favour of an armistice.

On 14 June, the political discussions were suspended because the government was again on the move—this time to Bordeaux—and because it had been agreed with Churchill at Tours to take no definitive decisions before Reynaud received a reply to his telegram appealing to Roosevelt for help. There was no one so desperate on the Allied side as to believe that the Americans were suddenly about to enter the war, but the approach to Roosevelt served various purposes. For the British it was a delaying tactic to win a few more precious hours. Those favouring an armistice hoped that a negative reply from Roosevelt would deprive their opponents of a valuable trump card. In Reynaud's eyes, the telegram was 'for the record', as Bullitt put it, a gesture for the history books.

By the morning of 15 June most members of the government had arrived in Bordeaux. Although at least the government was now in one place rather than scattered around the Loire, this also made it easier for Reynaud's opponents to concert their activities. The Mayor of Bordeaux, Adrien Marquet, was very favourable to them, and did all he could to smooth their path: Laval was given a suite in the best hotel, the Splendide (which meant kicking out the Queen of Portugal), and an office in the Town Hall. The British Ambassador, on the other hand, was quartered 50 km outside the city (until Mandel found him a hotel closer at hand). In the crowded streets of the city, teeming with refugees, rumours spread fast, hatreds were magnified, and xenophobia and anti-semitism were rife.

Although no answer had yet been received from Roosevelt, the government met again on the afternoon of 15 June. Before the meeting Reynaud had another stormy encounter with Weygand. Reynaud said he wanted to follow the Dutch example where the commander-in-chief had declared a ceasefire in the field while the government went abroad to continue the struggle. Weygand told Reynaud he would disobey such an order. His view was that the Dutch analogy was inappropriate, since a monarch could be said to represent the nation in a way that was inconceivable of the head of some ephemeral Third Republic government: '[O]nce the head of government in France has gone,' alleged Weygand, 'he is soon replaced and forgotten.' Weygand claimed that Reynaud was trying to shift responsibility for the defeat from the politicians to the military; he, of course, was trying to do the opposite. Weygand had now moved into open defiance of the government, but Reynaud hesitated to dismiss him—though he now excluded him from cabinet meetings.

At the cabinet meeting following this altercation, four hours of discussion made no progress towards reaching a decision—the fact that the government was supposed to be waiting on Roosevelt seemed to have been forgotten—until Chautemps offered a way forward. He observed that if the government were to go abroad, it was necessary to prepare public opinion by establishing that any proposed armistice terms were unacceptable. Otherwise departure abroad would seem like desertion. Chautemps's solution was not formally to request an armistice but to ascertain what the potential conditions of an armistice would be. Although Chautemps, one of the great political fixers of Third Republic politics, presented his proposal as a means of helping the government to continue fighting, in reality this was entirely disingenuous since for the past three weeks he had been privately expressing his view that France should get out of the war. This ingenious compromise seemed to meet with the approval of the majority of the government. Reynaud, who could see that it was a slippery slope—as he pointed out, there was no difference between asking for the *terms* of an armistice and asking for an armistice—said he preferred to resign rather than accept it. In the end, Reynaud agreed that he would ask the British if they would allow France to proceed down this path. After the meeting, Weygand, who had been pacing up and down outside the room, launched another attack on Reynaud, screaming at him at the top of his voice in the presence of several eyewitnesses.

On the morning of 16 June, Reynaud conferred with the Presidents of the Senate and Chamber, Jules Jeanneney and Édouard Herriot, about the legal aspects of moving the government abroad. There was another cabinet meeting at 11 a.m. Pétain threatened to resign unless the government agreed to ask for an armistice at once, but he was prevailed upon to wait at least until the British view had been ascertained. The meeting was adjourned until 5 p.m. After it Reynaud had another violent row with Weygand, who again refused to obey orders. At about midday, Roosevelt's reply to Reynaud's telegram finally arrived. He offered little more than sympathy, but the key question now was how the British would react to Reynaud's request of the previous evening.

The British government was unsure how to respond. To refuse outright might have been the best way of reinforcing the position of the anti-armistice faction. But if the French government decided to go ahead with an armistice anyway, the British would have lost any leverage over it. So London's initial reaction was to accede to the French request providing that beforehand the French agreed to transfer their fleet into British ports. Almost as soon as this decision had been communicated to Reynaud in the early afternoon, it was overtaken by a telephone call that Reynaud received at 4.30 p.m. from London. At the other end of the line was de Gaulle, who was in London liaising with the British about a move to North Africa. Speaking from 10 Downing Street, de Gaulle read down the telephone to Reynaud a project to transform the Anglo-French alliance into a complete political union between the two countries. This extraordinary document had been drawn up hastily in London, with the enthusiastic support of Churchill, in the hope that it would reinforce the position of the anti-armistice group. Reynaud himself seemed buoyed up with hope on hearing the proposal. He quickly came down to earth once the cabinet reconvened at 5.00 p.m. The idea of Franco-British union fell on stony ground. Why, said Pétain, should France want to 'fuse with a corpse'? Discussion reverted to the Chautemps proposal and the armistice. Reynaud, sensing that the tide of opinion was running against him, announced that he wished to confer with the President of the Republic, and that the meeting would reconvene at 10.00 p.m.

Seeing Lebrun alone, Reynaud told him that since there was no longer a majority in the cabinet against an armistice, he had decided to tender his resignation. Having failed to dissuade Reynaud from this course, Lebrun called in Herriot and Jeanneney, the Presidents of the two Chambers of Parliament, to consult them, in conformity with the Constitution, as to whom he should appoint to succeed Reynaud as premier. They were both hostile to an armistice, and had also been worked on by Spears and Campbell. They counselled Lebrun to keep Reynaud, but not it seems very vigorously. In the end, seemingly convinced that he could not resist the pressure for an armistice, Lebrun decided that he had no alternative but to appoint Pétain. When the ministers reassembled at 10.00 p.m., they were informed that Reynaud had resigned and Pétain had been asked to form the next government.

## 16 June: Reynaud's Resignation

Reynaud lived for the rest of his life with the knowledge that his resignation had let in Pétain and removed the final obstacle to the signing of an armistice. Over the next twenty years, he offered ever more convoluted justifications of his conduct in these dramatic days.

In the hours immediately after his resignation he seems almost to have been in denial about the implications of what he had done. Spears was amazed to discover that Reynaud was still expecting to attend a meeting planned to take place between himself and Churchill at Concarneau in

Brittany on 17 June. It was quickly indicated to him that since he was no longer head of the government the meeting would not proceed. Churchill, who had just boarded the train at Waterloo when the news of Reynaud's resignation came through, abandoned the trip. 'I returned to Downing Street with a heavy heart', he writes. The only conceivable reason that Reynaud can have had for thinking that a meeting might still occur between himself and Churchill was the possibility that Pétain's government might have been presented with armistice terms that were too harsh to be acceptable, thus allowing Reynaud to return at the head of a new government committed to fighting from abroad. Reynaud subsequently claimed that he had nursed such an idea, but if this is really true, he was indulging in serious wishful thinking.

The real question, however, is whether Reynaud had really been obliged to resign. He did so because he apparently believed that the majority of the cabinet was against him. Since no formal vote had been taken, it is impossible to know for sure if this was true, but three ministers from his government—two of them his supporters and one an opponent—later testified that there would probably have been a small majority opposed to seeking an armistice. In the face of this evidence, after the war Reynaud changed his own defence. He argued that what mattered was not so much the number of his opponents as their political weight. What did a numerical majority matter if the minority included figures of the stature of Pétain, Chautemps, and Weygand (who was not, of course, in the cabinet)?

Reynaud did have the support, from outside the cabinet, of both Herriot and Jeanneney, whose positions gave them a certain weight, but they did not push his case very forcefully. Jeanneney, aged 76, was quite frail. President Lebrun also seems to have been opposed to an armistice, but he lacked the courage of whatever convictions he had. Within the government, one of the most vociferous opponents of the armistice, de Gaulle, was only an extremely junior minister who was anyway absent in London on 16 June. The politically most important member of the government to be opposed to an armistice was Georges Mandel. About his strength of character and convictions there was no doubt, but he played a somewhat background role in the final crisis. Mandel had started his career as Clemenceau's political hatchet man in 1917–18—'I fart and Mandel stinks' was how Clemenceau put it—and went on to be an independent conservative MP in the interwar years. He was devoted to Clemenceau's memory and to the style of uncompromising patriotism he represented. Like Clemenceau, he was instinctively Anglophile and he was one of the politicians in whom the British put most hope in these final days. But Mandel had also inherited

Clemenceau's bottomless contempt for the folly of humankind. Spears's memoirs are peppered with Mandel's caustic observations on his fellow politicians. Of Lebrun, he observed: '[H]e raises his hands to heaven and weeps.' Of Chautemps, he said: '[I]n that wonderful voice of his he depicts the misery of the refugees in their cars. He always ends by giving a heartrending account of the poor old grandmother in the back seat weighed down with babies and a cage full of canaries.'[35] But Mandel had none of the inspirational qualities that allowed Clemenceau to believe that only he could overcome the deficiencies of his fellows. He had been a brilliant number two, but never a leader. If Clemenceau was galvanized by his cynicism, Mandel was paralysed by his.

Mandel is the only Frenchman for whom Spears seems to have had unreserved admiration, but even he found Mandel's cold unflappability, his strange fishy eyes, most disconcerting: 'He was so detached that when he spoke he might have been a biologist informing a colleague of the strange antics of some lower form of animal when submitted to an unusual test.' Baudouin, an enemy, had the same impression: 'a fortress of contempt whose eyes of ice are amused to observe in his colleagues fear and a mediocrity which exceeded even his most pessimistic expectations'.[36] Mandel was also inhibited by the fact that he was Jewish. In the increasingly xenophobic and anti-Semitic atmosphere of Bordeaux, a Jew who argued in favour of leaving French territory was liable to be accused of desertion.

In the end, then, Reynaud felt himself very much alone in June 1940. His resolution was certainly worn down systematically by some of his closest advisers such as Baudouin and Villelume. As early as 26 May, Spears had identified Villelume as 'the nigger in the fence [sic] as far as Reynaud is concerned'. He was 'the pessimist who, fat and sly, sits next door to him, pouring defeatism in his ears.... If he is half as dishonest as he looks, he has Fagin beat by furlongs.'[37] There was also Mme de Portes, who in these last days seems to have been everywhere. Bullitt, who resented the fact that he did not enjoy the same rapport with Reynaud as he had with Daladier, told Roosevelt on 6 June that Reynaud was 'completely dominated' by de Portes. On the next day Reynaud tried to get her to leave the room when he was sending his telegram to Roosevelt, 'but she came right in and when he ordered her out of the room, refused to go'. The only job to be done now, Bullitt concluded, is 'flattering the King's mistress'.[38] On 14 June, Mme de Portes, in the company of Villelume, took the extraordinary initiative of going to see the American diplomat Anthony Biddle. Implying falsely that they were speaking for Reynaud, the two of them told him that the military situation was now so serious that Reynaud believed his telegram

17. Georges Mandel (1885–1944).
Spears, who admired him,
commented: 'If it was possible to like a
fish I should have been fond of
Mandel. For he was like a fish if you
could imagine one with straight
damp locks of black hair hanging like
seaweed over its gills.'

appealing to Roosevelt for help was now out of date and should be ignored.
An armistice was the only solution. Biddle offered Mme de Portes a
handkerchief to dry her tears, but did not believe what she had told him.

On the next evening (15 June), while de Portes and Villelume were
dining with Reynaud, the discussion became so heated that Reynaud ended
up throwing two glasses of water over her. When Spears, at the Château de
Chissay, asked to see a particular telegram from London, it could not at
first be found, and then supposedly turned up in her bed. On 16 June, while
Spears was talking to Reynaud, she kept poking her head round the door.
At the very least, this constant pressure on Reynaud must have been wearing. The First Secretary of the US Embassy, Freeman Matthews, who on
one occasion had Mme de Portes 'an hour weeping in my office to get us to
urge Reynaud to sign an Armistice', wrote afterwards: 'Mr Biddle and I saw
Reynaud at least four times a day during his last few days as Prime Minister; never once did we see him that Hélène de Portes was not just coming
out of or going into his office.' As Reynaud himself once put it: 'Ah! You do
not know what a man who has been hard at work all day will put up with to
make sure of an evening's peace.'[39]

Reynaud was at the end of his tether, and his mood oscillated alarmingly.

On the morning of 13 June Spears thought he showed 'every sign of resolution and firmness'; by the evening he looked 'ghastly, with a completely unnatural expression, still and white'; on 14 June he seemed 'forlorn . . . too tired and bewildered to be rational'; he seemed 'pale and washed out' after the meeting on 15 June, and 'still nervously exhausted' the next morning; but immediately after his resignation he had 'the barely suppressed gaiety of a man relieved to be shed of a terrible burden'. Others noted the same. As de Gaulle wrote later: 'only those who were eyewitnesses of it can measure what the ordeal of being in power meant during that terrible period. It was a tragic spectacle to see this man of such worth unjustly crushed by events beyond his control.'

Reynaud's elaborate apologias ultimately do him more harm than what was probably the truth: although wobbling occasionally (as on his return from London on 26 May), he was genuinely opposed to the armistice but lacked the inner conviction that there was a viable alternative to it. If Reynaud had rejected the armistice and gone abroad with the government, a dissident government formed by Pétain on French soil would certainly have enjoyed greater moral authority in the eyes of the French public. No Third Republic premier in June 1940 could have counted in the balance against Pétain once he and Weygand had decided to save the reputation of the army at the expense of the reputation of the Republic. If Reynaud had gone abroad he would, unlike de Gaulle, have been able to claim the legal status of a head of government, but like de Gaulle, he would have had to reconquer a genuine legitimacy for himself. Reynaud's tragedy in 1940 was that, having failed, in an impossible situation, to be the new Clemenceau, he also missed the chance to be de Gaulle. Reynaud never forgave himself for that.

# 4

# THE FRENCH PEOPLE AT WAR

## 17 June 1940: Georges Friedmann in Niort

AT midday on 17 June, the day after Reynaud's resignation, Pétain made his first radio speech as Prime Minister:

At the request of the President of the Republic, I assume the leadership of the government of France starting today. Certain of the affection of our admirable army, which has fought with a heroism worthy of its long military traditions against an enemy superior in numbers and in arms. Certain that it has through its magnificent resistance fulfilled our duties towards our allies; certain of the support of the war veterans whom I had the honour to command; certain of the confidence of the entire French people. . . . It is with a heavy heart that I say to you today that it is necessary to cease fighting. I have this evening approached the enemy to ask if he is ready to try to find, between soldiers, with the struggle over and in honour, the means to put an end to the hostilities.[1]

When this speech was printed in the papers the next day, the words 'cease fighting' were changed to 'try to cease fighting'. Since an armistice had not yet been signed, to order soldiers to stop fighting already would have destroyed the last shreds of bargaining power left to the French government. Even so, few who heard Pétain's broadcast can have had any doubts that the battle was over.

There is a famous French film of the autumn of 1940 depicting a village community gathered around the radio to hear Pétain's speech. The reality was very different. As the German wave crashed over France, the French people, whether soldiers in retreat or civilian refugees, found themselves washed up all over the country. Lieutenant Georges Friedmann, in civilian life a philosopher, found himself in Niort; south of the Loire:

At half past midday, during lunch, Pétain announces the cessation of hostilities. The overture of negotiations for an armistice. I was expecting it. But still it is a terrible shock. That idiot L. can't resist throwing in his opinion: 'the politicians have fled the ships like rats.' But the others say nothing, devastated. Ten men remain together silently face to face, and once the meal is over they get up without having said a word.

A few days later Friedmann reflected on the deeper meaning of what he had witnessed over the last six weeks:

A whole country seems suddenly to have given itself up. Everything has collapsed, imploded. The 'refugees' (how few of them really deserve the name), the runaways, the panic-stricken, the pitiable herds of civilians are still in the village streets, the town squares and the roads, mixed in with the debris of the most powerful army—so we were told—in Europe. One sees women perched on gun carriages, where dishevelled ordinary soldiers are mixed up with civilians. It is true that not all images of these weeks have been so shameful and I know that one could find others. But I am convinced that they would not be the dominant ones.... Today, among many French people, I do not detect any sense of pain at the misfortunes of their country: during the days of this perfectly pure summer in these villages, towns and camp stations of Limousin, Périgord, and Guyenne, among so many civilians and soldiers ... I have only observed a sort of complacent relief (sometimes even exalted relief), a kind of base atavistic satisfaction at the knowledge that 'for us it's over' ... without caring about anything else.[2]

Friedmann's words certainly seem to match the experience of Captain Georges Sadoul, in civilian life a writer and journalist, who found himself on 16 June in Sully-sur-Loire. In front of the church he spotted a group of refugees who had been sleeping on straw in front of the porch:

I get down from the lorry. A woman speaks to me. I answer her. Then there are thirty of them at me, asking my advice, because I am a man, because I am in uniform, and because for hours they have found no one who can tell them anything.... One woman, red with anger and excitement, shouts out: 'what are you waiting for, you soldiers, to stop this war? It's got to stop. Do you want them to massacre us all with our children ... why are you still fighting? That Reynaud, if I could get hold of him, the scoundrel!'[3]

The kind of scenes witnessed by Friedmann and Sadoul took place all over France in the last days before the armistice. They suggest that, whatever the errors of France's military leaders, the deficiencies of its allies, or the defects of its political system, another possible reason for the defeat of 1940 was that the French people, whether soldiers or civilians, were not prepared to sacrifice themselves for the cause of the country as they had been in 1914. This was certainly the view of Gamelin, who managed to find the time on 18 May to draft a report for Daladier on the causes of the German breakthrough. Exempting himself from any responsibility, Gamelin pinned the blame for the defeat on the ordinary soldier:

The French soldier, yesterday's citizen, did not believe in the war.... Disposed to criticize ceaselessly anyone holding the slightest amount of authority, and encouraged in the name of civilization to enjoy a soft daily life, he did not receive the kind of moral and patriotic education which would have prepared him for the drama in which the nation's destiny will be played out.... The regrettable instances of looting by our troops at numerous points on the front offer manifest proof of ... this indiscipline.... Too many of them have failed to do their duty in battle.[4]

To what extent was this criticism justified? In what ways was the attitude of the French population different from 1914?

## Remembering 1914

The comparison with 1914 was in many people's minds when war was declared in September 1939. William Bullitt wrote: '[T]he whole mobilisation was carried out in absolute quiet. The men left in silence. There were no bands, no songs. No shouts of "On to Berlin" and "Down with Hitler" to match the shouts of "On to Berlin" and "Down with the Kaiser" in 1914.' In 1914, the words 'To Berlin' had been chalked on the sides of many trains; in 1939, Georges Sadoul saw them only once on the side of a lorry, but he saw many others daubed with the words 'goodbye to love' or 'here go the men without women'.[5]

1914 was more than a memory. Most newly mobilized soldiers in 1939 found themselves passing through the killing-fields of that previous conflict as they set off to join their units. Private Gustave Folcher, a farmer from the Languedoc, had to cross almost the whole country to join his regiment on the Moselle. Looking out of the window as his train headed towards Metz, he saw 'a huge cemetery with the crosses laid out in lines, left over from the war of 1914, which doesn't do much to cheer us up'. Some weeks later, while on a training exercise, he visited an American cemetery near Thiancourt (near Belfort):

It is in silence that we leave this immense field of rest thinking of the thousands of men who sleep there, so far from their families, of their sad fate and of that which awaits us, for it is not encouraging for us in the situation in which we find ourselves to see almost everywhere these vast cemeteries of white or black crosses.[6]

Georges Friedmann was drafted into an ambulance unit near Laon. Travelling between Rheims and Laon on 10 September 1939, he noted:

We journey through all these villages, hills and forts whose names I had so often read as a child in the communiqués during the last war. Our driver, a prosperous local farmer from the area, knows every inch of the land. Here, he tells us, a section of *chasseurs* was destroyed by a machine gun nest; there a massive, a monstrous hole, its sides quite bare, reminds him that two companies were killed by a German mine in 1916; and along the road, here and there, we pass large fields planted with neat crosses.... All these names that were for me only names, fill with images: Craonne, Berry-au-Bac, le Chemin des Dames.

A month later Friedmann had a very disturbing encounter. Having set off on an expedition to pick mushrooms, he and a companion came across a lumberjack, about 60 years old, who seemed not to understand anything they said:

Then suddenly he begins to speak, in rapid and jerky phrases, in a dull voice, and tells us that he had been in the war. He had been at the Somme, in Alsace, at Douaumont (Verdun), where he was buried for a whole night in a shell hole. The next morning he could hardly hear any more: he was told that he would hear again once he was far from the shells. But it got worse and worse. He never heard again. He looks at our uniforms for a moment. And then, laying aside his axe, with an astonishing agility, he throws himself on the ground, mimes an attack, crawls forward, takes a branch to serve as his gun, puts it to his shoulder, fires, and then slowly, cautiously raises his head, as if in a trench, to see the result, loads his weapon, charges forward, throws himself to the ground.... This man of the forest relives his combats, perhaps he has lived with them, and only with them, for 25 years.

They ask if he has an invalidity pension, but he cannot hear the question. They try writing the question, but he cannot read. They leave him with a 'reflex "au revoir" which is lost in the night'.[7]

## A Pacifist Nation

If this individual, eternally immured in his memories of the war, was a particularly sad relic, there were few French men or women in the inter-war years who did not live to some degree in the shadow of the Great War. 1.3 million Frenchmen had died in that conflict, and over 1 million survivors had been left as invalids. There were over 600,000 widows and over 750,000 orphans. The bodies of many who had died in the conflict were never recovered. At Verdun, scene of the most murderous battle of the war, a massive ossuary was built to commemorate those 300,000 soldiers whose bodies had never been found or identified. In every one of the 30,000 towns and villages of France, war memorials were built to honour the dead. These memorials still have the power to move us today; so much the more must this have been the case in the 1930s when they were so new, and so many living people remembered the names inscribed upon them.

Unlike Britain and Germany, France had also suffered from the fact that the war had largely been fought on its territory. By 1918 many cities in the north-eastern region of the country had been reduced to rubble; much rich agricultural land resembled a lunar landscape. One observer wrote in 1919: '[I]t is only after travelling day after day in an automobile through village after village and town after town, often where nothing is standing erect more than a few feet above the ground, that one can begin to have any conception of the enormousness of the destruction.' The war zone was, in the words of another post-war witness, 'a desert . . . corpses of horses, corpses of trees covering the corpses of men'.[8] Some villages had disappeared forever. Still today there are fatalities almost every year from farmers coming across live shells. While the tracks for France's high-speed train were being laid in 1990, 23 tonnes of unexploded shells were recovered in the Somme department. The rebuilding of this devastated area was one of the most remarkable achievements of the much-criticized Third Republic. By 1927 reconstruction was complete. Those ten years saw the rebuilding of some 800,000 farm dwellings, 20,500 public buildings, and 61,000 km of roads; over 3 million hectares of land had been cleared of barbed wire, trenches, and shells.

It is hardly surprising, therefore, that France had emerged from the war a profoundly pacifist society. Pacifism took various forms. There were ideological pacifists, especially among left-wing intellectuals and Socialists, who subscribed to a philosophical rejection of war in any circumstances. Such was the case, for example, of the novelist Jean Giono, who had been gassed in the war and almost lost his sight. 'There is no glory in being French,' wrote Giono, 'there is only one glory: to be alive.' In 1937 he published a collection of articles, *Refus d'obéissance*, which advocated desertion if war broke out. Pacifism of this kind was also widespread among the public sector workers, especially the postal workers and the 100,000 members of the primary schoolteachers (*instituteurs*) union (SNI). Among those who contributed to the SNI newspaper was the writer Léon Emery who coined the phrase 'rather servitude than war'.

One of the most famous pacifists was Émile Chartier (known as Alain), whose position as teacher of philosophy at the famous Parisian *lycée* Henri IV gave him enormous influence over generations of young intellectuals, many of them, like Jean-Paul Sartre, destined for the elite École Normale Supérieure (ENS). If one ideology prevailed at the ENS in the inter-war years, it was pacifism. A big issue among students was whether they would

agree to undergo the special training course (Préparation Militaire Supérieure (PMS)), which allowed those pursuing higher education to perform
their military service as officers. The PMS was obligatory in institutions
like the ENS, but in 1928 a majority of pupils signed a petition protesting
against this. The future philosopher Raymond Aron, a signatory, recalls
that he purposely failed his PMS course. Many *instituteurs*, who would
normally have been expected to furnish a large contingent of reserve
officers, also refused to do the PMS.

Those who subscribed to this uncompromising pacifism placed it above
patriotism or Republicanism or indeed any ideology. Their patriotism had
died in the mud of Verdun. But this extreme position was held by only a
small minority, although an influential one. Most people subscribed to a
kind of bruised patriotism that went hand in hand with a profound sense of
the horror of war and a desperate desire to avoid it at almost any cost. This
was the spirit of the Armistice Day ceremonies, which took place each year
around the war memorial of every community in France on 11 November. It
was sentiments of this kind that inspired the leading peasant organizations
and war veterans associations. They did not reject patriotism, but they lived
in the hope of reconciliation with Germany. This idealism was exploited by

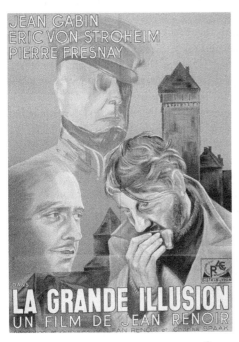

18. Jean Renoir's *La Grande Illusion*,
one of the most popular films of
1937, was the culmination of a
whole series of inter-war anti-war
films, starting with Abel Gance's
*J'Accuse* (1919). The 'Grand Illusion'
is the idea that war solves anything.
The film was banned in 1939

the Nazi regime, which sent an envoy to Paris to encourage pro-German feeling in France. This was Otto Abetz, a former German art teacher with a French wife. In 1934 Abetz organized a meeting between Hitler and two French war veterans' leaders; in 1935 he set up a Franco-German Committee (CFA), which published a review and organized cultural and youth exchanges.

Pacifism and sympathy with Germany also existed in inter-war Britain. What was specific to France, however, was another current of pacifism born out of a sense that France's vital energies had been sapped by the war. This was a pacifism rooted in exhaustion, in deep pessimism—or realism—about whether France could survive another bloodletting on the scale of the Great War. The French birth rate had been declining since the beginning of the nineteenth century. In 1800 France was the most populous country in Europe; by 1900 it had been overtaken by Germany and Britain. Thus the French casualties of about 4.1 million men in the Great War represented 10.5 per cent of the working male population—a higher proportion than in any other belligerent nation except Serbia. Even that uncompromising French nationalist, Georges Clemenceau, had declared after signing the Versailles Treaty that no treaty would guarantee France's security if the French people did not start to have more children. It was these kinds of considerations that underlay the 'realism' of many French conservatives in the 1930s. The conservative deputy Louis Marin (who was in fact to be one of the members of Reynaud's government who opposed the armistice) declared at the time of Munich that France could not permit itself the luxury of a Battle of the Marne every twenty years.

These different strands of pacifism all came together at the time of the Munich agreement. A petition, headed 'We don't want war', was produced in September by the leaders of the SNI and the postal workers' unions. It obtained some 150,000 signatures. Trade unionists like the SNI leader André Delmas worked behind the scenes with conservative politicians like Flandin to lobby against war. When Daladier landed at Le Bourget after returning from Munich there was a large crowd to acclaim him. Chamberlain was equally popular. There was a brief vogue for buying Chamberlain umbrellas—which people called 'mon chamberlain'—and one paper set up a fund to buy him a country house in France. An opinion poll in October 1939, the first ever undertaken in France, showed that Munich was approved by 57 per cent of the population.

Munich was the high point of inter-war pacifism. The fund to purchase a house for Chamberlain closed after a month with only £1,500 received, and the supply of umbrellas outstripped demand. From the start of 1939, the

19. Crowds cheering Daladier after Munich. He is shown here standing in his car in front of the Madeleine Church. When Daladier's plane, returning from Munich, approached the airport, he was convinced the crowds had come to boo him. When he saw that the opposite was true, he muttered: 'the idiots'

balance of public opinion shifted dramatically, and the all-out pacifists, instead of representing the most radical wing of the moderate pacifist majority, found themselves isolated. The congresses of the two biggest war veterans' associations, which had been ardently pro-Munichois, registered a more belligerent stance in the spring of 1939. The peasant press that had been fervently pacifist in 1938 was no longer so in 1939. In May, the former Socialist Marcel Déat, an ardent pacifist, wrote an article entitled 'Do you really want to die for Danzig?' His appeal was largely ignored or condemned. Within the Socialist Party, Blum's supporters now triumphed over the pacifist wing at the Congress of May 1939. Already the poll taken after Munich had shown that 70 per cent of the respondents favoured resisting further German demands. In July 1939 another poll showed that 70 per cent of the population was ready to resist a German move against Danzig, by force if necessary. There were many reasons for this change of mood: the feeling, after March 1939, that Hitler had proved he could no longer be trusted; the patriotic mood created by Mussolini's sabre-rattling demands for French colonies; the economic recovery that had started at the end of 1938; the popularity of Daladier. When war was declared in September 1939, the pacifist movement, so powerful a year earlier, seemed to have collapsed entirely. A manifesto calling for 'immediate peace' was published by the anarchist Louis Lecoin ten days after the declaration of war. The thirty-one signatories included all the usual suspects of the pacifist left, but after it was published many of them retracted their support, claiming that they had been misled about the use he intended to make of their names. Giono was put in prison for tearing down mobilization posters. The fact that pacifism could no longer be expressed openly did not mean that it had entirely disappeared on either right or left. On 30 August 1939, the headline of the extreme right-wing newspaper *Je suis partout* proclaimed 'Down with War. Long live France!'. In the Socialist Party, pacifists like Paul Faure went into a kind of internal exile. Another Socialist, Ludovic Zoretti, ran a semi-clandestine newspaper, *Redressement*, which expressed the unreconstructed pacifism of many Socialists. But these were isolated voices which certainly, for the moment at least, expressed the view of only a small minority. France in 1939 was still a pacifist society, but one which had accepted, reluctantly, the necessity of war.

## Going to War: 'Something between Resolution and Resignation'

The French people may not have demonstrated great enthusiasm for war in 1939, but they did not show much opposition to it either. As in 1914, the number of soldiers refusing the call-up was tiny. 'Resolution', 'gravity', and 'calm' were the words most frequently used by the Prefects to describe the attitude of the population. 'Something between resolution and resignation' reported the Prefect of the Rhône. William Bullitt's comment, quoted above, contrasting the situation in 1939 with 1914 went on to say of 1939 that 'there was no hysterical weeping of mothers and sisters and children. The self-control and quiet courage has been so far beyond the usual standard of the human race that it has a dream quality.' The British Ambassador talked of the population's 'quiet determination'. Of course such observers often saw what they wanted to see and their testimonies must be treated with caution. In plotting the evolution of opinion towards the war one must be sensitive to rapid shifts of mood, and to differences between different sections of the population.[9]

Even after the declaration of war, many people still hoped for peace. As one observer wrote of the war as he left to join his unit: 'We knew war was coming since it was bound to come, but at heart one thought it might not come. And now 90% of people still think that it will be possible to reach an arrangement. I think so too. We must.' But if people hoped for peace, they were determined to fight if it had to be war. That is certainly the impression one receives from the memoir of Gustave Folcher. Assigned to the 12th Regiment of Zouaves,[10] Folcher had spent much of the Phoney War on exercises, moving around frequently and eventually being assigned in March to a sector of the line behind the Ardennes. During these months his life consisted of long marches and endless digging. His exhaustion, homesickness, and boredom were relieved by companionship and by the excitement of seeing a region of France he had never visited before. He found many of the villages of the Moselle region dirty and unappealing, but the countryside often attractive. The events that really mattered in his life as a soldier were a proper night's sleep, a comfortable bed, a chance to put on clean clothes, 'good coffee with rum served by nice young girls'. What is striking about his narrative is the narrowness of its horizons. The military leaders, the politicians, the enemy, the principles for which the war is being fought—none of these intrude. The war is accepted as a job to be done. Sartre noted a similar indifference to the world outside his unit: 'I've never heard anyone mention Gamelin here. Never—not even to say something bad about him. He doesn't exist.'[11]

This was also how many regimental commanders read the mood of their men. The colonel commanding the 77RI observed in January 1940: 'Good morale. Not at all expansive, they give the impression of having little enthusiasm for this war. . . . But they are loyal, and like any good farmer, resigned to good and ill fortune, and one can be certain that they will hold out and will bring honour to the regiment.'[12] Was this so different from the world view of the *poilu* of 1914–18?

## Phoney War Blues

As the waiting war dragged on into winter, all those reporting to the government on the mood of the population detected a slump in morale. Among civilians, resentment was fuelled by rising prices (despite Reynaud's efforts). Peasants were angry that workers, often young, were being drafted from the front to the factories, while farms were allowed to fall into ruin. Once again it seemed that the peasants were being used as cannon fodder. There were floods of letters denouncing individuals who had obtained transfers from the front on allegedly fraudulent grounds. The mood in the factories was no better, even if they seemed a privileged haven to those outside them. Owing to Reynaud's tax increases many workers in the arms industries were now putting in between 60 and 70 hours a week with little financial reward. A non-skilled worker in the Paris region who had previously earned about 400F for a 40-hour week now found himself earning 420F for 60 hours. Wage levels were pegged but prices were rising. In October 1939 the CGT and employers had negotiated an agreement (the Majestic Accords) on industrial cooperation, but the reality of the factory floor was still one of class revenge for 1936. One diarist commented in February: 'I observe every day social divisions and class resentments which complicate and sully the conflict.'[13]

Among the soldiers at the front, the mood by December was reported to be one of 'veritable demoralization'. The winter was the coldest since 1889—temperatures fell to −24°C in the east—and there were not enough socks and blankets to go round all the soldiers. Most debilitating of all for morale was a growing sense of lassitude and boredom after months of forced inactivity. This problem was less serious in the front-line regiments, where troops were kept busy with intensive training, but for the reserves this was not always possible owing to the lack of sufficient modern equipment. Much time was spent digging defences with spades.

Three diaries from the period tell a similar story. First that of Jean-Paul Sartre:

26 November 1939: all the men who left with me were raring to go at the outset but now they are dying of boredom.

20 February 1940: The war machine is running in neutral; the enemy is elusive and invisible. . . . The whole army is waiting in that 'hesitant, timid' attitude the generals wanted to avoid like the plague. . . . And the truth is that this waiting . . . hasn't failed to have its effect. . . . Many people are hoping for an 'arrangement'. Only yesterday a sergeant was telling me, with a gleam of insane hope in his eyes: 'What I think is, it'll all be arranged, England will climb down'. Most of the men are fairly receptive to the Hitler propaganda. They're getting bored, morale, is sinking.

Secondly, Private Fernand Grenier:

15 November: Inactivity . . . The newspapers are less and less read; doubt has entered into people's minds; they believe less and less what the papers say . . . The total lack of organised distraction, the monotonous routine of this dull army life means that the tiniest, most insignificant government announcement arouses discontent.

27 November: very few military exercises. The men are getting bored.

Thirdly, Georges Sadoul:

13 December: The days pass, interminable and empty, without the slightest occupation, without any other obligation beyond presence at the roll-calls in the morning and at midday.... The surprising tranquillity of the front ought to reassure us, help us to put up with our semi-captivity, which is at least without risks. But it only irritates us more. Why not send us home since we are doing nothing and there is nothing to do? ... The officers, mainly reservists, think no differently from the men on this point. One feels they are weary of the war. They say and repeat that they would like to go home.

End January: militarily speaking we are doing literally nothing.... We are huddled around the stove, only going out for the two daily roll-calls. We are only provided with damp wood to heat ourselves.... We are so numbed with apathy and cold that many of us do not bother to wash, or to shave, to put on our shoes or even to undress properly when going to bed.... Departures on leave, and return from leave, are all that structure this life without incident. Most people return with their morale even worse than before.[14]

Sadoul's unit of reservists, made up primarily of Parisians, was perhaps not representative in its composition, but the army services monitoring the soldiers' correspondence picked up similar impressions. One typical letter of 20 February 1940 read: 'nothing new here. I am bored to death. All we do is wait. But wait for what? This is the life of an imbecile and I am beginning to be completely fed up with it. Oh, let it end soon.'[15] Thus, Sadoul was probably right when, having met other soldiers in the train during his leave, he reflected that 'our little microcosm ... is the barometer of a general mood'.

This deterioration of morale, both in the army and among civilians, was not ideologically motivated. The government was obsessed by Communism, but the effect of Communist propaganda was negligible. The Communists produced an underground copy of their newspaper L'Humanité (banned since September 1939) and a special newspaper for soldiers that was just a cyclostyled sheet. In fact although the Communists argued for an immediate peace on the grounds that the war was an imperialist conflict and against the interests of the French workers, they did not advocate revolutionary defeatism, desertion, or fraternization with the enemy (at least as long as the war was not against the Soviet Union), and told their members to obey orders and perform their duty—which seems to be what most of them did (Grenier and Sadoul were both Communists). But the relentless anti-Communist propaganda must have been enough to make some ordinary Communists wonder in what sense this was *their* war.

As for the factories, subsequent allegations that Communist-inspired workers carried out sabotage were largely groundless. The Communist Party did not in fact advocate sabotage, although it did urge the workers to protest against working conditions and slow down production. The only proven case of sabotage took place in the Farmann factory. It was the work of a tiny group of Communists—two of them brothers—acting on their own initiative. Three of them were shot on 22 June, just before the signing of the armistice. It is impossible to say if the production difficulties in certain arms factories were due to political motives. The shortfall in aircraft production in the Phoney War was attributed by one general to 'the nonchalance of the large majority of workers and the lack of authority of the cadres'.[16] But the most striking fact about the Phoney War was the total lack of industrial unrest: in the factories the labour force had never worked harder. In the whole of the Phoney War, only two cases of labour unrest were registered in the Renault factory. The mood, however, was certainly not one of enthusiasm. Even a very conservative employer like the steel magnate de Wendel worried that the logic of Reynaud's tax levies was operating as a disincentive to effort.

## Why Are We Fighting?

The Communist Party had been so weakened by government repression and by defections in the wake of the Molotov–Ribbentrop Pact that its anti-war propaganda had little impact. More serious, however, was the ineffectiveness of official propaganda in favour of the war. The army spent time organizing entertainments for the troops, but failed to explain why the war was being fought in the first place. Answering this question was supposedly the task of the Propaganda Commissariat, which had been created by Daladier in July 1939. It was headed by the writer Jean Giraudoux, who had made his reputation in the 1920s with works denouncing militarism and in favour of Franco-German reconciliation. His best-known work was the anti-war play *The Trojan War Will Not Take Place* (1935).

This was a curious pedigree for someone whose responsibility was to organize propaganda against Germany, and it was generally agreed that Giraudoux's Commissariat was a disaster. He recruited a galaxy of intellectual luminaries—the writer André Maurois, the director of the Bibliothèque Nationale, Julien Cain, the historian Paul Hazard—but he was no organizer, and his headquarters at the Hotel Continental was a den of intrigue, gossip, and infighting. Maurois soon gave up in disgust. The fastidious and literary tone of Giraudoux's radio broadcasts either passed over the heads of his listeners or alarmed them, as in his broadcast of

27 October evoking the 'the Angel of Death' stalking over the sleeping armies.

But Giraudoux did not have an easy task and was not to blame for all his problems. He did not have ministerial status, and his budget was small (minuscule compared to Goebbels's). The army did not take propaganda seriously. While the German High Command employed good photographers and released thousands of pictures to the press, the French army was more secretive; the press often had to be content with dull photographs of Parisians strolling in the Champs Élysées (it is also true, of course, that the Germans at least had some victories to boast about).

Giraudoux's main handicap, however, was that the government provided no guidance as to how it wanted him to present the war. A generation brought up on memories of First World War propaganda lies (*bourrage de crâne*) was predisposed to be suspicious. Sartre noted:

The public is so used to the idea of official lies that the speeches of Daladier and Chamberlain affirming their 'unshakeable resolution etc.' leave them cold.... There is an a priori suspicion towards the most innocent news in the papers—which derives from what they have been told about the '*bourrage de crâne*'.

Patriotic rhetoric on the model of 1914 would not have worked in 1940. As Folcher recounts: '[T]he CO, on parade, makes a little speech, in which he declares that our fathers in the other war, the Great one (this one presumably being the Small one), went to the trenches singing; which caused one of the men to reply that the few who returned came back crying.' Attempts to revive the famous First World War song La Madelon were totally unsuccessful. The most popular song of the Phoney War was the wistful love song 'J'attendrai' ('I will wait, day and night / I will wait always / I will wait your return'). Obscene songs were also popular. On one occasion Sadoul heard soldiers singing the tune of La Madelon but with the words 'Madelon! Madelon! Madelon!' replaced by 'Du croupion! Du croupion! Du croupion!' ['Arse, Arse, Arse']; on another occasion someone in the barracks who tried to sing Madelon and then the Marseillaise was shouted down on both occasions.[17]

What, after all, were Britain and France fighting for after the collapse of Poland? Presenting the war as an anti-Fascist crusade was ruled out by the government's desire to avoid any provocation of Italy (and to avoid alienating French conservatives). In a broadcast in October 1939 Daladier specifically declared that this was not a war against Fascism; the censors were instructed to bar any slighting references to Mussolini. In the end the ineffectiveness of propaganda reflected the divisions and uncertainties of the French people.

One vivid illustration of the failure of propaganda was the impact of the pro-German broadcasts by the French journalist Paul Ferdonnet broadcasting from Radio Stuttgart. Hitherto an insignificant figure on the fringes of the extreme right, Ferdonnet acquired notoriety when the government revealed his existence in October. The most effective theme of his broadcasts was that Britain would fight to the last Frenchman: 'Britain provides the machines, France provides the men.' It does not seem that many people actually heard the broadcasts—though it is surprising how much they are mentioned in diaries and memoirs of the period—but they contributed to a sort of psychosis about the existence of a fifth column. Ferdonnet would broadcast a piece of military information, and when it proved to be correct the rumour spread that he was being fed information by a team of spies, although he knew nothing that could not be gleaned from the French press. Rumours of his omniscience were demoralizing, and soldiers who had not heard his broadcasts often wrote home to announce, completely fallaciously, that some recent manoeuvre of their regiment had been announced beforehand on Radio Stuttgart. The British consul in Marseilles reported at the end of December:

The expression of dissatisfaction to be heard in the market places not infrequently takes the form so familiar to us from the German broadcasts that I fear German propaganda has had some success with the meridional people.... There are even some who refuse to believe that British troops are on the Western front and declare that no reliance can be placed in the newspapers.[18]

The government was fully aware of the poor state of morale, and Daladier's obsession with Finland was partly due to his need to offer the French population some kind of military success. Despite the capitulation of Finland, the mood did begin to improve during the spring. This had nothing to do with the replacement of Daladier by Reynaud, who was not popular in the country. After Reynaud took over, Sartre noted: 'The men here are reproaching Reynaud for not having said a word in his broadcast address about "the heroism of our valiant soldiers". "That Daladier, he'd never have missed that out!" they complain sadly.' The improvement in morale may have owed as much to the weather as anything else. The monitors of correspondence noted of one regiment on 23 April that only 13 out of 5,864 letters revealed an unsatisfactory attitude. In all the surveys of correspondence between 25 April and 10 May army morale was described as 'excellent', 'very good', or 'good'. Given that this positive estimation included the

55DI and the 71DI, both of which were to collapse dramatically at Sedan, one might question the value of such surveys. Obviously it is impossible to reach any kind of scientific precision with a notion as subjective and nebulous as 'morale'. Moods can change very quickly according to circumstances. The attitude of soldiers whose disaffection was born largely of boredom and lack of motivation could change overnight once the enemy attacked—once inactivity was replaced by a clear and palpable danger. What happened then would depend on how prepared the soldiers were to carry out the tasks allotted to them.[19]

## The French Army in 1940

The French army was not a monolithic organization.[20] There were huge differences in fighting quality between the active units, the twenty Series-A reserve divisions and the eighteen Series-B reserve divisions. After a period of active military service (eighteen months from 1923 to 1930, one year from 1930 to 1935, two years from 1935[21]), each adult male was liable for twenty-seven years' further service: three years in the 'ready' reserve, sixteen in the first line reserve (A-Series), and eight in the second line reserve (B-Series). Overall there was supposedly up to ten weeks' reserve training.

The introduction of one-year service had complicated the task of training conscripts in time. They were incorporated biannually in two contingents so as to ensure that France was always defended by half a contingent of partially trained men. But this meant that at any one moment the army was dealing with three categories of soldier. The presence in every unit of men at different stages of training disrupted tactical organization. Furthermore the real training period was considerably less than a year, taking account of days lost in the break between the two annual contingents, in the induction process, in holidays, agricultural leaves, and so on. It was estimated in 1930 that 18 per cent of the riflemen in an average regiment had never fired a rifle and one-quarter had never thrown a grenade. Sartre noticed during the Phoney War the 'respectful terror' with which a fellow soldier handled an 'unloaded and obsolete' revolver; Fernand Grenier observed that only two out of twenty men in his unit knew how to use the grenades they received in June 1940.

The army was particularly worried by the quality of its reserve officers and NCOs. Reserve officers were supposed to take refresher courses, and were given financial incentives to do so, but many did not bother. Many men whose level of education would normally have led them to be officers served only as common soldiers because, owing to the anti-militarism prevalent among intellectuals and *instituteurs*, they had refused to perform their PMS. Jean-Paul Sartre and Raymond Aron, two intellectuals very representative of their generation, had both done their military service as ordinary soldiers in the meteorological section. An exercise in 1934 to test a representative reserve division, the 41DI, concluded that the reserve officers and NCOs were unprepared, and the men unfit and demoralized by poor leadership. Recruitment was organized geographically. This was supposed to overcome some of the problems caused by short active service, since it allowed units to acquire cohesion by training together over time. The reality was different. The principle of geographical recruitment was often breached for practical reasons. For example, rural Breton units received drafts from cities to increase the supply of literate NCO material, armoured battalions required a certain proportion of men with driving licences, and so on. Once soldiers joined the reserve, however, they came under the authority of their local mobilization centres, which did not send reservists back to their former active comrades if this involved dispatching them long distances for brief training periods. Whatever cohesion did exist on mobilization frequently disappeared as a result of all kinds of shifts of personnel such as the dispatch of 100,000 mobilized workers to industry during the Phoney War, or the decision in December 1939 to move younger soldiers on the Maginot Line to mobile units and to move older soldiers to fortress duties. This broke up well-trained fortress crews for the dubious advantage of mixing younger soldiers with the B-Series soldiers. Thus, to quote one historian of this subject, the ideal of a cohesive reserve army ready to spring into action on mobilization was in reality 'an army of makeshift units—constantly shifting their personnel, never testing their wartime organisation and resigned to training in ad hoc units and with borrowed equipment—led by inexperienced junior officers and NCOs'.[22] Private Grenier observed that the 100 men in his company of engineers came from the north, the east, the Alps, the Midi, and Paris. One detachment of six men comprised one Savoyard who had done his active service in Syria, one from Épernay, one from Marseilles, Grenier himself from Paris, and two drunkards (of unknown provenance).

The Phoney War should have allowed time to overcome these training deficiencies. With many weaker divisions, however, the opportunity was often squandered either owing to lack of equipment or because there was an insufficient sense of urgency. Pierre Lesort, a reserve officer posted in March 1940 to the 120th Infantry Regiment of the (subsequently infamous) 71DI[23] (part of the Second Army), was shocked by what he found. His company lacked training or equipment, and their living conditions were squalid. He did his best to improve the training of the machine-gunners in his section, but the experience was dispiriting:

The ambiance strikes me as very lax as regards discipline; one must remember what sort of life these men have been leading for the last six months, shivering in this mud. The material conditions are bad; men are on straw on the ground, the walls are dirty and things are strewn up everywhere.... The platoon has been under the command for 4 months of a deplorable sergeant and everything has been allowed to go to seed; the men have got used to doing nothing, the two camps are revolting... like a gypsy encampment... the trouble is that we lack every kind of material, even planks to make beds.... Luckily morale doesn't seem too bad; the men have accustomed themselves passively to the appalling conditions in which they are living, and the only problem is to drag them out of their inertia. Unfortunately we lack the time to do the work to improve the living conditions since we have the whole time to carry out fatigues for the engineers, to dig trenches, unload sacks of cement.

A few weeks later things had got worse:

I am absolutely disgusted by this company. All my efforts come to nothing except that I am seen as an interferer ... I am after all only a platoon commander.... Unfortunately it is impossible to instil a sense of esprit de corps, discipline and work into a section in the middle of this dump of a company. In my section there are one or two individuals who are just thugs.[24]

Corap was extremely worried about the state of his Ninth Army soldiers. In February he worried about 'slackening of discipline in certain billets ... soldiers insulting and sometimes attacking local inhabitants'. In the next months he noted 'an unacceptable slovenliness, men badly turned out, not saluting or saluting sloppily, nonchalance and inactivity'; he received reports of widespread drunkenness and of soldiers causing scandals in stations by singing the Internationale.[25] These descriptions of the Ninth Army certainly seem to bear out the impressions of the British General Sir Alan Brooke, who had watched a parade of Ninth Army troops in November 1939: 'Seldom have I seen anything more slovenly ... men unshaven, horses ungroomed ... complete lack of pride in themselves or their units. What shook me most, however, was the look in the men's faces, disgruntled and insubordinate looks.'[26]

## Soldiers at War I: 'Confident and Full of Hope'

'This time it's the real war; so much the better since at last we can see the end.' 'If you knew how confident and full of hope I am.'[27] These two comments come from letters written by soldiers of the 21DI between 11 and 13 May as they headed into Belgium after the German invasion. They should remind us that the soldiers' demoralization during the Phoney War represented not so much hostility to the war in itself as boredom caused by waiting for a war that never seemed to come. Thus, many soldiers greeted the news of Germany's invasion of Belgium with relief.

The confidence displayed by these soldiers, of course, assumes an ironic hue in the light of what was about to occur, but in fact the story of the French army in 1940 cannot be reduced to the disastrous events on the Meuse. There were many examples where French soldiers, properly armed, properly trained, and properly led, fought just as effectively and courageously as their celebrated *poilu* forerunners.

This was certainly true of the two DLMs of General Prioux's cavalry at Hannut on the Belgian plain on 13 May (the same moment that the Germans were breaking through at Sedan). This was the first tank battle of the war, and it was won by the French in difficult conditions. There is some dispute as to the exact numbers of tanks arrayed on each side. The most recent French authority claims about 650 German tanks and 320 French, but if the light German tanks (Panzer I and Panzer II) are not included among the German forces, the French enjoyed superiority. Some historians also criticize Prioux for deploying his tanks in too linear a fashion, and displaying insufficient manoeuvrability. But all accounts agree that the French fought well, although the 3rd DLM, which suffered the brunt of the attack, had only recently been formed. Despite the Germans enjoying total air superiority, the French fulfilled their mission (which was of course to act as a decoy, but they could not know that).

Once Prioux had fallen back, the task of holding the Germans in the Gembloux gap fell to the newly arrived divisions of the First Army, in particular the First Moroccan Division and the 1st Motorized Division. The former was an only partially motorized unit that had covered 135 km of the journey on foot. The last soldiers only arrived on the morning of 14 May and were still preparing their positions, under enemy air attack, when the German tanks moved against them. Encounter battles of this kind were precisely what Gamelin had wanted to avoid, but for two days the Germans tried to break the line without success. The French held firm thanks to the determined resistance of their infantry and the effective performance of their artillery. This was a rare example of infantry stopping an armoured division in open country, without air support. When the French fell back on 16 May, it was not because they had been beaten but because the Germans had broken through on the Meuse.

Even on the Meuse, apart from the case of Guderian at Sedan, the German crossings were not as easy as is often suggested. The most effective French resistance occurred at Monthermé between 13 and 15 May when a thinly spread French defence (the Half Brigade of Tirailleurs Coloniaux) held off a Panzer division for two days until the collapse of the French resistance on their flanks made the position untenable. Rommel's crossing at Dinant also encountered strong resistance, although the defenders were not in an easy situation. At one moment Rommel had even feared that some of his troops were about to lose their nerve. Even after his men had established a foothold on the other side of the river on the night of 13–14 May, the French fought hard despite the breaching of their defensive line. There was no panic. For the second time Rommel had to throw himself into the thick of the battle in order to prevail. One of his company commanders, Captain Hans von Luck, wrote: 'His command tank was hit and the driver put it into a ditch. Rommel was slightly wounded, but hurried forward on foot—in the midst of the enemy fire. . . . It made a strong impression on all the officers and men.'[28]

It would be wrong to assume that, even once the Germans had broken through the three bridgeheads, their advance westwards was simply a mopping up operation. We should not forget, for example, the very fierce resistance of the 3rd DCR and 3rd DIM at Stonne to the south-east of Sedan between 15 and 25 May. Hard fighting was still going on here when the Germans had reached the Channel.[29] Tenacious resistance was also demonstrated by the remnants of the First Army caught in the jaws of the German trap and knowing that the outcome was predestined. In Lille, about 30,000–40,000 soldiers of the First Army held off massively superior German forces between 28 May and 31 May, despite being entirely surrounded and relentlessly bombarded by artillery fire. The Germans had to fight their way through the suburbs while the French held on wherever they could—in factory buildings, apartment blocks, behind improvised barricades—until all ammunition was exhausted. One regimental commander, Lieutenant-Colonel Dutrey, committed suicide rather than surrender. Although they may not have realized it, these soldiers had held off the Germans long enough for the BEF and part of the French army to reach the Dunkirk bridgehead.

The bridgehead of Dunkirk itself was defended between 29 May and

4 June by about 8,000 soldiers left over from the 12DIM (one of the divisions of the First Army which had been at Gembloux fifteen days earlier). Their commanding officer, General Janssen, was killed on 2 June. The miracle of Dunkirk, we should remember, was made possible by Gort's foresight, Hitler's loss of nerve, British resourcefulness, and French heroism.

## Soldiers at War II: 'The Germans Are at Bulson' (13 May)

The story was of course different at Sedan on 13 May. This sector was defended by the 55DI of the Second Army. Many soldiers in this B-Series division had performed their military service up to twenty years previously. Only 4 per cent of its officers were regulars. Training during the Phoney War had been hampered by shortages of material. The major deficiency was in anti-aircraft weapons and anti-tank guns. The standard density of anti-tank guns in defence was meant to be ten weapons per km, but in this sector it was less than four per km. In the end, however, this hardly mattered, since the division had collapsed before German tanks crossed the Meuse in significant numbers.

On this sector of the line the Germans enjoyed significant local superiority: the first line of resistance on the left bank of the Meuse, between Wadelincourt and Bellevue, was very spaced out along 10 km of the bend in the river. The 55DI's sister regiment, the 71DI, was considered to be barely ready for battle. Originally it had been placed on the right of the 55DI, but it was withdrawn for training in April. On 12 May it was ordered forward again, and these troop movements only caused confusion at such a crucial moment. One unit that played a key role in the defence was the 147th Fortress Infantry Regiment, under the command of Lieutenant François Pinaud. This unit found itself bearing the brunt of the German attack on 13 May. Of the four main crossings made by Guderian's XIX Panzer Corps, three were in the 147th's sector. Pinaud's unit comprised B-Series troops, mostly from the Ardennes and Aisne regions, and from Paris. One-third of them had originally been conscripted from 1918 to 1925, another third from 1926 to 1925. This meant that the average age of an ordinary soldier was 31 and a captain 42. Their level of training was not high. To remedy this, the men had been rotated through training sessions, but once these were over they were not always returned to where they had originally been stationed. Thus, although the 55DI as a whole had been in the Sedan region for months, Pinaud's men had been moved around a lot. When the Germans attacked none of the nine companies under his command was occupying a position it had been in for more than a month.

Even taking account of all these problems, there is no doubt that the performance of this regiment, and of the division in general, was exceptionally poor. To explain this, it is impossible to overestimate the impact of the eight-hour aerial bombardment that preceded the German crossing. Nothing had mentally prepared the men, cowering in their shelters, for this. If the bombardment did not succeed in destroying the French bunkers or gun emplacements, its psychological impact was incalculable. In the words of General Ruby, Deputy Chief of Staff of the Second Army:

The gunners stopped firing and went to ground, the infantry cowered in their trenches, dazed by the crash of bombs and the shriek of the dive-bombers; they had not developed the instinctive reaction of running to their anti-aircraft guns and firing back. Their only concern was to keep their heads well down. Five hours of this nightmare was enough to shatter their nerves and they became incapable of reacting against the enemy infantry.

One significant material effect of the bombardment was to destroy telephone communications. This cut the defenders off from each other, since they were not allowed to use radios in case their messages were picked up by the enemy. Their sense of isolation aggravated the psychological effects of the bombardment. Some men were reported to be stunned to the point of derangement, as sometimes occurred after particularly heavy artillery bombardments in the First World War. Especially unnerving were the screaming Stuka dive bombers, hurtling down on the cowering French defenders, their sirens screeching: 'The noise, the horrible noise! . . . You feel the bomb coming even if it falls 50 or 100 yards away. You throw yourself on the ground, certain of being blown into thirty pieces. And when you realise that it is only a miss, the noise of this shrieking shatters you.'[30]

Then there was the demoralizing sense that the sky was empty of British or French planes:

A hundred and fifty German planes! It is breathtaking! The noise of their engines is already enormous, and then there is this extraordinary shrieking which shreds your nerves. . . . And then suddenly there is a rain of bombs. . . . And it goes on and on and on! . . . Not a French or British plane to be seen. Where the hell are they! . . . My neighbour, a young bloke, is crying. . . . Nerves are raw. . . . Few men are actually hit, but their features are drawn, tiredness rings their eyes. Morale is affected. Why are our planes not defending us? No one says it, but everyone is thinking it.[31]

For those watching from the other side of the river the effect was hardly less dramatic. One German sergeant reported:

Squadron upon squadron rise to a great height, break into line ahead and there, the first machines hurtle perpendicularly down, followed by the second, third—ten, twelve aeroplanes are there. Simultaneously, like some bird of prey, they fall upon their victim and then release their load of bombs on the target. . . . It becomes a regular rain of bombs, that whistle down on Sedan and the bunker positions. Each time the explosion is overwhelming, the noise deafening. Everything becomes blended together; along with the howling sirens of the Stukas in their dives, the bombs whistle and crack and burst. . . . We stand and watch what is happening as if hypnotised; down below all hell is let loose! At the same time we are full of confidence . . . suddenly we notice that the enemy artillery no longer shoots . . . while the last squadron of Stukas is still attacking, we receive our marching orders.[32]

The first Germans crossed the Meuse at 4 p.m. on 13 May. For the French defenders, this was the moment of truth. As Alistair Horne writes:

Suddenly the great, complex stratagems of both sides, in which armies are moved around like chess pieces, become reduced to the isolated actions of one or two

20. The German Ju 87 dive bomber, popularly known as the 'Stuka'. The pilots would swoop down at 70 to 80 degrees from an altitude of 10,000 feet and pull out of their dive at 3,000 feet or lower. The aircraft were fitted with sirens which emitted a high-pitched shriek

men. . . . The success or failure of such lone combats leads to the success or failure of a platoon, from a platoon to a company, from a company to a regiment, and so on until the whole battlefield is in flux and the day is decided.[33]

The troops of the 147th Fortress Infantry Regiment, already demoralized by the aerial pounding, were unlucky enough to be facing the tough troops of the 1st Rifle Infantry Regiment commanded by Lieutenant-Colonel Balck. The speed with which the Germans moved up the river bank and took the first French bunkers suggests that the resistance was weak and the defenders badly demoralized. This was only the beginning. Some individual infantrymen had already started fleeing during the early afternoon, but a few hours later panic spread to the artillery. Some time after 6 p.m., the commander of the 55DI, General Lafontaine, who was at his command post behind Bulson, a village 4.5 km south of Sedan, heard shouting outside. He went out to see what was happening. As General Ruby tells the story:

A wave of terrified fugitives, gunners and infantry, in cars, on foot, many without arms but dragging kitbags, was hurtling down the Bulson road screaming 'The tanks are at Bulson.' Some were firing their rifles like lunatics. General Lafontaine and his officers rushed in front of them, trying to reason with them and herd them together, and had lorries put across the road. . . . Officers were mixed in with the men. . . . There was mass hysteria. All of them had supposedly seen tanks in Bulson.[34]

Lafontaine thought that he had stopped the flood, but he was to discover that it had spread elsewhere behind the lines when he decided to move his command post to the village of Chémery, 8 km south-west of Bulson. Arriving in Chémery at about 7.15 p.m. he found the village crowded with soldiers fleeing south from Sedan by the other north–south road in a state of indescribable panic, lighting the powder trail of rumour as they fled further south. About 37 km south-east of Bulson, at Flaba, was the command post of the X Corps artillery (the 55 and 71DI were both part of the X Corps). Its commander, Colonel Poncelet, was visiting a subordinate unit when the rumour that German tanks were close reached his command post. At about 7.45 the decision was taken to move to an alternative post. Poncelet quickly realized that there was no need for this and returned to his post, but by then most of its communications equipment had been destroyed in the flight.

The 'Bulson rumour' also spread east: by 10.30 p.m. it had reached Rethel. By dawn the next morning soldiers in flight were milling around Vouviers, many of them looting farms to satisfy their thirst and hunger. One eyewitness reported:

They seemed so eaten up by fear that they terrified each other during their retreat with more and more fantastical stories, as if they wanted to forbid themselves any hope of return. . . . Many were without their bags or arms and they did not seem concerned to recover them. They only wanted to get away.[35]

Overall some 20,000 soldiers fled in the Bulson panic. Although it started among the artillery, eventually every type of unit was affected. But the collapse of the artillery, traditionally the glory of the French army, was particularly significant for an army that placed such emphasis on the importance of firepower. The sight of this panic also had a catastrophic effect on the morale of other units that were at the same time being sent forward to reinforce the front line.

Why did it happen? The rumour that German tanks were at Bulson was quite false. No German tanks had crossed the Meuse at this stage, and it was to be six more hours before they did. The origin of the rumour is unclear. Some suggest, with no evidence, that it was started by German fifth columnists. More probably, some fleeing French soldiers had mistaken French tanks for German ones. The decision to move Lafontaine's and Poncelet's command posts certainly contributed to the sense of chaos. When no one answered the telephones in these deserted command posts there was understandable alarm. In Lafontaine's case the move was apparently intended to allow him to organize a counterattack more effectively, but it contributed to the soldiers' sense that they were being abandoned by their commander. 'We have been betrayed', 'our officers have abandoned us': such phrases were on the lips of many of the fleeing soldiers. Poncelet committed suicide on 24 May, apparently acknowledging his unwitting role in the disaster.

The exact origins of the Bulson rumour will never be known. But in more general terms it is not hard to explain the collapse of the 55DI—and to do so one does not need to invoke any kind of rottenness in the French body politic. These were ill-trained and ill-equipped troops, not originally intended for battle duty, whose cohesion had been weakened by frequent swapping of personnel, and who had found themselves facing an aerial onslaught for which they were mentally and materially unprepared in every respect. They were the wrong men in the wrong place at the wrong time.

## Soldiers at War III: The 'Molecular Disintegration' of the 71DI

The collapse of the 55DI was followed on the next day by that of the 71DI, another B-Series division. One of its regiments (205RI) had already been sent in for a counterattack on the evening of 13 May. The soldiers' spirits were not raised by encountering fugitives coming in the other direction shouting 'Don't go forward! The Boches are there!' In the end, on the next morning, the 205RI was ordered to fall back before it had even fought owing to the failure of the counterattack that had been undertaken by General Lafontaine in the early morning.[36] This withdrawal further confused the men, and turned into a rout. Two other regiments of the 71DI (246RI and 120RI) were dispersed into companies to form defensive points (*points d'appui*) facing west along the flank of the German advance. These units were isolated from each other—communications with the divisional commander, General Baudet, had broken down—and some could see enemy tanks moving along the road to their south, that is behind them. Increasing numbers of men could see no alternative but to escape before it was too late.

In many accounts of the Fall of France, the fate of the 71DI figures as an even more humiliating development than that of the 55DI on the previous day, since most of its units had not even fought at all. There was no single moment of panic as occurred at Bulson. Rather there was what several historians describe as a kind of 'molecular disintegration'; the division is seen as having 'vanished into thin air' (*volatilisée*). It is all too tempting to see its unhappy end as symbolic of the supposed demoralization of the French army in 1940. In one notorious incident, which figures in many accounts, Colonel Costa of the 38RA, seeing men of the 71DI in flight, tried to block their way and reason with them, but met with the response: '[W]e want to go home and get back to work! There is nothing to do! We are lost! We are betrayed!'

Here it is necessary to remember how different the smooth and simplifying narratives of military history can be from the muddled and messy reality of battle. Phrases like 'molecular disintegration' or '*volatisée*' are only metaphors. What did this actually mean for the soldiers who experienced these events? Pierre Lesort, whom we have already encountered in the Phoney War, was caught up in them as a part of the 120th regiment of the 71DI. With painstaking scrupulousness he has tested his own memories, and his contemporary letters, against subsequent historical accounts. In the end he finds that none of them successfully captures the reality of his experience. The often-repeated anecdote of Colonel Costa turns out to be a classic case of historical 'piggybacking', as Lesort traces it back from historian to historian, from Henri Amouroux (1976) to William Shirer (1969), to Alphonse Goutard (1956), and so on until he finds its origin in a somewhat polemical work written during the Occupation by a strongly pro-collaborationist author, Paul Allard. So tainted an original source should certainly make one suspicious of the accuracy of this otherwise entirely unverifiable anecdote, but even if it were true, only a massive historical sleight of hand can make it stand for the 'truth' about the 18,000 men of an entire division or even the 3,000 in a regiment.

On 13 May, Lesort's detachment found itself manning one of the defensive points in the hills north-east of Angecourt above the Meuse. German air bombardment started at around 10 a.m. Of the description of this event by General Ruby, as quoted above here (and by many other historians), Lesort observes:

I have no idea where General Ruby derived his own personal observation of the front lines on the ground itself; I only know that he was deputy chief of staff of the Second Army whose HQ was at Sennuc about 40 km to the south of the Meuse at Sedan. I can only say what I saw, heard, lived and have kept in my memory.... I saw very well, about 800–1000 metres on my left, an artillery battery ... which never stopped firing at the diving Stukas which ceaselessly attacked it: I can still see the little round clouds which its guns created in the sky around the swirling planes which continuously dispersed and returned.... As for the reactions of the machine-gunners in my company, we never stopped shooting desperately at the planes.... It must be said that this control of the sky by the Germans for these two days made the men discontented and impatient. At the start it was just a sort of grumbling: 'Christ, there are only German planes, what the hell are ours doing?' But on the following days ... one felt the growth of a kind of helpless resentment which corroded our need to find reasons to hope. But on the evening of 14 May it only needed two French fighters to appear in the sky behind us chasing and bringing down two German planes to sweep away that sense of humiliation which can be such a dangerous internal enemy for the infantryman who knows he is so badly armed against planes, artillery and tanks.

When the men saw the planes, a cheer went up. Then, on the evening of 14 May, they heard that the Germans were at Angecourt and that the entire battalion was to fall back towards the village of Yoncq. Lesort's detachment of about twenty men was ordered to move. As they set off at about 3 a.m., his feelings were mixed:

Thirst, fear, solitude ... And yet, despite all this, a memory of a certain light-headedness? First, no doubt, because of the confidence, which seemed mutual, between my machine-gunners and me ... Confidence also, of another kind ... How to describe it? In events? In the future? In the French army? I was certainly none too optimistic for the immediate future. I had been too angry over the last few months, about the weakness of the means at our disposal and the indifference of too many of our leaders. I was not really surprised that the Germans had broken through on our left; I knew only too well the men and arms in our poor division. . . . But I did believe in the existence of a genuine organized 'second position', and above all in the presence, behind us, of reserves composed of better armed divisions, notably of mechanized and armoured units. From my narrow vantage-point of head of an infantry section, as dawn broke, we were going to remain here until at H hour, in accordance with our mission . . . we would fall back at the fixed moment, in silence or under fire, leaving behind some dead (among whom might be me), but the survivors would rejoin solid lines which had been formed behind the units which had been outflanked, they would take their place in their companies, and they would be used again in the battle which was beginning.

After five hours zigzagging through the woods, and avoiding the roads as much as possible, laden with equipment and almost crazed with thirst, they reached the village of Yoncq in the early hours of 15 May, to find that it was under attack from German tanks. Briefly caught up in the fighting between the Germans and the French defenders above Yoncq, they continued their journey south-west, having received some indications about the location of their battalion.

We arrived at a cross-roads, somewhere between Neuville and Buzancy [this puts them about 35 km south of Sedan]. On the road coming from our right (thus from the north) appeared a procession of small groups and isolated individuals. An immediate impression of total disorder and shameful despair. Belongings pushed on bikes, helmets and guns out of sight, and the appearance of dazed vagrants . . . How many men? A few dozen?

By the side of the road a man was standing alone, immobile. Wearing a black cap and short cassock: a military chaplain . . . I approached him to ask if he had any idea of the whereabouts of my unit, and when he looked round at me I saw that he was crying. I asked him my question, but he did not know. I didn't insist. I had other things to do than offer sympathy. Had he perhaps tried to talk to these men in flight? I don't know. . . . What I recall is my feeling: fear of contagion for my own men, and so a desire to get away; I didn't want to wait around; my men picked up their arms and went on marching with me, and we continued our journey west. It was a strange road, so deserted at times, and then suddenly encumbered by convoys going in either direction . . . an immense racket of engines, human voices and neighing horses. And above all this, in the sky, the enemy planes were humming, passing over, disappearing, returning.[37]

Finally, after some thirty-six hours, late on 16 May they made contact with their regiment near Boult-aux-Bois.

Gustave Folcher found himself in exactly the same sector, and his account, written quite independently, is in many respects similar to Lesort's. His regiment was part of the 3rd North African Infantry Division, which was a unit of regular soldiers forming part of the Second Army. On 13 May, they were on the high ground above the Meuse, slightly to the south-west of Sedan, when the aerial bombardment began:

It was terrifying to see those machines diving at us, spitting out their bombs with a shrieking which, we assumed, was made by the bombs as they fell. In any case the noise was terrible, and despite ourselves we were far from reassured. We quickly dug a hole and made a kind of parapet with the stones and earth. There we felt safer . . . and we even became bolder, and each time the planes came back we emptied our guns at these balls of fire which seemed to mock our poor rifles. . . . One thing surprised us, something we hadn't at first thought about in the panic of the morning, and now which was on everyone's lips: what were the British and French planes doing? How come there was not a single one to be seen?

On the night of 13 May they were ordered to fall back, and they arrived in the early hours of 14 May at a village they later ascertained to be Yoncq. They also discovered that the enemy was very close:

Day was breaking; however, no precise order was given, we stayed waiting in the village . . . What to do? No one knew. Our lieutenant, commanding the company, was the most affected by all this. He was completely incapable of giving any orders; turning from one group to another, stammering without uttering a coherent word. So finally we took the initiative ourselves, for the sun which was starting to light the crest of the hill reminded us that at any minute this hole of a village could become our tomb. So my section, with sergeant Vernhet in command, decided to leave the village.

They took up a position on the hills behind the village, hidden as best they could, waiting for the attack:

To think we were going to engage combat in these conditions against motorised vehicles, without a hole to shelter in, without any installation, while for four months we had modernised, prepared our trenches, which snaked between the blockhouses and the fortified positions, with reserves of food, telephone, blankets, nothing missing. To have abandoned all that to engage combat in the open fields, without shelter, without trenches, only a few kilometres from our trenches on the other side of the Meuse. . . . The sun was disappearing behind the hill and we thought that the moment was going to arrive; everyone was ready, the finger on the trigger, to fire at the first sight of the enemy. . . . Night fell and we had the joy, the great joy, of at last seeing the first French plane turning above the hills at a very low altitude. It was certainly welcome, the first one since the start of the fight, displaying its tricolour emblem above us, while since the beginning we had seen thousands of German black crosses. It gave us our courage back . . . and there was almost an ovation which greeted it.

During the night their thirst became so bad that Folcher went down to the village to fill up their flasks at the fountain. A lieutenant arrived to inspect with a staff officer. He saw that the section was not commanded and issued orders. This improved the mood. But the next morning the men's spirits fell again when instead of the enemy they saw the dreadful sight of soldiers fleeing in chaos past the village (among them presumably Lesort, not in flight, but in search of his battalion).

They told us terrible things, unbelievable things. . . . Some had come from as far as the Albert Canal. . . . They asked for something to eat and drink; poor lads! . . . The stream went on endlessly; it was a piteous sight. Ah, if those enthusiasts who go and watch the magnificent military parades in Paris or elsewhere, could have seen on that morning this other army, the real one, not the army of parades and music, perhaps they would understand the real suffering of the soldier.

Soon afterwards, in the afternoon, the enemy assault began:

On the fringe of the wood, to the left and the right of the road, the first tanks made their appearance in large numbers. Our artillery redoubled its fire, concentrating everything now on one side, now on the other. Two tanks are hit and burn, a mortar shell scores a direct hit on a third and that also bursts into flames. The others, facing this violent barrage, turn and shelter in the forest. It is here that the scene changes. The enemy artillery comes into play and a hail of bullets starts to rain down. Too long to begin with, they burst behind us, but the range soon adjusts so that they rain down on us. I make myself small, as small as possible in my trench. Some fall so near that the trench trembles and the earth starts to collapse. It calms down a little and I stick my nose outside and spot a large tank, coming from I don't know where, which is going to arrive right at the cross-roads in my field of fire. What can I do? Quickly I take out my normal magazine which I replace with one of our armoured bullets and I wait for the precise moment when it is going to come onto the cross-roads. I am not too confident as to what is going to happen, for I realise, and this is what makes me tremble, that if I miss, this formidable machine, spitting fire from everywhere, will come right over me, and we shall be lost. I also know that even armoured bullets don't do very much harm to it. All this races through my head in an instant. In spite of this I'm still cool, and just at the moment when I'm going to let loose my first volley, a shell bursts on its front; immediately the engine stops and two men get off the vehicle. Half a minute later, some men from the platoon nearby take them prisoner without any resistance. It is a 25mm anti-tank gun, placed behind me and with the same line of fire as me, which stopped it. He really made me pleased, above all in not missing, for I had the impression that I was for it.

Despite this lucky escape, by the early hours of the morning it was clear that things were going very badly.

Suddenly a lieutenant, I don't know which, and without any previous order, gives out a kind of 'every man for himself' directive. In five minutes, he announces, the withdrawal must have got over the hill. It's abrupt and immediately there is a general panic, everyone thinking of his own skin.

Folcher got away to fight another day, until finally he was taken prisoner in June.[38]

These two narratives tell similar stories. They describe the experiences of two small detachments of soldiers trying to hold together and respond to the most adverse conditions while everything seems to be disintegrating around them. They show the terrifying impact of the German air superiority, the alternating waves of hope and despair, the soldiers' sense of being thrown into a conflict for which they were not prepared, and the importance of leadership for men who found themselves isolated and cut off from their commanders.

Ultimately it is impossible to generalize about the performance of the French army in 1940. Certainly, in general it was the B divisions that performed least satisfactorily, but even here considerable differences are observable as one looks below divisional level. It seems impossible to relate these differences to the social composition or geographical origin of different units. One should be wary of accepting the contemporary prejudices of the French High Command, often repeated by historians, which view 'sturdy' Norman or Breton peasants as more reliable than soldiers of urban, especially Parisian, origin—just as in 1914 there were similar myths about the unreliability of troops from Provence—although it does seem that in 1940 North African—especially Moroccan—troops fought particularly well.

In the 71DI there was nothing to choose between the 246RI, composed primarily of men from the Paris region about whom doubts had been expressed before 10 May, and the 120RI, formed mainly of rural troops from the Ardennes and Aisne. Another B-Series division that performed badly overall without ever really fighting was the 61DI of Corap's Ninth Army, which was made up mainly of Norman peasants, and had been previously considered to display good morale and discipline. The reasons for its discomfiture derived as usual from the circumstances. Required to hold the Meuse sector north of Givet, it was not involved in the initial fighting further down the river. The division was, however, destabilized by Corap's decision to pull his line back on 15 May.[39] Lacking coherent orders for the organization of this withdrawal, and without sufficient vehicles to carry it out fast enough, the troops moved back through the woods in confusion, only to find that Reinhardt's Panzers had already reached the line to which they were supposed to be retreating. This made it easy enough for the Germans to mop them up in small groups.

## The Exodus

One recurrent theme in the narratives of both Folcher and Lesort, and of innumerable other accounts of these events, is the devastating psychological impact of witnessing, and being swept up in, the great wave of civilian refugees that instantaneously became known as the 'Exodus'. Let us quote another soldier trying to keep his head while so many around him seemed to be losing theirs:

We overheard these conversations exchanged between fugitives at every point where two roads crossed . . . 'Where are you coming from?' 'The south.' 'What, are the Germans already in the south?' 'Yes, of course. And you?' 'From the east.' 'But there're everywhere, then.' And they would ask us what to do. We didn't know what to reply. And the pitiable herd would continue on its way almost without hope. Can you imagine the effect this had on our morale?[40]

The biblical term 'Exodus' seems entirely appropriate for this extraordinary phenomenon, which swept across the country from the north-east to the south. One writer described it as resembling a geological cataclysm. It is the Exodus which transforms the events of 1940 from a mere military defeat to something approaching the disintegration of an entire society. No account of the Fall of France can avoid asking what the Exodus reveals about the state of mind of the French people in 1940.

Starting with the arrival of Belgian refugees in mid-May—'I would never have believed that there were so many refugees in Belgium' remarked one observer[41]—the Exodus quickly spread to northern France: Rheims by 16 May, Soissons by 20 May, Compiègne by 28 May, Senlis by 29 May. In June it spread further south: Paris between 6 and 12 June, Chartres on 15 June. It is estimated that the population of Lille fell from 200,000 to 20,000, Tourcoing from 82,000 to 7,000, Chartres from 23,000 to 800. Cities in the south saw their population swell alarmingly: Bordeaux from 300,000 to 600,000, Pau from 30,000 to 150,000, Brive from 30,000 to 100,000. It is estimated that between six and eight million people abandoned their homes and took to the roads. Friedmann, travelling back from the front, found himself moving through a kind of desert until occasionally, as he left the main arteries, he came across villages that were like little oases which had not yet been abandoned, perhaps because they had not yet heard what was happening in the villages around them.

21. The civilian exodus, starting from Belgium and then moving like a wave across northern France, provides some of the most poignant images of France's defeat. Describing what he saw from the air, St Exupéry wrote: 'somewhere in the north of France a boot had scattered an anthill and the ants were on the march'

Some refugees headed for the Loire in a desperate hope that safety lay on the other side of the river; most just followed the vehicle in front of them without any idea where they were headed. Those who had cars seemed at first to be the lucky ones, until they ran out of petrol and had to abandon their vehicles and possessions by the side of the road and continue on foot. Many people had loaded their possessions on to horse-drawn carts; others pushed wheelbarrows or even prams. This was the sight which greeted Gustave Folcher as his unit retreated through Verdun:

People are thronging the roads, panic-stricken, despite the late hour; it's not yet night but soon will be. The women, the kids, the old, lug trunks, suitcases, bundles, wheelbarrows, carts; everything jams up the roadway and forces our transports to slow their pace and in some cases to stop completely. We try to chat to the civilians and immediately we understand. The people are half mad, they don't even reply to what we ask them. There is only one word in their mouth: evacuation, evacuation.

And a bit further down the road:

What is most pitiful is to see entire families on the road, with their livestock that they force to follow them, but that they finally have to leave in some cattle-pen. We see wagons drawn by two, three or four beautiful mares, some with their young foal which follows at the risk of being crushed every few metres. The wagon is driven by a woman, often in tears, but most of the time it's a kid of eight, ten or perhaps twelve years old who leads the horses. On the wagon, on which furniture, trunks, linen, the most precious things, or rather the most indispensable things, have been hastily piled up, the grandparents have also taken their place, holding in their arms a very young child, even a newborn baby. What a spectacle that is! The children look at us one by one as we overtake them, holding in their hands the little dog, the little cat or the cage of canaries which they didn't want to be separated from.[42]

One of the most poignant aspects of the Exodus for a people whose inhabitants were so tied to the land was the fate of the animals: dead horses along the side of the road; cows lowing in pain because they had not been milked for days; abandoned bird-cages; stray cats and dogs. On 12 June, a Swiss journalist in Paris came upon a herd of abandoned cows in central Paris whose streets, empty of cars, echoed with the sound of their bellowing.[43]

Often refugees, arriving in a locality they believed to be safe, frequently found it had already been abandoned, often in terrible haste, uneaten meals still on the table. Sadoul compared the refugees to locusts as they descended upon communities whose inhabitants had themselves fled without the time to take their belongings. Looting certainly occurred, if there was time for it. One observer wrote: 'Further on, in another locality, we saw people rushing into a food shop. What was going on? Was it a panic? No, it was just a shop owner, a woman, terrified by the bombing, who had told people: "I'm off. I'm leaving the doors unlocked. Take what you want."[144] Describing the Exodus is easier than explaining why it occurred and what at the deepest level it tells us about France in 1940. It is tempting to characterize the French as gripped by an irrational panic, a kind of collective trauma, revealing the underlying fears of a population that had from the start not been psychologically prepared to face the strains of war. Another reading would be to see the Exodus as a perfectly rational response by defenceless civilians to the consequences of a series of military disasters for which they were not responsible, but whose consequences they wanted, quite understandably, to escape. Because the authorities had not predicted a German breakthrough of such speed, and on such a scale, there were no contingency plans for the civilian population except in the border areas. The military were inclined to see evacuation as a capitulation rather than as an orderly way of regrouping the civilian population. The result was that civilians, lacking any instructions from the authorities, were forced to take matters into their own hands. In the week after Germany attacked, the population of Rheims witnessed a steady flow of refugees from Belgium streaming through their city. With little guidance from above, the citizens of Rheims were forced to take matters into their own hands. The military did not finally order an evacuation until 19 May, but by then only about 5 per cent of the population was still there. As for the rest of the department, no evacuation was ordered until 2 June. By then, in many localities, only livestock were left to receive the news.

Rheims, like much of the north-east of France, had been occupied in the First World War. There was a regional folk memory of German 'atrocities', some apocryphal and some not, in the previous conflict, and this understandably influenced the way people responded to the invasion of 1940. Simone de Beauvoir in 1940 came across terrified refugees in western France with stories of having encountered children whose hands had been severed—one of the most famous atrocity scares of 1914. Some young women refugees in 1940 covered themselves in mustard to avoid being raped. As well as the memories of the previous war, the population had been fed with inter-war scare stories about the effects of bombing. For all these reasons, it was hardly surprising that people wanted to escape from the advancing Germans before it was too late. If the conflict was again going to be four years of stalemate, this time they wanted to be on the right side of the front line.

It should be remembered too that in 1914 there had also been a panic of a similar nature, albeit on a much smaller scale. In 1914, about 400,000 Belgian refugees had fled to Holland and about 200,000 into France, whilst about 400,000 French civilians had fled further into the interior of France. In the last two weeks of August 1914, before the French victory on the Marne, a wave of panic had spread across parts of the country that lay in the path of the German troops. In the Aube, on 8 September, the Prefect reported that 'the unfortunate emigrants coming from the Ardennes . . . are spreading terror in the localities through which they pass by the stories they tell of their misfortune'.[45] There was also an exodus from Paris in the early days of September 1914. One observer wrote on 3 September 1914: 'yesterday's panic has been getting worse among those who are late to join the exodus, on hearing that the gates of Paris will be closed every evening at 7.00 and that from tomorrow no car will be allowed to leave the city. This was the signal for a desperate flight'.[46] Before the situation could get any worse, the victory on the Marne reassured the population, and stemmed the panic. In 1940 there was no victory to do the same.

## Soldiers at War IV: 'Sans esprit de recul' (5–10 June)

Despite the Exodus, in those regions of France not immediately threatened by the German advance, there was no panic. Indeed during May and the first days of June, there was a remarkable increase in armaments production. There were more planes with the armies by the end of the battle than there had been at the beginning: 2,343 as opposed to 2,176 on 10 May—but unfortunately many of these still lacked parts and had not yet been tested for combat. No less remarkable than the productivity of the workforce was the tenacity with which the French army continued to fight in the first two weeks of June, despite the terrible blows that it had suffered in the previous three weeks. Soldiers' letters opened by the censors revealed a striking improvement in morale at the start of June. Many of these letters were couched in a language of simple patriotism reminiscent in every way of 1914. To take three examples from soldiers of the 31DI on 2 and 3 June before the Somme battle:

For my part I can't wait to kill the largest possible number of Boches.

We are really tired, but we have to be here, they will not pass and we will get them [on les aura].

I have an unlimited confidence in myself and I feel sure God will protect me until the end . . . I will be proud to have participated in the Victory of which I have no doubts.

An infantryman of the 28DI wrote on 28 May: 'It seems that the Germans have taken Arras and Lille. If this is true, the Nation must rediscover its old spirit of 1914 and 1789.' A member of de Gaulle's 4th DCR, which had carried out a number of counterattacks at Abbeville at the end of May, wrote: 'In fifteen days we have carried out four attacks and we have always been successful, so we are going to pull together and we will get that pig Hitler.'[47] This was not just bravado. The Germans themselves were impressed by how hard the French fought on the Somme and Aisne. This battle was almost certainly lost in advance owing to the Germans' quantitative superiority, but the initial French resistance was so strong that Weygand briefly wondered whether the line might after all be held.

There are various reasons for this improvement in French fighting capacity. First, Weygand's combative style initially had a galvanizing effect after the torpid and distant leadership of Gamelin. Second, soldiers who had experienced German air attacks in early May had become partially inured to them, at least to the shrieking of the Stukas. Third, the High Command had belatedly altered its tactics. Abandoning the orthodoxy of the continuous front, Weygand adopted a 'chessboard' defence system made up of 'hedgehogs', points of resistance centred on a natural obstacle like a wood or a village, and protected all round by artillery. The gunners were now instructed to fire at tanks on sight, as if firing a revolver, rather than, as French doctrine previously prescribed, being employed only for concentrated fire under centralized control. This gave greater flexibility to the defence.

Once the Somme/Aisne line had been breached, there was no organized defensive line in existence. Even so, there were still examples of tough French resistance on the plains of central France between the Seine and the Loire, and then at various points on the Loire itself. For example, a battalion of the 109RI fought off the Germans on the Loire between Jargeaud and Châteauneuf; for two days the cadets of the Cavalry School at Saumur held the bridges at Saumur until on 19 June all their ammunition had run out. It is worth noting that the 109RI was a unit containing an exceptionally high concentration of known left-wing activists, while the cavalry officers of Saumur were drawn from the most conservative members of society. These pockets of last-ditch patriotism were to be found across the political spectrum.

It is striking that while German losses for the campaign as a whole were remarkably light—27,074 killed, 111,034 wounded, 18,384 missing—in the first stage, from 10 May to 3 June, the casualty rate was 2,500 per day. In the second phase, from 4 June to 18 June, when one would have expected the French troops to have been entirely demoralized, it rose to almost 5,000 per day. The high casualties on the French side also disprove any allegations that the French did not fight tenaciously in 1940. No systematic official investigation of the number of French soldiers killed in the Battle of France was undertaken after the defeat. Until recently, the most generally accepted figure was between 90,000 and 120,000, with most authors inclining towards the higher figure, but a recent review of the available evidence has suggested a rather lower figure of between 50,000 and 90,000, and tending towards the lower end.[48] These are still, however, significant numbers.

It is true that the number of French prisoners was very high—something like 1.5 million—but probably as many as half of these were captured in the six days between Pétain's 17 June broadcast, announcing that the government would be seeking an armistice, and the actual signing of the armistice itself on 22 June. There is no doubt that after Pétain's speech French resistance collapsed. Most people knew after hearing Pétain that an armistice was imminent. What in that case was the point of fighting on? This kind of attitude was encouraged by the government's announcement on 18 June that all centres of population above 20,000 were to be declared open cities. Where soldiers wanted to fight on they found themselves spurned, even attacked, by civilians. Most people were now desperate to end the fighting. Georges Friedmann was not wrong in his observations on the mood of the French population in the last days before the armistice.

But this mood was not characteristic of the nation as a whole during the entire previous ten months. It would be more fitting, then, to end with two more favourable comments on the fighting qualities of the French—comments that are all the more telling in that they come from outside observers who had no predisposition to be favourable to the French. The first comes from Hitler himself, writing to Mussolini on 25 May:

Very marked differences become apparent in the French when their military ability is evaluated. There are very bad units side by side with excellent ones. On the whole the difference in quality between the active and nonactive divisions is extraordinarily noticeable. Many of the active units have fought desperately, the reserve units are for the most part obviously not equal to the impact of battle on morale.[49]

The second comment comes from Sir Ronald Campbell, whose desperate attempts, with Spears, to keep the French government in the fight had left

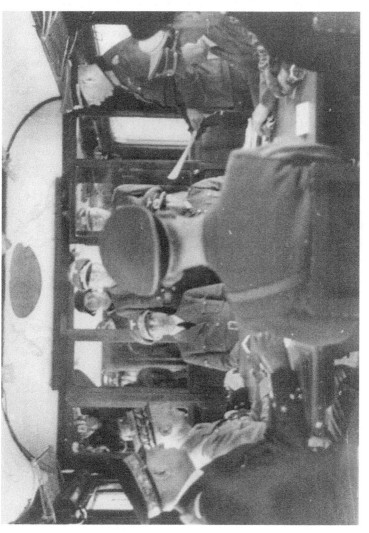

22. The signing of the armistice between France and Germany on 22 June 1940. On the left, opposite Hitler, is the French representative General Huntziger. To rub in France's humiliation, Hitler had the ceremony take place in the railway carriage where the armistice of 1918 had been signed after Germany's defeat

him bitter and exhausted. But his last report from France on 27 June refused to condemn an entire nation for the mistakes of its leaders:

Coming to the crux of the matter, the reason of the French collapse, I find myself unable to give a simple answer. It seems incredible that the great French army should have crumpled up in the way that it did. At the outbreak of the war I am convinced that the spirit was excellent. By the end of the year men coming home were saying that, whilst they had been ready to die for their country, they were not ready to sit about doing nothing indefinitely. As the months went by German propaganda, cleverly and insidiously conducted, played further havoc with the morale of the troops. . . . The question may be asked whether there was something rotten in the state of France. It is also a difficult question to answer by a straight 'yes' or 'no'. In conversation with me a number of Frenchmen (M. Reynaud among them) ascribed the collapse in part to the abuse of the democratic system: life in France was too easy; facilities and favours were too readily obtained. Whilst there may be something in this, I do not accept it as an explanation of what occurred. From all accounts the mass of the French people was sound. It never had a chance to prove its worth. I should rather describe France as a man who, stunned by an unexpected blow, was unable to rise to his feet before his opponent delivered the 'coup de grâce.'[50]

# PART II

## Causes, Consequences, and Counterfactuals

Ah, the blueprint that historians will draft of this! The angles they will plot
to lend shape to the mess! They will take the word of a cabinet minister, the
decision of a general, the discussion of a committee, and out of that parade
of ghosts they will build historic conversations in which they will discern
far-sighted views and weighty responsibilities. They will invent agreements, resistances, attitudinous pleas, cowardice.

(A. de Saint-Exupéry, *Flight to Arras* (Penguin edn. 1961), 87)

Such as we are, we can be certain that history will mention us, will dwell on
us. It will put a great full stop after 1940, and 1941 will begin a new chapter.
We will be in that chapter. We will say: 'I was there, such and such a thing
happened to me.' We will be interrogated. We will be quoted. Our ailments
will be studied; our words will cast light or cause scandal. The most silent
among us will be asked to speak. We will have the honour of quotation
marks.

(Paul Morand, *Chroniques de l'homme maigre* (1941), 162)

It has become a habit to look for signs of decomposition in the France of
1922–1935.... Our epoch is in the process of constructing a representation
of itself to cut the ground from under the feet of historians.

(Jean-Paul Sartre, *War Diaries: Notebooks from a Phoney War, November 1939–
May 1940* (1984), 175)

# 5

# CAUSES AND COUNTERFACTUALS

## July 1940: Marc Bloch in Guéret

AFTER the signature of the armistice, Marc Bloch, a middle-aged professor of history, temporarily residing near Gueret in the south-west of France, set about putting down on paper his own impressions of the catastrophe that had befallen France. Bloch was an internationally celebrated medieval historian. He had served in the French army with great distinction in the First World War. Decorated four times, he ended the war as a captain. Called up again in 1939, at the age of 53, he had witnessed the débâcle at close hand, and he felt a burning need to record what he had seen while it was 'still fresh and living' in his memory.

Bloch had spent most of the Phoney War with the First Army. Initially, thanks to his linguistic abilities, he had been assigned to the Intelligence Branch as liaison with the British. Here he witnessed at first hand the lack of comprehension between the British and French. In the eyes of the French, the British soldiers were lecherous and rowdy, and the British officers distant and snobbish. Frustrated by this posting, Bloch was relieved to be reassigned to a new position as the officer in charge of the army's petrol supplies. Since the First Army was the most motorized of all the French forces, this was a post carrying great responsibility. Bloch quickly mastered his new task, and, like most other soldiers, he spent much of the Phoney War bored, cold, and frustrated by inactivity. He whiled away the time by starting work on a history of the French people. This was the book that eventually became his *Apology for the Historian*.

On 10 May 1940, Bloch was in Paris. He rushed back to the front and rejoined the First Army as it moved into Belgium. Five days later, the armies began their retreat back towards the French frontier along roads clogged with refugees. Despite the chaos of the retreat Bloch managed to ensure that petrol was always available, and equally that none of the petrol depots under his responsibility fell into enemy hands: 'the whole line of our retreat from Mons to Lille was lit by more fires than can ever have been kindled by Attila'. Eventually he found himself, with other remnants of the First Army, in Dunkirk. In this 'ruined town with its shells of buildings half-visible through the drifting smoke', he set about organizing the evacuation of his men. It took 'superhuman doses of charity not to feel bitter', as 'ship after ship carried their foreign companions to safety'. Bloch wrote:

I can still hear the incredible din which, like the orchestral finale of an opera, provided an accompaniment to the last few minutes which we spent on the coast of Flanders—the crashing of bombs, the bursting of shells, the rat-tat-tat of machine guns, the noise of anti-aircraft batteries, and as a kind of figured bass, the persistent rattle of our own little naval pom-pom.

Bloch himself left Dunkirk on the evening of 31 May on a British ship, the *Royal Daffodil*. Immediately upon his arrival at Dover the following morning he was transported by train to Plymouth, from where he returned to Cherbourg later that evening.

Back in France, Bloch spent the first two weeks of June in northern France, first in Normandy and then at Rennes in Brittany. He was angry and frustrated that he and his men were not being effectively reorganized so that they could take part in the fighting again. On 17 June Rennes was bombed; on the next day it was rumoured that the Germans were about to arrive. In order to avoid being taken prisoner, Bloch found himself some civilian clothes, made contact with an academic colleague in the town, booked into a hotel, and pretended to be in Rennes on academic business. The Germans did not suspect that this grey-haired and respectable-looking gentleman had been in the army a few days earlier. It was clear also that the Germans had quite enough prisoners already without tracking down all those soldiers who might be evading them. At the end of the month, once the railways were running again, Bloch rejoined his family in Guéret.

These were the events that Bloch recounted in his manuscript, under the heading 'One of the vanquished gives evidence'. In the last section, entitled 'A Frenchman examines his conscience', he tried to analyse the causes of the disaster. His pages seethe with anger at the folly, incompetence, and human weaknesses he had witnessed on the French side. He is particularly critical of politicians, army leaders, junior officers, journalists, and teachers. Nor does he spare academics like himself who 'out of mental laziness' had gone back to the 'tranquillity' of their studies after 1918 and allowed France to head down the path to destruction. Although himself a man of the moderate left, Bloch was as critical of the self-interested narrow-mindedness of the working class as of the egoism and class hatred of the bourgeoisie. The essential thesis of his book, however, is that the fundamental causes of the defeat were intellectual: France had become an intellectually ossified and sclerotic society.

Having completed his manuscript, Bloch put it away until France should once again be free and it could be published. He never lived to see that day. During the Occupation, Bloch joined the Resistance, becoming one of the organizers in the Lyon area. As well as fighting the Germans, the Resistance was very concerned with drawing up reforms for liberated France. Bloch himself drafted far-reaching proposals for reform of the educational system to be implemented after Liberation. These were published in one of the clandestine Resistance newspapers. Bloch was arrested by the Germans on 7 March 1944. After being imprisoned and tortured, he was shot on 16 June, a few days after the Allies had landed in Normandy.

In 1946 Bloch's autopsy of the defeat was finally published as the book *Étrange Défaite* [Strange Defeat], not a title he had chosen. Bloch had written without access to documents, interpreting his experiences in the light of his insights as an historian. What makes his essay so fascinating is that Bloch was one of the leading lights of the so-called 'Annales' group of historians (so named after the review *Annales* founded by Bloch and his friend Lucien Febvre in 1929). These historians wanted to move historical writing away from its traditional concentration on political events (*histoire événementielle*) in order to study the 'total' history of a period over a long time-frame (*la longue durée*). 'Annales' historians were more interested with the long, slow history of deep structural continuities than with the superficial discontinuities of politics. Yet the 'event' of 1940 imposed itself too urgently for Bloch not to feel the imperative, as a citizen, to try to explain it. This has led one commentator to suggest that the impact of 1940 had in effect led Bloch to abandon Annales history: 'when Bloch analyses the defeat, it could be any historian writing about a period of national crisis. . . . He talks about individuals, their intelligence, stupidity, courage, patriotism, virtue, honesty . . . he talks about destiny, fate, chance, fall of the cards, surprise.'[11] Conversely, many other readers of *Étrange Défaite* take a rather different view, interpreting Bloch, in his confrontation with the historical event of 1940, as having rejected contingency in favour of a quest for deep structural causes to explain it.

## Historians and the Defeat

However one wishes to interpret Bloch's account, it remains the starting-point for most historians in their search to understand the causes of the defeat, even if they use his arguments only as a foil. In the first years after the Liberation, the problem for French historians who might have wished to test or develop Bloch's intuitions was that the debate on 1940 had become highly politicized. One of the first acts of the Vichy regime of Marshal Pétain had been to set up a tribunal at the small town of Riom, not far from Vichy itself, to try those it blamed for the defeat. The defendants included Léon Blum, Daladier, Pierre Cot (in his absence), and Gamelin. Given that three of these figures had been leading members of the Popular Front, it was clear in which direction Vichy was pointing the finger. The Riom trial, which finally opened in February 1942, was suspended two months later before a judgement had been reached. It had become a public relations disaster because Daladier and Blum succeeded in turning the tables on their accusers and demonstrating the flimsiness of the charges against them.

At the Liberation, it was the turn of Pétain and other members of the

23. The caption reads: 'Riom . . . Let's have a laugh.' It refers to the trial of those whom Vichy held responsible for the defeat. The cartoon shows Gamelin (in uniform) and (clockwise): Daladier, Blum, Mandel, Reynaud. Mandel and Reynaud were not tried at Riom, but were imprisoned by Vichy. Mandel was assassinated in 1944

RIOM ...          RIONS...

Vichy regime to find themselves on trial, not only for their activities during the Occupation and their role in the events of 1940. In addition, the French Parliament set up a Committee in August 1946 to enquire into 'the political, economic and diplomatic events that, from 1933 to 1945, preceded, accompanied and followed the Armistice, in order to establish the responsibilities incurred'. In the event, this Committee, despite its broad remit, concentrated primarily on the events of 1940. The starting date of its investigation —1933—three years before the Popular Front came to power, contradicted Vichy's assertion that everything had started to go wrong after 1936. Over the next four years, most of the major actors in the events of 1940 came to testify before the Committee. There were more than one hundred hearings. Nine volumes of evidence were published. The first volume of the Committee's report, published in 1951, and covering only the period up to 1936, highlighted the responsibilities of the army command. The subsequent volumes were never produced because the Committee lapsed at the end of the parliamentary session in 1951, and was never reconstituted.

Although there were specific reasons why neither the Riom trial nor the post-war Committee ever finished their work, their failure also seems

24. Reynaud, standing on the right, and Weygand, standing on the left, fought out their quarrel of 1940 once again in 1945 at the trial of Pétain. The Marshal himself, slumped in a chair on the right, his kepi on the table in front of him, refused to testify

symbolic of the magnitude of the task they faced. The mountain of material amassed by the Riom court and then the Committee has been mined by historians ever since. Soon historians were also able to start exploiting the memoirs that began to pour out in the decade after 1945. First off the mark was Gamelin with three volumes of memoirs between 1946 and 1947, then Reynaud with two volumes in 1947, and Weygand with three volumes between 1952 and 1955. Lesser known, but hardly less important, figures also produced their testimonies. Among these were Jacques Minart (1945), who had been on Gamelin's staff at his headquarters in Vincennes; General Prioux (1947), Commander of the First Army's Cavalry Corps; General Ruby (1948), Deputy Chief of Staff of the Second Army; General Charles Grandsard (1949), Commander of the Second Army's X Corps (which included the ill-fated 55DI).

Even if the archives were closed for many years to come, historians certainly did not lack documentary material to begin studying the Fall of France, but almost no histories of the event appeared in France in the thirty years after the end of the war. Two notable exceptions, neither by professional historians, and both appearing in 1956, were Jacques Benoist-Méchin's *Soixante jours qui ébranlèrent l'occident* [Sixty Days Which Shook the West] and Colonel Adolphe Goutard's *La Guerre des occasions perdues* [The War of Lost Opportunities], both of which were translated into English. Benoist-Méchin's book, three volumes long, was extremely well documented, but it certainly did not pretend to objectivity. Its author had been a hard-line supporter of collaboration with Germany during the war and an unapologetic Fascist sympathizer. He was therefore extremely hostile to the defunct Third Republic, which he saw as bearing fundamental responsibility for the defeat. Goutard's approach could hardly have been more different. As his title implied, his view was that the defeat was due not to the decadence of the French people or the defects of the Republic, but to the mistakes of its military commanders. For Goutard, this was a war that could have been won.

The lack of any other important French studies of the Fall of France at this time was symptomatic of a more general reluctance among the French historical profession to write contemporary history. In this period, the Annales school was becoming increasingly influential and increasingly obsessed with studying long-term socio-economic trends. This was especially true of its dominant post-war figure, Fernand Braudel. Under Braudel's influence Annales became more dogmatic in its rejection of the 'event'. Braudel argued that the significant turning-points in history were linked to economic cycles. This meant, as he argued in a lecture in Mexico in 1953, that the real moments of discontinuity in France's nineteenth- and twentieth-century history were 1817, 1872, and 1929. In this reading of French history, 1940 was a purely epiphenomenal politico-military occurrence. Braudel had come to prominence in 1949 with the publication of his massive study of the Mediterranean in the age of Philip II. Having researched the book for fifteen years, Braudel began to write it entirely from memory while a prisoner of war in Germany between 1940 and 1944. He had thrown himself into the task almost immediately upon arriving at the camp. In July he wrote to Lucien Febvre: 'I am working flat-out on the 16th century; rather absurd at such a time but so consoling' ['chose absurde mais si douce']. At the very moment that Bloch was confronting the 'event', Braudel was fleeing it—perhaps because, unlike Bloch, his confinement in a camp offered no immediate prospect of acting upon 'events'. Looking back thirty years later on his development as an historian, Braudel was quite explicit about this relationship between contemporary history and his own choices as an historian:

My vision of history took on its definitive form without my being entirely aware of it ... partly as a direct existential response to the tragic times I was passing through. All those events which poured in upon us from the radio and the newspapers of our enemies, or even the news from London which our clandestine receivers gave us—I had to outdistance, reject, deny, them. Down with events, especially vexing ones! I had to believe that history, destiny, was written at a much more profound level.[2]

Many historians in France at this time were, of course, not part of the Annales group. Political and diplomatic history was being written at the Sorbonne; contemporary history was being written by the group of historians working in the Committee for the History of the Second World War, which had been set up immediately after the Liberation. This Committee produced an important journal that was the first scholarly review anywhere entirely devoted to the history of the war. But although not entirely neglecting the defeat of 1940, most of the Committee's research in the 1950s and 1960s was devoted to the study of the Resistance. In the 1960s, when General de Gaulle was in power, the attitude of official archivists was certainly not encouraging towards historians who might want to study the causes of the defeat. The Gaullist regime did not want to dwell on this dark episode in France's history.

In the 1970s, after de Gaulle's death, these official attitudes relaxed somewhat. French archival laws became more liberal after 1975, and historians were less prone to see their task as glorifying the Resistance. This, however, led them to focus not on 1940 but more and more on Vichy and collaboration. As one historian comments: '[B]y the mid-1970s there was scarcely a scholar in France with any interest in 1940.'³ The defeat still remained a touchy subject. Pierre le Goyet, a senior historian in the French Army Historical Service, had his career cut short because in 1975 he published his book on Gamelin without official authorization.

In the absence of major French studies on 1940, the field was left open to British and American writers. Three influential books appeared in English at almost exactly the same time: Guy Chapman's *Why France Collapsed*, published in 1968, and Alistair Horne's *To Lose a Battle: France 1940* and William Shirer's *The Collapse of the Third Republic: An Inquiry into the Fall of France in 1940*, both published in 1969. Of the three writers, Chapman, the author of several excellent books on French history, was the most knowledgeable about the political background of the Third Republic, but for various reasons he chose in his book to concentrate almost exclusively on the detailed military narrative of 1940. The result is a book that is both spare in style and dense in content, but one that never really ends up satisfactorily answering the question in his title: 'why?'

Shirer, who had been an American foreign correspondent in both Berlin and Paris during the inter-war years, took a very different approach. His enormous book devotes hundreds of pages to the domestic political background in France. Written with the same light touch that made his history of the Third Reich a worldwide success, the book is extremely readable, but it is marred by a certain exasperated condescension at the ineptitude of the French and their creaky political institutions. Shirer has both the qualities and the limitations of a first-rate newspaper reporter. At times he almost seems to be suggesting that everything might have been all right if only France had been a bit more like America. The result is an unremittingly bleak account of the last years of the Third Republic, which is depicted as having been in a state of terminal decline: 'its strength gradually sapped by dissension and division, by an incomprehensible blindness in foreign, domestic and military policy, by the ineptness of its leaders, the corruption of its press and by a feeling of growing confusion, hopelessness and cynicism in its people'. The French defeat was 'a collapse of the army, the government, the morale of the people'.

Horne's book is not entirely free of the same underlying assumptions. Previously the author of excellent books on the siege of Paris in 1870–1 and the Battle of Verdun in 1916, Horne spent much less time on the politics than Shirer. As a military narrative of the events of 1940, his book is one of the best ever written, but when he does discuss the social and political background of the 1930s, he is prone to a somewhat moralistic reading, in which the Third Republic appears as irremediably decadent. For example, his description of the French army leaders: '[L]ike the lotus-eating mandarins of Cathay behind the Great Wall, the French Army allowed itself to atrophy, to lapse into desuetude.' Or his comments on the effects of the Popular Front: 'a newly acquired instinct for disobedience, a disdain for authority of all forms ... which was certainly to bear moral fruit in 1940'.[4]

The books of Shirer and Horne, both translated into French, had considerable influence in forming popular views of the Fall of France. Less widely known, because published only in the form of articles, were the writings of the Canadian historian John Cairns. Offering a critique of the inadequacies of the existing literature, as well as providing detailed studies of Franco-British relations in the war, Cairns pointed the way towards a more sophisticated understanding of the causes of the Fall of France. He argued that analysis of the event had to be separated from the polemics that had immediately followed it; that the Third Republic needed to be treated historically and not merely as the prelude to the débâcle; that the defeat must be put in the context of the Franco-British alliance and not seen as a purely French event; that even General Gamelin deserved to be considered by history 'as fairly as it considers every commander on whom finally the sun did not shine'.[5] In short, Cairns argued that it was necessary to rescue the history of the defeat from the view that France was terminally decadent in 1940.

In the end Cairns has never written the book on 1940 that his articles seemed to promise, but his work provided the agenda for a number of 'revisionist' works, which started to appear from the 1970s. These works can be called revisionist in the sense that they tried to escape from the paradigm of 'decadence' in their view of the Third Republic. For example, the Canadian historian Robert Young argued in 1978 that French policy in the 1930s was a rational attempt to match objectives with resources. In his view the French prepared intelligently for a long war that would exploit Allied economic superiority. The Israeli-American historian Jeffrey Gunsburg in 1979 offered a remarkably favourable assessment of French military planning in the 1930s. The British historian Martin Alexander in 1992 even assumed the seemingly hopeless task of trying to rehabilitate General Gamelin. Alexander argued that Gamelin had struggled to modernize the French army in the face of overwhelming difficulties. Even if he had to conclude that Gamelin was not entirely successful, Alexander's purpose was to move beyond over-simplifying accounts of the period constructed around contrast between, on the one hand, a few visionaries like de Gaulle, and, on the other, a French High Command that was hidebound, conservative, and impervious to what was going on in the rest of Europe. Analysing the complex constraints—diplomatic, economic, and financial—under which the governments of the later Third Republic operated, all these historians concluded that France's leaders did not perform badly.

These revisionists could not of course ultimately gainsay the fact that France was defeated. Some explanation needed to be offered for that fact. One approach, followed especially by Gunsburg, was to emphasize the *Allied* dimension of the defeat. For Gunsburg, however well the French planned their war and however competent their leadership, nothing could compensate for the fact that in 1940 their allies were able to offer them very little. Secondly, some historians argued that, despite the best efforts of French leaders in the 1930s, France did suffer from underlying political and economic weaknesses that proved insuperable. In other words, there were underlying structural causes of the French defeat, which required to be identified rather than passing inappropriate moral judgements on the state of France or of the French people as a whole. Thirdly, it was possible to argue that ultimately the defeat of 1940 was a primarily military phenomenon caused by military miscalculations which were only related tangentially, if at all, to the political and social background.

While these revisionist works began appearing outside France, most French historians remained remarkably uninterested by the events of 1940. There was, however, a growing interest in modern and contemporary history, and some of this did have important implications for the understanding of the defeat. In 1978 the august Fondation Nationale des Sciences Politiques published two volumes summarizing the proceedings of a conference devoted to the Daladier government of 1938–9. This was the first attempt to study Daladier's government in detail and see it as an important moment in the recovery of French national self-confidence on the eve of the war rather than as just another episode in the game of Third Republic musical chairs. In 1982, the historian Robert Frankenstein published a very technical study of the way in which the French governments had financed rearmament in the 1930s. This book destroyed one old right-wing *canard* by showing that it was under the left-wing Popular Front that French rearmament had begun in earnest. More generally it showed what considerable efforts the Third Republic had made towards rearming France in the late 1930s.

Despite the revisionist implications of these works, the best-known book on the lead-up to the war to appear in France at this time took a very different approach. This was a 1979 study of French foreign policy in the

1930s by the doyen of French diplomatic historians, Jean-Baptiste Duroselle, whose title seemed to say it all: *La Décadence*. Where exactly Duroselle thought the 'decadence' lay was not entirely clear, but one theme of his study was that there had been a failure of political leadership in France. The sub-text of the book seems to be that France lacked a figure of the stature of Clemenceau (or indeed de Gaulle). For Duroselle the assassination of Louis Barthou in 1934 removed the last French politician with the necessary vision and will to stand up to Nazi Germany. In the same spirit, in 1980 Henri Michel, the leading historian of the Committee for the History of the Second World War, wrote of the defeat as 'the outcome of a long process of disintegration affecting all the activities of the French nation'.

From the early 1980s onwards, important studies have been produced by the staff of the Historical Services of the various armed forces. These have added hugely to our understanding of the state of the armed forces on the eve of war, but, because military history continues to be looked down upon by most French university historians this work has not always had the wider impact it deserves or been integrated into a wider picture. The military history of the war has been somewhat ghettoized in France, and its practitioners are themselves not always sensitive to complexities of the political context. For example, a recent useful history of French tanks in 1930, produced under the aegis of the Army Historical Service, tells us that the Third Republic was characterized by 'political instability (42 governments from 1920 to 1940) rendering a coherent defence policy vain'.[6] In fact, despite the political instability of the 1930s, Daladier had been continuously Minister of Defence since 1936, irrespective of the government, and since he worked well with Gamelin, who had been in charge of the army since 1935, they provided a team that offered considerable continuity and coherence in defence planning for four crucial years. That they may have made many errors of judgement is another matter altogether.

One book that stood apart from any other (though interestingly it came from a historian writing from outside the academy) was the massive two-volume work by Jean-François Crémieux-Brilhac, entitled *Les Français de l'an 40* [The French People in 1940] (1990). As a young man during the war, Crémieux-Brilhac had been with the Free French in London and his book was clearly driven by a personal need to understand the events of his own past. It contains pioneering research on the state of French morale in 1939/40, and superb analyses of the economics of rearmament and of the French political background. Crémieux-Brilhac's study provides no simple answers, but it certainly offers a much more positive account of French morale than had any other author previously. For that reason alone, if one had to situate his book historiographically, it would be in the revisionist camp, but it is in reality too nuanced to be pigeon-holed in any way.

It remains a curious fact that the most extreme revisionist studies have come from outside France. The most recent example was the publication in 2001 of a book by the American historian Ernest May, robustly entitled *Strange Victory*. The burden of May's argument is that militarily France was in all respects in a superior position to Germany in 1940—in computer simulations of the likely outcome France wins!—and the defeat was almost entirely attributable to the dramatic failure of the intelligence services to predict the location of the main German attack. But for this fatal error, France should and would have won. This may be a revisionist bridge too far, but the argument has some force.

Many French historians, despite Crémieux-Brilhac's work, still tend somewhat lazily to fall back on crude stereotypes about the Third Republic, almost as if, as a profession, they have unconsciously assimilated the Gaullist idea that the Fifth Republic has finally cured France's constitutional ills. This makes it harder for them to view the Third Republic in an entirely positive light. Thus, a recent much-read textbook by the French historian Serge Berstein invokes the 'drama of the 1930s which in retrospect seems to have led the country inevitably to the tragedy of 1940'.[7] A recent French collection of excellent scholarly essays on 1940 opens with the words: '[E]veryone knows that the conduct of the war of 1939–40 by a deliquescent Republic was disastrous.'[8] The conduct of the war may have been disastrous, but is it really accurate to say that, except in retrospect, the Republic in 1939 was 'deliquescent'?

The ancient historian Pierre Vidal-Naquet has written, in a different context, that 'history is not tragedy. To understand historical reality, it is sometimes necessary not to know the end of the story.'[9] It is certainly true that, when the outcome is known, the narrative tends to write itself too smoothly. In narratives of 1914, Joffre's massive bulk functions as a symbol of his imperturbable moral solidity; in narratives of 1940, the fact that the 'portly' General Corap was so fat as to have difficulty getting into his car serves as a symbol of his sluggishness in responding to the German breakthrough. If we did not know the end of the story, the inter-war Third Republic could be depicted as an extraordinary success story. The reconstruction of the north-east of France during the 1920s was certainly one of the greatest achievements of any country in inter-war Europe. Despite the turmoil of the following decade, between 1934 and 1938 the Third Republic succeeded in seeing off the threat of Fascism, carrying out significant social reforms, and launching ambitious programmes of rearmament.

Clearly France was a very divided country in the 1930s, but writing the history of these years as an inexorable road to decline, leading inevitably from the Stavisky riots in Paris in February 1934 via Munich in September 1938 to the signing of the armistice at Rethondes in June 1940, fails to take account of the remarkable recovery that occurred in the twelve months following Munich. The reassertion of national self-confidence and governmental authority between September 1938 and September 1939 is every bit as striking as the rapid deterioration in France's situation between 1930, when it was seen as the '*île heureuse*' because the economic crisis had not yet struck, and 1932 when it was on the way to becoming the sick man of Europe. In 1938, Daladier was one of the most popular prime ministers France had ever had; by the outbreak of the war his government was already one of the longest lasting in the history of the Third Republic, the economy was recovering so rapidly that Paul Reynaud could justifiably talk of an 'economic miracle', and the rearmament effort was at last taking effect.

## Counterfactuals I: 1914

Although it might be true that the situation in 1939 was healthier than it had been a few years earlier, one is of course starting from a low base. What if the comparison is made not between 1939 and say 1934 but between 1939 and 1914? The result of such a comparison is less telling than one might expect: if for a moment we imagine a German victory in 1914—something that came close to happening—it would not be difficult to construct a political and social narrative that explained why that event was fated to occur. To begin with 'morale', many years ago the historian Jean-Jacques Becker demonstrated that despite the popular image of mass enthusiasm and crowds baying 'To Berlin', the prevalent mood in 1914 was sombre. The words which recur most often in the contemporary accounts are 'consternation', 'tears', 'sadness', and 'resignation'. In cities, the mood was more bellicose, but they also witnessed the largest demonstrations against the war. Some kind of anti-war meeting was recorded in thirty-six departments; the biggest, in Montluçon, attracted some 30,000 participants. In the end this opposition came to nothing, and the proportion of those refusing the call-up was about 1.5 per cent—more or less the same as in 1940.[10] Becker notes that even once the war was underway, in the first days French morale was 'extremely fragile . . . reacting a bit like a weathervane to the gusts of wind'. As we have already noted when discussing the Exodus of 1940, morale reached a low point in August 1914 as the Germans advanced on Paris and the government fled to Bordeaux. As for the fighting qualities of the troops in 1914, it was claimed in the autumn that the XV Corps, made up mainly of meridional troops, had been extremely unreliable. Many monuments to defend the reputation of the XVth were subsequently erected in Provence. The reliability of this particular allegation is questionable but it is certain that there were some cases where morale was very suspect in 1914.

What about the political situation in 1914? One must not underestimate the extent of class conflict in the decade before 1914, which witnessed extremely high levels of strike activity. In the 1900s there was a trade union movement committed, at least in theory, to the doctrine of revolutionary syndicalism and to anti-militarism. Three-year military service, which had been introduced in 1913, was one of the main issues at the 1914 elections. The left-wing parties, which won those elections, had pledged to repeal that law and were only stopped from doing so by the outbreak of war. So frightened was the government of anti-war feeling on the left that it had a list of about 2,500 trade union activists and others who were to be arrested when war broke out.

As far as comparisons of political leadership are concerned, when Duroselle comments that the team of Lebrun–Daladier in 1939 was hardly comparable in quality to that of Poincaré–Clemenceau,[11] he forgets that that team was not in place until November 1917, more than three years after the start of the war. In 1914, the premier was the ineffectual René Viviani, who was constantly on the edge of a nervous breakdown; Poincaré, the President, had only limited opportunity to influence policy; and Clemenceau refused to join any government that he did not lead. Daladier and Reynaud were figures of almost Napoleonic stature if compared to Viviani, whose main preoccupation during the whole month of July, when Europe headed towards the abyss, was the trial of Madame Joseph Caillaux, the wife of one of France's leading politicians, who had shot a newspaper editor dead some months earlier. It is true that there was greater political unity in 1914 than in 1939, but there was also a lot of backbiting and infighting.

As far as relations between the Allies are concerned, we have already seen that structures of coordination were much more rapidly set up in 1939 than in 1914, when they barely existed at all. Of course such structures did not guarantee that in human terms relations would be cordial, and we have seen that often they were not. But the relations between General French, Commander of the BEF in 1914, and General Lanrezac in command of the French Second Army in 1914, were every bit as bad as those between Gort and Blanchard or Weygand in 1940. When French and Lanrezac first met on 17 August 1914, no interpreters were present in order to preserve secrecy, although each man could barely speak more than a few words in the other's language. French tried to ask whether the Germans were going to cross the Meuse at Huy, but had trouble with this almost unpronounceable name, which needs almost to be whistled. Eventually he spat the word out, and an exasperated Lanrezac replied: 'tell the Marshal that in my opinion the Germans have merely gone to the Meuse to fish'. This very much set the tone for the future.[12] The ubiquitous Spears, who was acting as a liaison officer between the two armies, remarks of Lanrezac that he 'invariably tended to prefer retreat to battle'—showing that his skills at acerbic commentary were already well honed. Although the Allies did learn to work with each other, relations between Haig and Pétain in 1918 were also atrocious, and Pétain had not forgotten this in 1940.

As far as military planning is concerned, Joffre's infamous Plan XVII of 1914, which involved an offensive into Lorraine, was quite as disastrous as Plan D in 1940. Joffre completely misread the German intentions and was slower than Gamelin in 1940 to realize a terrible mistake had been made. The French General Staff's understanding of the nature of modern warfare was every bit as bad in 1914 as in 1940, if not indeed worse. The British military writer Fuller described Joffre as a 'tactically demented Napoleon'. It was not only Joffre who was at fault. The 24-year-old lieutenant de Gaulle wrote in September 1914: '[A]ll the wounded officers are agreed on the profound reasons for our early drawbacks ... inadequacy ... of too many of the divisional and brigadier-generals who did not know how to use the various arms in liaison with each other.' Joffre had to sack so many generals in the summer that he gave the new word '*limoger*' to the French language (the disgraced generals were exiled to Limoges, where, Spears tells us, 'they were popularly supposed to while away the time by playing melancholy games of bridge together'). Finally, it should be noted that in 1914 France suffered from a serious inferiority in armaments, especially artillery. French military spending in 1938 was in real terms 2.6 times what it had been in 1913.

In short, France was less ready for war in 1914 than in 1939. But in 1914 there was time to adapt, thanks to the victory of the Marne. That victory can be explained by a German mistake—when von Kluck wheeled his armies to the east of Paris thus exposing his flank to counterattack—and possibly by the Russian alliance: Moltke diverted six army corps to the eastern front on 25 August 1914. In 1940 there was no Russian alliance and no German mistake—except Hitler's 'halt order' of 24 May. This was a terrible miscalculation, which allowed the British to salvage a large part of the BEF, but did not much help the French.

## Counterfactuals II: Britain's Finest Hour

Even if it is true that France was better prepared for war in 1914 than in 1939, it could certainly be argued that, whereas many deficiencies were quickly overcome in 1914, in 1939 France's situation deteriorated during the Phoney War. These eight months saw political infighting, popular demoralization, and problems with armaments production. If a link is to be made between France's political and social conditions and the defeat, it can be more convincingly done by looking not so much at the last years of the Third Republic in general as at the very specific conditions of the Phoney War. This has led the Canadian historian Talbot Imlay to offer a suggestive middle way position between the 'decadence school' and the 'revisionists'. While rejecting the proposition that France was doomed to defeat once the war broke out, he argues that the defeat was not just the result of a series of military blunders. It resulted from the failure of France's political leaders to seize their opportunities during the Phoney War. In this view France's defeat was explained not so much by long-term structural deficiencies as by the conjunctural problems of the Phoney War. In the days preceding the German attack, the Reynaud government was mired in political crisis while the rearmament effort was stymied by the liberal economic choices that had been adopted after Munich. These choices were themselves imposed by the need to rally conservative support, but did not in fact prevent many conservatives from feeling distinctly lukewarm about the war. In short, political and economic factors pulled the government in contradictory directions. In this interpretation, Reynaud's advocacy of schemes like the Caucasus operation were signs of desperation, an attempt to escape from his domestic dilemmas before they doomed France.

To reinforce his point, Imlay contrasts French inadequacies during the Phoney War with the more successful policies pursued by the British. The problem, however, about linking the defeat to France's difficulties during the Phoney War is that it would in fact also be easy to highlight many similar difficulties in Britain during the Phoney War, or as many people revealingly called it, the 'bore war'. If for a moment we imagine a second counterfactual—British defeat in 1940—there would be no difficulty in demonstrating the inevitability of this event.

To begin with propaganda, British performance in the first months of the war was generally agreed to be a disaster, quite as bad as Giraudoux's efforts in France. The first Minister of Information, Lord Macmillan, was so ineffectual that he was replaced in January 1940 by Lord Reith, formerly the head of the BBC. Reith himself was no more successful and was moved in May 1940. A particularly bad impression was created by one government poster that proclaimed: '*Your* courage, *your* cheerfulness, *your* resolution will bring us victory'. The organization Mass Observation, which attempted to monitor public opinion, found that people resented the distinction between 'your' and 'us', as if ordinary people were being asked to sacrifice themselves for their leaders.[13] When it came to propaganda, however, the greatest criticism was reserved for the BBC, whose broadcasts seemed stale and boring. Many people tuned into the Radio Hamburg broadcasts of William Joyce, popularly known as 'Lord Haw Haw', formerly a member of Oswald Mosley's British Union of Fascists. The Listener Research Department of the BBC found in January 1940 that 30 per cent of the population listened to his broadcasts. The rumours spread by people listening to Lord Haw Haw began to cause great concern to the Ministry of Information. By March the novelty had worn off, and only one-sixth of the population listened regularly to Lord Haw Haw, though only one-third said they never listened at all.[14] For a while the phenomenon of Lord Haw Haw was as disconcerting to the British authorities as the equivalent case of Paul Ferdonnet broadcasting to France on Radio Stuttgart. If Ferdonnet has gone down in folk memory as a somewhat sinister figure and Lord Haw Haw as a faintly ridiculous one, that is due to what happened subsequently.

During the Phoney War, British morale was no better than French. One historian suggests that between September 1939 and May 1940 British morale was probably lower than at any other time during the war.[15] Mass Observation concluded its study of the subject in 1940 by reporting:

A strong feeling in the country that the wretched war is not worth going on with ... looking back we can suspect that Hitler has won News-Round 1 in this war. He's been able to give his own people a tremendous success story—Poland—but he has also made millions of people bewildered. Bewilderment is the first step to suspicion.

The Socialist intellectual Beatrice Webb wrote in her diary on 5 October 1940: 'Everyone I speak to seems utterly bewildered and downcast, far more so than in the early days of the last war. There is no war enthusiasm—at most, a dull acquiescence.'[16] All this was encouraging to those groups lobbying for an end to the war. During the inter-war years there had been a strong feeling that Germany had been badly treated at Versailles, and traces of this remained in 1939. In the mid-1930s pro-German sentiment was stimulated by Hitler's future Foreign Minister, Ribbentrop, who visited London first as an unofficial envoy and then as Ambassador. Ribbentrop attempted the same role of seduction in London as Otto Abetz in Paris. Unlike the charming Abetz, the vulgar Ribbentrop certainly put many members of the British elite off, but he was not entirely unsuccessful. He played both on fear of war and anti-Communism. Among fervent anti-Communists was Lord Rothermere, proprietor of the *Daily Mail*, who had started purchasing estates in central Hungary as a refuge in case of revolution. Rothermere visited Hitler in December 1934. Like Abetz, Ribbentrop exploited the sense of comradeship and hatred of war felt by war veterans. He organized a visit to Germany in July 1935 by leaders of the British Legion. Abetz's Comité Franco-Allemande had its equivalent in the Deutsch-Englische Gesellschaft. More important than this was the Anglo-German Fellowship founded by the merchant banker Ernest Tennant, another friend of Ribbentrop, which had quite a bit of support among businessmen.

Among the many prominent British figures who visited Hitler in the 1930s were the pacifist Lord Allen of Hurtwood (January 1935), the pacifist Liberal peer Lord Lothian (January 1935 and April 1935), the former Prime Minister, David Lloyd George (1936), the former Labour leader George Lansbury (April 1937), and the Duke and Duchess of Windsor (October 1937). Two particularly fervent admirers of Hitler were the Duke of Buccleuch and Lord Brockett, both former conservative MPs, who attended Hitler's 50th birthday celebrations in 1939.

By 1939 most of these people had certainly lost their illusions about Hitler, apart from ultra-pacifists or hardcore Nazi sympathizers. The latter included *The Anglo-German Review*, edited by the *mutilé de guerre*, C. E. Carroll, with a circulation of about 12,000; the Link, founded in 1937 by Admiral Sir Barry Domvile, a former director of Naval Intelligence, and having about 4,300 members in 1939; the National Socialist League, founded by William Joyce and John Beckett, both former members of the BUF. Even more obscure were the British People's Party, founded in April 1939; the Nordic League—one of whose leaders declared in 1939 that he saw his mission as 'spreading the Gospel of Hate of the Jews'; and the Liberty Restoration League with the Duke of Wellington as its President. In May 1939 a speaker at a British People's Party meeting asked: 'Why should British lives be sacrificed to prevent Danzig, a German city, going back to Germany?'[17] It would clearly be absurd to inflate the importance of these fanatical groups, but it is worth remembering that even in France most of the most extreme pro-Nazis had repented or fallen silent after March 1939. If Marcel Déat's article 'Mourir pour Danzig' has left more traces in the history books than the speeches of the British People's Party, it was because of Déat's subsequent activities during the war. At the time the article fell largely on deaf ears and only served to demonstrate Déat's isolation. A number of British pro-peace activists continued to lobby during the Phoney War. They were particularly active amongst members of the House of Lords and included the Duke of Westminster, Lord Londonderry, the Duke of Buccleuch, Lord Tavistock (who succeeded to the title of the Duke of Bedford in 1940), Lord Redesdale (father of the notorious Mitford sisters, one of whom, Diana, was married to Oswald Mosley, and another of whom, Unity, fell in love with Hitler and tried to kill herself in 1940), Lord Brocket, Lord Mottistone, the Earl of Galloway, and the Earl of Mar. These were all figures of the right, or even the extreme right, some of whom had been in the Anglo-German Fellowship or the Link. There were also peers inspired more by a commitment to peace than attraction to Fascism. They included the former Labour MP Lord Arnold, the former Labour MP Lord Ponsonby, and the lifelong Labour pacifist Lord Noel-Buxton. On 11 September a meeting of anti-war peers took place at the house of the Duke of Westminster; a meeting a week later was also attended by some MPs. Just as Pétain's first Vichy governments had more representatives of the military than any French administration since Marshal Soult in 1832, any equivalent administration in Britain would probably have contained more peers than any other government since the Duke of Grafton's in 1776.

There were also a few right-wing pro-peace figures in the House of Commons. Several of them were members of the secret Right Club, formed by the MP Captain Archibald Ramsay in May 1939 to cleanse conservatism of Jewish control. This group had eleven MPs. More significant than these right-wing extremists was the Parliamentary Peace Aims Group, organized by the maverick Labour MP Richard Stokes. Consisting of about thirty MPs, mostly Labour, and ten peers, the group met weekly. It pressed the government to seek out the possibilities of a negotiated peace. There was much coming and going between these people and intermediaries who claimed to be in contact with moderates in the German government. Stokes, who was in Istanbul in January 1940, had a meeting with Germany's Ambassador, von Papen. Tavistock had a meeting with Halifax in January and claimed to have secret contact with the German leaders via the German Embassy in Dublin. Others had contacts with Goering's agent Prince Max von Hohenlohe in Switzerland. Another indefatigable mediator was the Swedish businessman Birger Dahlerus who also claimed privileged access to Goering. Alexander Cadogan described Dalherus as 'like a wasp at a picnic—one can't beat him off'.[18]

Wasps are rarely fatal, and Cadogan's dismissive comment shows that the government did not take any of this too seriously. None of the pro-peace peers were first-rank, or even third-rank, political figures. They were associated with extreme right organizations, which had almost no following in the country. Cadogan argued that there was no reason to stop the 'halfwit' Lord Tavistock publishing a pamphlet outlining his views in February 1940 since the best way of discrediting his views was to allow him to express them. As for those in the Commons favouring negotiations, they were a small and isolated group. Nonetheless they cannot be dismissed as entirely without importance, since there was certainly some audience in the country for the idea of conciliation. Pacifism still had a considerable constituency on the outbreak of war. The biggest pacifist organization, the Peace Pledge Union, had about 136,000 members in September 1939. One of its leading members was the feminist and Socialist Vera Brittain, who remained an indefatigable propagandist for pacifist ideas throughout the war. She wrote a weekly 'Letter to Peace Lovers', which had 2,000 sub-scribers. On 7 October 1939 George Bernard Shaw wrote a letter to *The New Statesman* advocating peace (to the horror of Marc Bloch in France). This gave rise to considerable correspondence over the following weeks. In the next issue, 17 intellectuals, including Clive Bell, Vera Brittain, and John Middleton Murry, signed a letter of support. Members of the National Peace Council, including the very popular philosopher Cyril Joad, the socialist intellectual G. D. H. Cole, the actress Sybil Thorndike, and the actor John Gielgud, wrote to Chamberlain urging him to 'give sympathetic consideration' to a peace proposal sponsored by neutral powers. Pacifist opinion also had support from a number of leading clergymen including the Bishops of Chichester, Southwark, and Birmingham. Opposition to the war not only came from pacifists, however. The influential military expert Basil Liddell Hart believed in March 1940 that Britain should 'come to the best possible terms as soon as possible'; there was 'no chance of avoiding defeat'. To this end Liddell Hart opposed the war, fearing that a total German defeat would result in Soviet domination of the Continent and feeling that Hitler was essentially a reasonable statesman.[19]

The MP Harold Nicolson, an ardent supporter of the war, was dis-quieted by the number of defeatist colleagues whom he encountered. He detected an atmosphere of 'disillusion and grumbling', which he compared unfavourably with the mood in France. Visiting France at the end of October 1939, he commented, having met numerous leading French politi-cians: '[A]ll these conversations convince me that we are much too defeat-ist in London and that these people are absolutely confident of victory.'[20] In the light of subsequent events Nicolson's remark seems ironic, even absurd, but in fact the number of French *députés* actively lobbying for peace was not much larger than that of British M.P., doing likewise: there were about fifteen members of the 'parliamentary liaison committee' against the war and twenty-two had signed the motion on 3 September calling for a Comité Secret to discuss the issue of war credits. Of course figures like Flandin and Laval had greater weight than the members of the Peace Aims Group, and the peace faction in France had supporters within the government itself, like de Monzie and Bonnet. But even in Britain there were figures of political significance who, while not part of the peace faction, would have been ready to offer it support in the right circumstances. The most important of these was Lloyd George, who had been greatly impressed by Hitler when he met him in 1936. In October 1939 Lloyd George spoke in favour of negotiations with Germany in the House of Commons. After this he remained silent, but the Peace Aims Group kept in touch with him, and he was biding his time. In January 1940, he told the newspaper editor Hugh Cudlipp 'we shall lose the war'.[21]

Another figure who seemed ready at one stage to play the peace card was the press baron Lord Beaverbrook, who on 3 March invited to dinner three leading peace campaigners from the left-wing Independent Labour Party (ILP) and told them that he was prepared to support their peace appeal. The Foreign Office, which heard about this, reported that Beaverbrook was 'believed to be under the impression that there is a widespread feeling in the country in favour of a negotiated peace'. It was most embarrassing to Beaverbrook when this was revealed in 1941: by then he was a member of Churchill's War Cabinet.

As in France, there were also members of the government whose commitment to the war was somewhat half-hearted. Among these one could probably put the Prime Minister, Neville Chamberlain, himself whose initial reaction to Hitler's occupation of Prague had been to continue appeasement. It was the intervention of his Foreign Secretary, Lord Halifax, which convinced him of the necessity of abandoning the policy. But in the months leading up to the declaration of war he and his close adviser Sir Horace Wilson had clearly not entirely given up hope that a final concession might be enough to stop Hitler. Another member of the government distinctly unhappy about going to war was the Parliamentary Under-Secretary of State at the F.O., R. A. Butler. In July he was arguing that the British should use their influence to make the Poles more amenable to German demands. In March 1940, when Roosevelt's envoy Sumner Welles was in Europe to explore the possibility of peace, Butler told the Foreign Secretary Lord Halifax that he would not 'exclude a truce if Mussolini, the

Pope and Roosevelt would come in'. Halifax replied: 'You are very bold . . . but I agree with you.'[22]

On 10 May, Neville Chamberlain was replaced as Prime Minister by Winston Churchill. Surely this is the point at which the comparisons with France must cease? Churchill was, history tells us, that great war leader France so sorely lacked. He, not Paul Reynaud, turned out to be the Clemenceau of 1940. As Daladier's biographer Elizabeth de Réau comments: 'Paul Reynaud did not succeed in creating a real War Cabinet, comparable to that which Churchill was to construct a little later.'[23] But there is a danger, yet again, of allowing one's perceptions to be clouded by retrospective knowledge.

In 1940 Churchill's position was far from secure. Like Reynaud, he was a maverick, distrusted for his impulsiveness and ambition; like Reynaud, he was in effect a man without a party. Nowhere was the suspicion of Churchill greater than within the Conservative Party. 'The Tories don't trust Winston,' as Lord Davidson wrote to Stanley Baldwin. He was distrusted for his 'disorderly mind' (Halifax), his 'inability to concentrate on business' (Chamberlain), his tendency to be 'rambling and romantic and sentimental and temperamental' (Cadogan). The view of Chamberlain's Private Secretary, John Colville, was that 'Winston will be a complete failure'. There was particular distrust of his entourage, 'gangsters' as they were commonly described. Chamberlain's Parliamentary Private Secretary Alec Dunglass—the future Prime Minister Alec Douglas Home—felt that the 'kind of people surrounding Winston are the scum'. The conservative MP 'Chips' Channon, a Chamberlain loyalist, wrote in his diary that the replacement of Chamberlain by Churchill made 10 May 1940 'perhaps the darkest day in English history'. At the end of that day he joined Butler, Dunglass, and Colville in drinking a champagne toast to the 'king over the water' [i.e. Chamberlain]. On the day Churchill arrived in the House of Commons for the first time as Prime Minister, the Conservative cheers for Chamberlain were much louder than for him. Throughout May Churchill continued to get a stony reception from the Conservative benches. This started to create such a bad impression, especially among American journalists, that party officials set about organizing a more enthusiastic reception for him.[24]

For these reasons, when he came to power Churchill was in far too weak a political position to be able to dispense with the services of the former 'appeasers'. His government was not dissimilar in composition to its predecessor, apart from the addition of Labour members. Chamberlain and Halifax were among the five members of his War Cabinet. The only prominent figure to be sacked was the Chamberlain loyalist Sir Samuel Hoare—

famous as the signatory of the Hoare–Laval pact in 1935—who was sent to be Ambassador in Madrid. This pleased Cadogan, who saw Hoare as the 'Quisling of England'. He took comfort from the fact that there were lots of 'Germans and Italians in Madrid and therefore a good chance of [Hoare] being murdered!'[25]

Churchill's position was not strong enough to prevent a major debate raging in the Cabinet between 26 and 28 May over the possibility of approaching Italy to sound out German peace terms. The dramatic background to these discussions was the failure of Weygand's plan for an Allied counterattack. There were five meetings of the British Cabinet to discuss this issue between 26 and 28 May. Halifax argued in favour of discovering what terms the Germans might be willing to offer: 'if . . . we could obtain terms which did not postulate the destruction of our independence, we should be foolish if we did not accept them'. The discussions became acrimonious enough for Halifax to consider resigning. He thought that 'Winston talked the most frightful rot'.

In the end Halifax's proposal was rejected: the French were told that there would be no approach to Italy. Churchill succeeded in persuading the Cabinet that Halifax's proposal was a 'slippery slope'. It would be wrong, however, to portray the debates within the British government as pitting a 'defeatist' Halifax, eager to make peace, against a 'resolute' Churchill, prepared to fight on to the bitter end. In the context of the events taking place in France it would have been irresponsible for the government not at least to consider its future position towards the war. In opposing Halifax, Churchill himself did not reject the prospect of one day approaching Germany about peace terms: '[A] time might come when we felt that we had to put an end to the struggle, but the terms would not then be more mortal than those offered to us now.' Churchill argued that, once Britain had shown that it was ready to fight on, and had done so, it would be in a better position to sue for terms than in its present condition of weakness. For Halifax, on the other hand, it might be possible to obtain more favourable terms before the total collapse of France than after it. No more than Churchill was he prepared to accept any terms that would compromise Britain's 'independence'. But he defined 'independence' in possibly less rigorous terms.

Even Churchill, however, was prepared to allow 'a restoration of German colonies and the overlordship of Central Europe', but 'never' a 'German domination of Europe'. According to Chamberlain, Churchill went as far as to say that 'if we could get out of this jam by giving up Malta and Gibraltar and some African colonies he would jump at it'. But he did not believe that this was the case. Nonetheless, although Churchill would not accept the idea of asking for terms, if he were told what they were, he 'would be prepared to consider them'. The difference between Halifax and Churchill was therefore not as stark as might be imagined in the light of Churchill's adoption in January 1943 of the policy of 'unconditional surrender'. That was a long way ahead in 1940.[26]

Of course it may be that Churchill in 1940 was adopting a more moderate position as a tactic to keep Halifax's support. It may equally be that Halifax was underplaying his own commitment to peace in order to win the Cabinet over to the idea of negotiations in the hope that once the government had embarked down this road it would find it hard to turn back: this was precisely the insidious strategy employed by Chautemps when he proposed that Reynaud agree to seek the terms of an armistice. Another view is that Halifax only supported the idea of peace feelers in order to avoid giving the French any grounds for recrimination.

Whatever the tactical undercurrents in the debate, one thing is certain: the idea of exploring the possibility of peace was seriously on the agenda within the British government at the end of May 1940, although it was never again discussed at such a high level or so intensively. For most of 1940 Churchill was still viewed with suspicion by his own party. On the day he delivered his famous 'finest hour' speech to the Commons, the Labour MP and minister Hugh Dalton noted: '[I]t is noticeable how much more loudly he is cheered by the Labour Party than by the general body of Tory supporters. The relative silence of the latter is regarded by some as sinister.'[27] After Dunkirk there was a press campaign against the so-called 'guilty men', the former appeasers, many of whom were still in the government. Churchill was worried about this. Summoning various press lords, he told them to stop the campaign because 'if he trampled on these men as he could trample on them, they would set themselves against him, and in such internecine strife lay the Germans' best chance of victory'.[28] Even admirers of Churchill had their doubts about him. Among these was the press proprietor Cecil King, who noted his disappointment on hearing a radio speech by Churchill on 18 June: 'a few stumbling sentences . . . the poorest possible effort on an occasion when he should have produced the finest speech of his life'.[29]

Churchill felt vulnerable enough to try to tempt Lloyd George into his government in order to stop his becoming a focus for discontent. There were rumours at the end of June that Lloyd George was hoping to become the British Pétain. But Lloyd George, who remarked to one visitor in June that Hitler was the 'greatest figure in Europe since Napoleon, and probably greater than him', rebuffed all offers. He told his secretary in October: 'I shall wait until Winston is bust.' Even within the government there were still those who had not entirely given up hope of possibly extricating the country from the war. On 17 June Butler had a conversation with Björn Prytz, the Swedish Minister, in London. Prytz reported him as saying that 'no opportunity for reaching a compromise peace would be neglected', and that 'no "diehards" would be allowed to stand in the way in this connection'. He also passed on a message, supposedly from Halifax, that 'common sense and not bravado' would govern British policy. Butler's off-the-cuff comments were taken more seriously than he had intended, and the Foreign Office was quickly forced to assure the Swedish government that there was no change of policy by the British government. Churchill warned Halifax that Butler's 'odd language' had given the Swedes a 'strong impression of defeatism'. Butler himself offered his resignation, agreeing that he 'should have been more cautious'.[30]

Butler's protestations of good faith were accepted, and it is likely that his remarks had been to some extent distorted. Butler was only a junior member of the government, but at the start of July, when the Pope was making suggestions about peace, Cadogan noted that 'silly old H[alifax] was evidently hankering after them'. In Madrid Hoare was reported to be 'forcefully arguing for a compromise' at the start of July. After a speech by Hitler on 19 July, Lord Lothian, the Ambassador in Washington, a long-standing advocate of appeasement, took it upon himself to find out, through the intermediary of an American Quaker, what the German peace terms might be. On 22 July he was reported as claiming that the German terms were 'most satisfactory'.[31]

Churchill, however, rejected any talk of this kind, and towards the end of the year his political position became stronger. In the autumn Neville Chamberlain was diagnosed with cancer, and Churchill replaced him as leader of the Conservative Party. The sudden death of Lord Lothian in December gave Churchill the opportunity to remove Halifax from the government by sending him to Washington (having first offered the post to Lloyd George). Halifax was replaced as Foreign Secretary by the long-standing 'anti-appeaser' Anthony Eden. Victories against the Italians in North Africa at the end of 1940 further bolstered Churchill's confidence. When Lloyd George made a somewhat defeatist speech in Parliament in May 1941, Churchill felt no need to conciliate him. He compared Lloyd George's words to the 'sort of speech with which I imagine the illustrious Marshal Pétain might well have enlivened the closing days of M. Paul Reynaud's cabinet'.

If 1940 was Churchill's finest hour, then, it had also been his most difficult. It was only in retrospect that it took on such a glorious hue thanks to the victorious Battle of Britain. The myth of Churchill was a result of victory, not its cause. Its main cause was geographical: the English Channel was a major obstacle to any successful invasion. Nor had Hitler made any serious plans to surmount that obstacle by preparing an invasion plan. After the defeat of France, which came faster than he expected, Hitler had believed that the British would sue for peace. It was only on 16 July that he issued a directive for the invasion, code-named Operation Sealion. Since the army had no landing-craft, the main role in preparing the ground for the invasion rested with the Luftwaffe. But the Luftwaffe had not been designed with a view to launching a separate air offensive. The odds were therefore stacked against the Germans in a battle to which Hitler was only half-committed. Already his thoughts were turning to an invasion of Russia. On 17 September, Hitler decided to postpone the invasion of Britain indefinitely.

That is not to say that Churchill's leadership played no part in the victory. As soon as he became Prime Minister, he succeeded in invigorating the government and inspiring the population in a way Reynaud signally failed to do in France. In August 1940 a poll showed that 88 per cent of the population approved of his leadership. Even so, one must be wary of investing Churchill's rhetoric with an aura that it did not necessarily have at the time. Of that gravelly voice, which seems in retrospect to embody the British fighting spirit of 1940, Halifax commented that it 'oozes with port, brandy and the chewed cigar'.[32] As for the effect of those speeches on the population at large, only five of the speeches Churchill made as Prime Minister in 1940 were broadcast and therefore heard directly by the people. Most of them were only heard in the House of Commons. It is true that Churchill's rhetoric, which only a few months earlier had seemed old-fashioned and ridiculous, even to his admirers, suddenly suited the national mood in a way it had never done before, but in the unlikely event that the Germans had succeeded in their invasion, Churchill's stirring words about fighting on the beaches would have taken on the same retrospective absurdity as Reynaud's often mocked rhetoric of 1940: '[W]e will win because we are the strongest.' It is in the light of defeat that Reynaud's rhetoric seems so hollow.

The effect of Churchill's speeches on morale is hard to calculate, as indeed is the impact of morale on victory. Public opinion can change very fast. British propaganda turned the Dunkirk evacuation into a kind of victory, and succeeded in hiding the fact that the mood of the returning soldiers was initially so poor that many of the men threw their equipment out of the windows of the trains that met them on their return to Britain. In monitoring morale throughout the war, the Ministry of Information concluded that it rose and fell according to the level of military success. Indeed morale continued to cause problems in the British army throughout the war. General Adam, visiting Italy in January 1945, found senior commanders 'obsessed with the problem of desertion'. Two British army training centres found in 1942 that most of the recruits 'lack enthusiasm and interest in the war and betray ignorance of the issues involved in it'. British soldiers who underwent Stuka bombardment for the first time in 1940 were no less alarmed than the French had been. One infantryman wrote: 'an attack by Stukas ... cannot be described, it is entirely beyond the comprehension of anyone who has not experienced it. The noise alone strikes such terror that the body becomes paralysed, the still active mind is convinced that each and every aircraft is coming for you personally.' In short, morale, in the British army as in the French, was volatile, and varied from unit to unit according to circumstances. One must resist the temptation to draw unwarranted general conclusions about the state of French—or British—society from so fluctuating a phenomenon.[33]

Neither of these counterfactual speculations—France losing in 1914 or Britain losing in 1940—must be pushed too far. The political divisions of France in 1939 were certainly much deeper than in 1914 or than Britain in 1940. The loyalty with which Chamberlain acted towards his successor Churchill stands in striking contrast to Daladier's petty behaviour towards Reynaud. The conflict between Reynaud and Daladier was nothing compared to the hatred which existed towards Blum in conservative circles. This made it impossible for Reynaud to consider taking Blum into his government, although the relations between the two men were very good. In mid-April 1940 the British Ambassador, Campbell, was embarrassed by the fact that on a visit to Paris Churchill had dined *tête-à-tête* with Blum: 'certain circles in Paris bitterly resent the fuss we make of Blum'. Campbell himself would have liked to see more of Blum but had 'to abstain since it is said in the salons which need to be kept sweet that the Embassy is very "red"'. A few weeks later Campbell reported that there was talk of creating a government of national unity made up of all former premiers but it came up against the 'Blum problem': 'it is extraordinary how one bumps up against this problem at every turn!'.[34] This made it very difficult for any leader to create the kind of political and social consensus that Churchill was able to achieve after May 1940.

The entry of leading Labour ministers into Churchill's government was

25. Blum was the subject of violent attacks in the right-wing press. This one appeared in the right-wing paper *Gringoire* on 18 January 1938. Under the title 'Invasion', it depicts Blum as a piper attracting an invasion of Communist and Socialist rats into France

to underpin this consensus and contributed importantly to the later suc-cesses of the British war economy. But even here contrasts between the two countries must not be drawn too starkly. Even if the French working class was as sullen and alienated as seems to have been the case, it is difficult to prove that this had any effect on production. In some respects the French war economy worked less well than the British one, but Reynaud's anti-inflation policies when Finance Minister were courageous and sensible. Many of the French production problems in the Phoney War were caused by the mistakes made at mobilization, and the effects of these were grad-ually being overcome. There is no single 'right' way to run a war economy. Both countries were feeling their way towards the most effective policies.

But even if one concedes that the French war effort did run into prob-lems during the Phoney War, it is difficult to link these directly to the kind of defeat that France suffered in 1940. If they had not been overcome, these problems might well have proved fatal, but we cannot know this since before it could dig in for the long war, France lost the short one. Even those who believe there was something fundamentally wrong with France in 1940 are hard put to show how this related to the short six weeks of fighting. They can argue only that France was like the victim of a violent murder who is subsequently found to have been suffering from an incurable disease, but they cannot show that the disease was the cause of the death in the form it took place. The defeat of France was first and foremost a military defeat—so rapid and so total that these other factors did not have time to come into play.

## The Other Side of the Hill: Germany

One way of answering the question why France lost is to examine German strengths rather than concentrate on French weaknesses. Taking a long-term perspective it is clear that France was a country in relative decline since the mid-nineteenth century, being rapidly outstripped by Germany both economically and demographically. Perhaps then we should be asking not why France lost in 1940—or 1870–1—but why it won in 1914–18. As the French diplomat Jules Cambon confided to a colleague in 1921: '[Y]oung man, remember this: in the immediate future the difficulty will be to slide France reasonably smoothly into the ranks of the second-rank powers to which she belongs.'[35]

France won in 1918 only thanks to its allies. Its leaders knew that this victory was a provisional and artificial one. Marshal Foch presciently described the Armistice of 1918 as a twenty-year truce. The Treaty of Versailles represented an attempt to embed France's temporary post-war dominance into something permanent despite the deeper structural trends of demography and economic power. If the situation unravelled even faster than the French had feared, it was because the British (and Americans) refused to underwrite the French position, and because France's finances were so badly undermined by the war. The value of the franc was falling rapidly in the first half of the 1920s. These two factors came together in 1923–4, when the French were unable to exploit their 'victory' over Germany in the Ruhr because they found themselves dependent on British and American loans to shore up their currency. The occupation of the Ruhr had merely succeeded in revealing France's weakness. French predominance in Europe was already over by 1924.

In the second half of the 1920s French governments made a virtue of necessity and embraced reconciliation with Germany. However idealistic the language in which Briand couched his policy, he was driven by realism: 'I make the foreign policy of our birth-rate', he once observed. Many of those in the 1930s who advocated appeasement of Germany and dis-engagement from Eastern Europe believed themselves to be the authentic heirs of Briand. But there was a point at which reconciliation became abdication, and that was a choice that French leaders and the French people, in their majority, were not prepared to accept. What is remarkable about France in 1939 is not the alleged defeatism and pessimism, which many observers claim to have detected in retrospect, but on the contrary the extraordinary confidence of the French political and military elites that it could win a war, and that to survive as a great power it had to do so. As Gamelin wrote to Daladier in December 1938: '[T]he question is whether France wishes to renounce its status as a European Great Power and aban-don to Germany hegemony over not only central but all of eastern Europe.'[36]

France's confidence was buttressed by the fact that the country had at last secured a British alliance. It was believed that in the long term the superior combined resources of the Allies would prevail as they had in 1918. In fact in the long run it could be said that this strategy was vindicated. The Allies had planned for a defeat for Germany in, probably, 1943; it came in 1945. When de Gaulle went to London in 1940 and declared that the defeat of France was only the first round in what was in reality a world war, he was remaining faithful to the entire Allied strategy. In this perspective, the Battle of France can be seen not as an episode disconnected from the war that followed, but as part of that larger conflict. In the Battle of France the Germans lost 1,428 planes—28 per cent of the total—and this signifi-cantly weakened the Luftwaffe before the Battle of Britain. What the Allies had not expected was that while they were preparing to win the long war, France would lose a short one. To some extent that defeat can be blamed on the deficiencies of Allied coordination—between Britain and France, between France, Britain, and Belgium. For example, the French believed that the Belgians were better prepared to defend the Gembloux gap than was in fact the case. Coordination between the BEF and the French was execrable once the retreat had begun. The key issue, however, was not lack of coordination, but the simple fact that the British could only offer very limited help in the early stages. Ironside commented on 17 May: 'I found that Greenwood was inclined to say "these bloody gallant Allies". I told him that we had depended upon the French army. That we had made no Army and that therefore it was not right to say "these bloody Allies". It was for them to say that of us.'[37]

That does not mean that the French reproaches against the British were all well founded. The British made a considerable contribution in the air, and did as much as was possible while retaining what was necessary for the security of the British Isles. The British lost a total of almost 1,000 aircraft in the Battle of France. And even if they had been willing to sacrifice even more, at the risk of jeopardizing their security for the sake of the alliance, there is no chance that this would have significantly changed the outcome of the battle. Despite German air superiority, the Battle of France was not won or lost in the air. As Air Chief Marshal Barratt, commander of the AASF, put it: 'the RAF could not win the war if the French infantry had lost it.'

Why did the French infantry lose it? Was German military strength so overwhelming, German military prowess so superior, that there was nothing France could have done about it? There are, it must be said, many myths about Germany in 1940, beginning with the elusive notion of 'Blitzkrieg'. The myth runs as follows: Blitzkrieg (lightning war) was a strategy conceived to allow Germany to overcome its industrial inferiority in relation to the combined economic strength of the Allies by winning a series of successive lightning knockout military victories. Another advantage of this method was to make it unnecessary for Hitler to shift the German economy onto a total war footing, something he was reluctant to do for political and social reasons. But in the view of the German historian Karl-Heinz Frieser, who has most recently and exhaustively studied the notion of Blitzkrieg, there is no validity in this account.[38] Blitzkrieg in fact emerged in a rather haphazard way from the experience of the French campaign, whose success surprised the Germans as much as the French. Why otherwise did the High Command try on various occasions, with Hitler's backing, to slow the panzers down, finally doing so on 24 May with the *Haltbefehl*? The victory in France came about partly because the German High Command temporarily lost control of the battle. The decisive moment in this process was Guderian's decision to move immediately westward on 14 May, the day after the Meuse crossing, wrenching the whole of the rest of the army along behind him.

Germany's success in France did lead to the adoption of Blitzkrieg at a politico-strategic level in 1941 with the invasion of Russia. Thus, to quote Frieser: '[T]he [French] campaign was an improvised but successful Blitzkrieg while that against Russia was a planned but unsuccessful one.' Blitzkrieg, at a politico-strategic level, was a backward-looking denial of the realities of modern industrial warfare. The war as a whole ended up more like the one that the Allies had expected to fight in 1940 than the one the Germans hoped to fight in 1941.

Where the idea of 'Blitzkrieg' did inform the campaign of 1940 was at the tactical and operational level. It derived from the 'infiltration tactics' pioneered by the Germans in 1918 as a way of breaking out of the stalemate of the Western Front. After a short and intensive artillery bombardment, groups of specially trained assault units or 'storm-troopers' had been sent, under cover of smoke and shells, to infiltrate the enemy lines, bypassing pockets of resistance if necessary. This tactic proved extremely successful, but insufficient mobility made it impossible to exploit the advantage gained sufficiently rapidly. In the 1920s, Guderian and others worked on how to overcome this problem by using modern military technology such as tanks, planes, and radio communications. One key element in their thinking was the need to develop close cooperation between different arms, especially between air and land forces.

Another source of Blitzkrieg was the writings of British military theorists like Fuller and Liddell Hart, who argued that modern technology could be used for the 'strategy of indirect approach'. The idea was to use armoured force to penetrate deep into the enemy rear in order to destroy its command and control systems. Instead of a clash of front-line troops aiming for a battle of annihilation, the objective would be to hit at the enemy's 'brain'. The campaign of 1940 certainly seems in many respects to have been a textbook example of Blitzkrieg in this sense, although it is unclear to what extent Guderian had been influenced, if at all, by the 'strategy of indirect approach'. Or was he more like Molière's M. Jourdain who wrote prose without knowing it? But one must not exaggerate the novelty of all the German methods in 1940. Apart from the crossing of the Meuse at Sedan, there were few, if any, examples where close air support— the combination of Stukas and Panzers—was decisive (it played no part in Rommel's crossing at Dinant where the Luftwaffe did not play an important role). And even at Sedan the initial success was, of course, due not to the tanks—which did not start to cross until the early hours of 14 May— but to the professionalism of a small number of infantry units, and to the inspirational leadership of a few infantry commanders like Balck and Rubarth.

Nonetheless one must not underestimate the vulnerability of the Germans in 1940. The German plan could so easily have gone wrong. During the crossing of the Ardennes, there were major traffic problems and infantry units got tangled up with one another. The Germans were very lucky that the French were so blissfully unaware of this and did not take the opportunity to bomb them, increasing the chaos. The German newsreels of the period depict young, bronzed, disciplined troops marching through the cornfields of France like conquering demigods. These images are so powerful that it is all too easy to characterize Germany as a ruthlessly efficient and militarized society in which every sinew was strained for war, with an imaginative and forward-thinking military command, and highly modernized armed forces. And yet almost all of these judgements are highly questionable.

It is a commonplace among historians of Nazi Germany that the regime's administration was chaotic and inefficient, not least in the organization of rearmament. Although the Germans had a considerable head start over the Allies in this respect, by 1940 the French armaments industry was in many areas out-producing the German. As far as the modernized army is concerned, the truth is that the German army in 1940 was more dependent on horse-drawn transport than the French one. Only sixteen of the German army's 103 divisions were fully motorized; and each infantry division required between 4,000 and 6,000 horses to transport its supplies from the railhead to the troops. Most of the German tanks at the start of the war were still light Panzer Is and IIs, and many of these had broken down during the Polish campaign. As for the cooperation between air and ground forces, in fact only one flying unit of the Luftwaffe was dedicated to this purpose, although the Stukas, which were intended for a wider range of operations, could be called upon to play this role. As far as the forward-thinking High Command is concerned, there were many high-level German commanders who were extremely worried by the audacity of commanders like Guderian.

What about German morale? William Shirer, at that time a correspondent in Berlin, noted in the days leading up to the declaration of war that people in the city looked 'dejected . . . grim and silent'. He detected 'almost a defeatism discernible in the people'. On 31 August he wrote: '[E]verybody against the war. People talking openly.' And two days later: 'I walked in the streets. On the faces of the people astonishment, depression. . . . No excitement, no hurrahs, no cheering, no throwing of flowers, no war fever. . . . There is not even any hate for the French and British.' Another observer on the same day saw small groups of Germans standing silently 'with faraway expressions'. These impressionistic observations are supported by the reports of the German security police between 1933 and 1939, which suggested that the Germans were 'not in an aggressive warlike mood but full of resignation, fear of war and longing for peace'. At a government press conference on 1 September 1939 journalists were instructed that there were to be no headlines containing the word 'war' in order to avoid panic in the population.[39] None of this is surprising: German soldiers too had fought at Verdun. The German High Command was worried after the Polish

26. Contrary to the myth propagated by the newsreels, which portrayed the German army as a sort of mechanized juggernaut, it was highly dependent on horses for transport. When Hitler moved against the Russians in 1941 his army had 3,350 tanks and 650,000 horses

campaign about the lack of fighting spirit demonstrated by certain units in Poland; Hitler lost his temper with Brauchitsch who told him that the German soldier in 1939 had not revealed the same qualities as that of 1914. It was for all these reasons that the German military leaders, even Guderian, saw the victory of 1940 as a 'miracle'.

## Explaining Defeat: 'Moving in a Kind of Fog'

The greatest German weapon in 1940 was not overwhelming military superiority but surprise. The failure of the French to predict the locus of the German invasion must rank as a failure of intelligence as dramatic as the American failure to predict Pearl Harbor or the Israeli failure to predict the Egyptian attack in 1973. There had in fact been ambiguous intelligence signals, but so often the history of intelligence in warfare supports the axiom that intelligence information tends to be sifted to reinforce received ideas rather than to overturn them. In June 1944 it took weeks before the German High Command accepted that Normandy was the real site of the invasion and not a diversionary tactic to cover the real attack that would come in the Calais area. The French intelligence services in 1940 did pick up quite a lot of information on the possibility of an Ardennes offensive—for example, on 13 March 1940 it was reported that a lot of bridging equipment was being assembled in Germany opposite the Luxembourg border, two days later that an increasing number of tanks were being deployed opposite south Belgium and Luxembourg—but even more about the possibility of a German move through Switzerland. The problem was how to distinguish genuine information from 'noise'. The cumbersome French command structure meant that there were no very clear mechanisms for the collation and centralization of intelligence information, especially after Gamelin split the headquarters up in January 1940. According to one historian 'no senior officer had the task of assimilating intelligence and relating it to operational planning'.[40]

The consequences of this intelligence failure in 1940 were exacerbated by the decision to gamble almost everything on the Dyle–Breda Plan. Why did Gamelin do this? One key motive was to bring in the Dutch and Belgians and weld them into the alliance; another possibly less openly avowed reason was to have an army between the British and the sea. Even if the Germans had attacked where Gamelin expected them to, his plan was risky because it exposed the French to fighting an encounter battle, something that went against French military doctrine. But the real problem was that the Germans did not attack in the right place. This meant not only that the sector on which the Germans concentrated their greatest forces was the least well defended but that part of what had been the central reserve—including two DLMs and some of the most mobile infantry divisions in the French army—was uselessly stranded deep in Belgium when the French most needed reserves to counter the Germans on the Meuse. For this decision, about which Billotte, Georges, and Giraud had all expressed reservations, Gamelin above all must be held responsible. He will have understood as well as anyone the force of Joffre's famous riposte to those who tried to argue that General Gallieni rather than he should be given credit for the victory of the Marne: 'I do not know who was responsible for winning the Battle of the Marne, but I do know who would have been responsible for losing it.'

It is the supreme irony of Gamelin's career that a man so cautious and rational should have taken—and lost—such a massively risky gamble. Perhaps it was Gamelin's very rationality and caution that let him down: he could simply not imagine that the Germans would take the extraordinary gamble of sending the bulk of their armoured forces through the Ardennes. But Gamelin sometimes seems to have been temperamentally unwilling to confront unpleasant realities, as if any problem could be finessed by charm, luck, and personal contact. Very characteristic in this respect were his expectations, based only on his secret and informal contacts with van den Bergen, that Belgium would suddenly abandon neutrality in 1939 because this was what would best have suited France.

On the other hand, Gamelin cannot be made a scapegoat for everything that went wrong in France in 1940. In the historical literature on 1940 poor Gamelin cannot win. Because, unlike Georges, he did not break down in tears, he is accused of passivity and detachment. He is accused by some historians of locking himself away at Vincennes, but during the first five days of the battle he visited Georges frequently—twice on 14 May necessitating about four hours of travel—which leads to his being accused by another historian of wasting too much time in this way.[41] In many respects Gamelin was the prototype of the general as administrator, with many of the qualities of those military managers such as Generals George Marshall, Alan Brooke, or Alexei Antonov who were the real architects of the Allied victory in 1945. It was Gamelin's tragedy that he did not have the chance to employ his undoubted qualities where they would have been most useful.

But the problems of the French army in 1940 went far beyond Gamelin. In 1914 Joffre's strategic mistake had been equally disastrous but there was time to remedy it. In 1940 there was too little time. The absence of Giraud's troops was not the only reason for this. One problem was that even once the

High Command had realized that the main German thrust was through the Ardennes, it still failed to read German intentions correctly. Georges operated initially on the assumption that the Germans would pivot south-east towards the rear of the Maginot Line, or possibly through the centre of the Second Army, but not that they would swing west into the right flank of the Ninth Army. Even when on the night of 13–14 May Georges did form a special detachment under General Touchon to close the gap between the French Second and Ninth Armies, he did not pay significant attention to the right flank of the Ninth Army. He may also have been lulled here into a false sense of security by the successful resistance of the French forces at Monthermé for two days. Thus, Georges's countermeasures played into the hand of the Germans and possibly aggravated the French situation once the Germans had broken through: there were almost no troops ready to place in their path. Georges had also been reluctant to move troops from behind the Maginot Line—possibly because of his fear that they might be needed to deal with an attack through Switzerland: this misplaced fear was another major intelligence failure.

More serious even than the French military's slowness to read the *direction* of the German attack was their incapacity to grasp the nature and speed of warfare as practised by the Germans in 1940. Even after the German break-through, the French were sure that it would eventually run out of steam, and allow them to plug (*colmater*) the gap. In the First World War, break-throughs of this kind had always slowed down owing to the exhaustion of the troops, and supply and logistical difficulties. From the beginning to the end of the battle, what is most striking about the French response in 1940 is its slowness—whether General Lafontaine's delayed counterattack at Sedan on the morning of 14 May, or General Flavigny's even more delayed attack on the next day, or the delay in sending the First DCR against Rommel, and so on. The first crossing of Rommel's men at Houx occurred before midnight on 12 May, but General Martin, in command of the XIth Corps (18DI and 22DI), was not told anything until 7 a.m. on 13 May, and Corap, who could not be contacted at first, did not know how serious the situation was until the evening.

The truth is that the French were faced with a kind of fighting for which they were completely unprepared—the opposite of the methodical warfare (*bataille conduite*) for which their doctrine prepared them. One striking difference between the two sides was the conduct of the senior commanding officers. The German commanders were closely involved in the battle, while their French counterparts usually remained in the rear. General Lafontaine of the 55DI, operating from his command post about 8 km behind Sedan, or General Huntziger, from his command post at Sennuc, about 45 km behind the line, were quite different from commanders like Rommel, throwing themselves personally into the fray. Of the four French regiments involved in fighting at Sedan, none lost its commander, whereas the Germans lost a number of key commanders. This was nothing to do with cowardice; it was a reflection of different doctrinal approaches: the 'methodical' battle required the senior commanders to stay in their command posts and keep their hand on 'the handle of the fan' rather than get too closely mixed up in the action; the German doctrine of 'mission oriented' tactics encouraged initiative on the part of lower-level commanders.

The fluidity of the battle between 15 May and 4 June was exactly the kind of warfare the French were least prepared to deal with. As General Prioux put it, the enemy was 'imposing his will on us and . . . we had lost the operational initiative'. The only solution would have been to organize a powerful thrust at the Germans by a concentrated force including the DCRs, but this force would have had to be ready by 16–17 May. The French lacked the logistical apparatus to coordinate their responses fast enough. The movement of troops was also severely disrupted by the German bombing and by the refugees who clogged the roads. There were too few radios; most communication was by messenger or telephone, both of which were easily interrupted. French deficiencies in communications were visible at every level, starting at the top. Gamelin's command post lacked a radio or even carrier pigeons. He either communicated by messengers (who were often the victim of accidents) or by time-consuming personal visits to command centres. Marc Bloch noted that the First Army headquarters often had no idea where its own corps were situated. In the resulting chaos, French command structures disintegrated; regiments were cut off from their divisional headquarters. As one soldier wrote: '[W]e had the impression of a total lack of coordination in the orders we received. We felt we were moving in a kind of fog.'[42]

British control and communications were no better: the whereabouts of Gort were often a mystery. As one British officer commented after the defeat: '[D]ecisions had to be made so very quickly and so often could not be confirmed on the basis of the information coming in. . . . The general moves the Germans made were so quick and where you may have a stable situation in the morning, by 7 o'clock or 8 o'clock in the evening, if you did not act and do something, the situation might be irretrievably lost.'[43]

The misadventures of General Prioux perfectly illustrate the confusion and communications breakdown on the French side immediately after the

German breakthrough. Prioux was one of the few French generals whose resolution did not falter throughout the disaster. Having fallen back from the Dyle with his Cavalry Corps, along with the rest of the First Army, he was eager to launch a counterattack on the German corridor from the north. One problem, however, was that his own forces had become very dispersed. While trying to reunite them, he also sought orders. From Valenciennes on 17 May, he phoned Georges and was told that he might be of use to the Ninth Army at Mormal, but that 'this was not an order and I was to do nothing without referring to the Army Group, which would perhaps have a different use for me'. This was indeed the case. Finding Billotte at Douai he was told that the First Army 'needs you' (Billotte also told him that France was heading for a catastrophe worse than 1870). At dawn on 19 May, Prioux was instructed to attack south towards Cambrai, which contradicted orders he had received the previous day. The order was anyway impossible to execute, since his tank brigades had not yet arrived despite having been ordered to do so. On the next day, trying to implement the instructions he had received, he dictated an order to attack towards the south-west of Arras. Then a few minutes later he was told to stay put instead. Prioux reflected ruefully that he had been at five different command posts in four days.[44]

There is no point in seeking out individual culprits. About thirty-five generals were sacked after the initial disaster, and Corap was selected as the most high profile sacrificial victim. But this was an entirely arbitrary choice. The performance of Huntziger's Second Army had been no better than that of Corap's Ninth. Corap had at least tried to draw attention to the problems of his sector before the German attack, unlike Huntziger, who had been extremely complacent. In October 1939, when hearing about the defeat of Poland from the French attaché in Warsaw, Huntziger had remarked: 'Poland is Poland . . . Here we are in France.' He is reported to have said, on hearing that the first Germans had crossed the river at Wadelincourt, 'that will mean all the more prisoners'. When the aerial bombardment started at Sedan his initial response was that the soldiers needed their baptism of fire. Although Huntziger had been sent important reinforcements in the form of the 3DCR and 3DIM on 13 May, he had failed to use them for a powerful counterattack. He may have owed his survival to the fact that on 15 May the Second Army at Stonne seemed to be performing somewhat better than on the previous two days, but that was only because the thrust of the German attack had shifted westwards. If Huntziger survived and Corap did not, it was because Corap had fewer protectors in high places. Huntziger went on to be a minister at Vichy.

Whatever the deficiencies of individual commanders, the real lesson of 1940 was the way in which almost the entire French High Command had been caught unawares by the new kind of warfare. If there were so many cases of French generals collapsing into tears it was because collectively—with very few exceptions—they had been utterly overwhelmed intellectually and psychologically. No one seems to have been more crushed by events than Blanchard who, according to Bloch, was urged by a corps commander: 'Do anything you like, sir, but for Heaven's sake do something.' Bloch himself observed Blanchard 'sitting in tragic immobility, saying nothing, doing nothing, but just gazing at the map spread on the table between us, as though hoping to find on it the decision which he was incapable of taking'. General Alan Brooke has an almost identical description:

He [Blanchard] was studying the map as I looked at him carefully and I soon gathered the impression that he might as well have been staring at a blank wall for all the benefit he gained out of it. He gave me the impression of a man whose brain had ceased to function, he was merely existing and hardly aware of what was going on around him. The blows that had fallen on us in quick succession had left him 'punch drunk' and unable to register events.[45]

## Army and Society

It is possible, then, to offer primarily military explanations for the Fall of France. And it must be remembered that in a battle the difference between success and failure can turn on very little. In 1914 France had survived very narrowly indeed; in 1940 the story was different. But can we stop there? As Michael Howard remarks in his history of the Franco-Prussian War: 'the military system of a nation is not an independent section of the social system but an aspect of it in its totality'.[46] In no society does the military operate entirely in a vacuum. In Marc Bloch's view, the French military had been intellectually outclassed, and he saw this as symptomatic of a more general intellectual sclerosis affecting France in this period. Such sweeping statements are difficult to verify, and Bloch's own original and pioneering work as an historian and creator of the Annales school is proof that certainly not all of French intellectual life was ossified in the inter-war years. Indeed there is a case for saying that this was one of the most culturally vibrant periods in modern French history.

Was the army somehow apart from this? It is easy to depict the French High Command as a complacent gerontocracy immured in its certainties and unwilling to rethink the future. Pétain told the post-war investigating commission that after 1918 'my military brain was closed'. But Pétain had no influence on French military planning in the 1930s, and there were, as one would expect, military conservatives and 'modernizers'—to the extent that these terms have any validity—in both Germany and France. Explaining why certain views and not others prevailed in each country requires us to consider the social and political context.

In France the 'modernizers' were certainly stymied by the delays in rearmament and the production bottlenecks. In 1936 the army still only possessed twenty-seven B tanks. Once these tanks did start coming on stream there was precious little time for training before they were thrown into battle. The French failure to exploit the full potential of the DCRs stemmed also from the commitment to the idea of the methodical battle. This commitment, however, was not just blind resistance to change. It was a response to the context in which the army had to operate. As one army manual put it: '[I]t is important to deliver methodical battles and avoid encounter battles. These, because of the uncertainties they bring with them, are not suitable for the employment of young troops who need, on the contrary, to be engaged methodically on the field of battle with all the necessary support of firepower.'[47] In other words, the 'methodical battle' was what the military considered necessary for an army composed primarily of short-service conscripts, badly prepared reservists, and overworked professionals—all posing problems which were exacerbated by the progressive reduction in army service between 1923 and 1930. The French military were undoubtedly suspicious of the fighting quality of their soldiers. Already in 1914 Joffre had hesitated to use reservists in the belief that they were not battle-ready. His mistake in estimating the size of the forces on the other side came from his belief that the Germans would act likewise.

The idea of a professional army on the lines proposed by de Gaulle was inconceivable in a political culture which since the nineteenth century had deeply distrusted the possible political ambitions of the army. A conscript army was considered the corollary of a democratic society. It should be remembered also that the military were operating within the context of a thoroughly pacifist—or at least peace-loving—society. Weygand recorded in his diary in 1933: 'France is profoundly pacific. . . . The army . . . is one of the means, the most important, that a country uses to support its policy. The old formula that it is necessary to have the army of one's policy has lost none of its validity.'[48]

In this context, putting the case for armoured divisions was something that had to be done with skill and tact. Daladier, for one, had never been entirely convinced about the desirability of B1 tanks: were they the kind of armaments that a democratic and pacific society required? The situation in Germany was very different. In the 1920s, the reconstruction of the Reichswehr, which had to proceed clandestinely, was carried out by the army without civilian interference; in the 1930s, it was the politicians who provided the impulse to war. The Nazi regime existed to make war. This is not to say that France was 'decadent', and that Germany was not, unless the kind of pacific and liberal values in which France's leaders believed are to be equated with decadence. In the circumstances one might indeed consider that the efforts achieved in France to prepare the country for war were remarkable—a testimony to the adaptability of French political institutions and to the quality of France's governing class.

It is true, however, that the memories left by the previous war, and the scars inflicted by the divisions of the 1930s were still so fresh that there were many people who were only half convinced that this was 'their' war. This was the case of many pacifists on the left, and many anti-Communists on the right. Had the early stages of the war gone better, however, it is quite possible that it would have become 'their' war, as seemed to be happening in the early days of June, and as happened in Britain during the Blitz, which transmuted a conflict that had been accepted without enthusiasm into a genuinely popular crusade. In both countries conditions were much more fluid and open-ended than they seem to us in retrospect. The way that the different social and political ingredients crystallized was to a considerable degree a *result* of the military situation. Many French politicians and intellectuals were haunted in the 1930s by a sense of the weakness of their country and the decadence of its political institutions. The recovery that had taken place in the year before the war was too recent for that mood of pessimism to have dissipated entirely. The sense of French decadence was shared by figures as far apart as the Fascist novelist Drieu La Rochelle and the liberal philosopher Raymond Aron. In his memoirs Aron wrote: '[D]uring the years of decadence, we felt France's ills personally.... What struck us all ... was the contrast between the paralysis of the democratic regimes and the spectacular recovery of Hitler's Germany.'[49] The sense of decadence was therefore not purely a retrospective shadow cast by 1940, but on the other hand it did not predetermine the responses to 1940, even if it explains why *some* people were able to resign themselves so easily to defeat: Drieu became an ardent collaborator, but Aron went to London. In Britain also there were many politicians and intellectuals who felt deeply alienated by what they saw as the drift and lack of imagination of the National Government, and the conservatism of British society. They were lucky enough to be able to find a home supporting the Churchill coalition in 1940. In other circumstances their alienation might have found other outlets.

It is certainly true that once the French army had been defeated, some French conservatives, and many others who felt alienated from the Republic for different reasons, readily found explanations for the defeat and were ready to embrace it almost with a kind of self-sacrificial fervour, seeing it as a chance to remake the nation in their image. This was the force of Charles Maurras's comment that the defeat was a 'divine surprise'. By this he did not mean that he had welcomed it, but that at least it had the beneficial result of bringing to power France's saviour in the form of Marshal Pétain. The politics of the 1930s do, then, matter in our discussion of the Fall of France—but they help explain the consequences of the defeat more than its causes.

# 6

# CONSEQUENCES

## June 1940: François Mitterrand at Verdun: 'No Need to Say More'

THE experience of Sergeant François Mitterrand in June 1940 was typical of that of many soldiers. During the Phoney War his unit, the 23rd Colonial Infantry Regiment, was stationed first in Alsace and then behind the Ardennes. Mitterrand found the boredom of the Phoney War deeply frustrating, and hated being a soldier. He lacked motivation and felt no commitment to the war. In a letter dating from the beginning of 1940, he wrote: '[W]hat would really annoy me is dying for values in which I do not believe.' Once the fighting started, his unit, which managed to hold together, was forced to retreat towards Verdun. It was near Verdun, on 14 June, that Mitterrand was wounded by a shell. He was carried off on a stretcher along a road teeming with refugees. The refugee column was attacked by German planes, and the stretcher-bearers ran off, leaving Mitterrand lying on the road looking up at the German planes in the sky above him. Over the next five days, as the French armies retreated, he was taken from military hospital to military hospital. In the fifth of these, near Bruyères in the Vosges, he woke up one morning to find that the Germans had arrived, and he was now a prisoner. Later Mitterrand wrote of these days: 'I was a defeated soldier in a dishonoured army, and I felt bitter towards those who had made that possible, the politicians of the Third Republic.'[1]

Mitterrand was transported to a prisoner-of-war camp near Kassel in Hesse. On his third attempt, he succeeded in escaping from the camp, arriving back in France in January 1942. He found employment as a functionary of the Vichy regime, working for the reintegration of prisoners of war who had been released from captivity. Gradually he gravitated from support for the Vichy regime towards active sympathy with the Resistance. By 1944 he was the leader of a Resistance movement of escaped prisoners of war.

Of all his experiences between 1940 and 1944, it was the defeat and imprisonment that had most marked Mitterrand. He claimed, in words rather similar to those of Sartre writing about his own imprisonment, that it was in the prisoner-of-war camp that he had his 'first real encounter with other men'. It helped him to move away from the aesthetic individualism that had characterized his adolescence. About the defeat, he later wrote: 'My sense of belonging to a great people (great in the idea that it constructed of the world and of itself, and of itself in the world, according to a system of values that rested neither on numbers nor brute force nor money) had taken some knocks. I had lived through 1940: no need to say more.'[2] As much as anything, it is the words 'no need to say more' that deserve attention. As the historian Stanley Hoffmann has observed: '[T]here is a stunning contrast between the proportions of the May–June 1940 catastrophe and the role it plays in the country's intellectual production.'[3] There seems to be no equivalent of what the historian Henry Rousso, in his book tracing the memory of Vichy in French national life since 1945, has described as the 'Vichy syndrome'—in political debate, in fiction, in films, and so on. A similar study of the defeat of 1940 would be rather short. In literature, the most notable works are the last volume of Jean-Paul Sartre's *Roads to Freedom* trilogy, which opens with the defeat, the novel *The Flanders Road* (1960) by Claude Simon, and the novel *A Balcony in the Forest* (1958) by Julien Gracq. There is also a powerful description of the retreat from Dunkirk in Robert Merle's novel *Weekend à Zuydcoote* (1972). Among films, there is really only Rene Clément's *Jeux Interdits* [Forbidden Games] (1952), which tells the story of a small girl who loses her parents in the Exodus during a German bombing raid. A peasant family takes her in, and she and the little boy of the family create a secret animal cemetery. Although their macabre and disturbing activities are presumably supposed to reflect the impact on two children of the national trauma, the film is really about childhood more than it is about the defeat—apart from the extraordinarily vivid images of the Exodus in the first half hour.

Perhaps one reason for the absence of a '1940 syndrome' is the long shadow cast by the 'Vichy syndrome'. The defeat was immediately followed by a series of harrowing new experiences—occupation, collaboration, deportation—which pushed defeat into the background. At the trial of Pétain, which was supposedly about his role in the signing of the armistice and the end of the Republic—that is the events of 1940—the discussion frequently strayed into the Occupation period. Who had said what to whom at Bordeaux in the last days of June seemed in 1945 to belong almost to another era. It interested people less than what had happened after 1940.

Similarly the parliamentary committee established in 1947 to look at the events in France between 1934 and 1940 never attracted much public attention. Obviously no nation wishes to dwell on its defeats. In 1945, the shame of defeat seemed to have been partially redeemed by the heroism of the Resistance—even if many fewer people had been involved in the Resistance than had fought in the army in 1940. Of course, some, like Mitterrand, who had fought in 1940, later participated in the Resistance. But many of the soldiers of 1940 were unable to do so because they spent the war in prison camps. When these prisoners returned in 1945, they soon felt that they were somewhat unwelcome spectres at the feast of Liberation and national self-congratulation. After the initial celebrations to mark their return, they found that their memories of the war jarred uneasily with the general mood. France after the Liberation needed heroes, not reminders of defeat. As one of the prisoners' newspapers put it: '[O]fficial France has forgotten you. A veil has even been thrown over those who died in 1940. France is ashamed of you.... Soon France will spit on your tombs.' The soldiers of 1940 found themselves ignored by the Resistance and despised by the surviving veterans of 1914–18. One former prisoner recalled: '[T]hese were men who were so humiliated that they spent their lives trying to wash away the stain of their humiliation.' Spokesmen for the former prisoners argued that the soldiers of 1940 had fought well but had found themselves in an impossible position. They also tried to link their role in 1940 to the subsequent emergence of the Resistance:

The prisoners must not have the feeling that ... in the eyes of the country they are the defeated ones while others gather the laurels of victory. For, if it is true that France has never ceased to be at war ... then the war is indivisible ... and it is only fair that those who succumbed in the first act of the drama take their rightful place in its final act.[4]

This reading of the war as a single unity meshed with de Gaulle's own interpretation of it. At the Liberation, de Gaulle, whose priority was national unity, hoped to put the occupation and the Vichy period in parentheses, and downplay those aspects of the occupation that had set the French against each other. De Gaulle argued that there had been an uninterrupted struggle of the French people against the Germans since 1940. Indeed de Gaulle went further, claiming that the war of 1939–45 was part of a thirty-year struggle between France and Germany that had begun in 1914. In this view, 1940 was a temporary setback in an ultimately successful conflict. All this might have made de Gaulle sympathetic to the plight

27. Crowds turn out on 1 June 1945 to greet the return of the millionth prisoner of war, Sergeant Jules Caron from Sisteron in the Basses Alpes. But once the welcome-home celebrations were over, the returned prisoners soon felt neglected and marginalized in postwar French society

of the prisoners of war. But it did not. De Gaulle had himself spent three years of the First World War as a prisoner. His five escape attempts had been unsuccessful, and he subsequently felt only shame and frustration about having been forcibly kept out of the action. De Gaulle's view in 1945 was that the prisoners would do better to keep quiet, rather than draw attention to themselves. On hearing about Mitterrand's Resistance movement of former prisoners, he allegedly remarked: 'a Resistance movement of prisoners? Why not a Resistance movement of hairdressers?' From the start de Gaulle's relations with Mitterrand were extremely frosty. When Mitterrand came to lobby on behalf of the returned prisoners in June 1945, he received short shrift. Perhaps Mitterrand's long-standing—and fully reciprocated—animosity towards de Gaulle derived in part from the different outlooks of two men towards their imprisonment—one of them resenting every minute that he had spent as a prisoner, and wanted in no way to dwell on the experience; the other of them counting it the formative experience of his life.

## Vichy: The Lessons of Defeat

If 1940 figures less prominently in France's memory wars than one might expect, this may be because it was an event too painful to contemplate. One is reminded of Gambetta's injunction about Alsace-Lorraine after 1870: 'think of it always, talk of it never'. It is clear that the reverberations of the defeat have been profound and long-lasting. On the other hand, it would be wrong to see it as a kind of French Year Zero, and fall into the temptation of attributing to it all the major changes in France since 1945. Post hoc is not the same as propter hoc.

Of the defeat's immediate consequences, however, there is no doubt. It was the precipitating cause of the collapse of the Third Republic and the setting up of the Vichy regime. And it set the agenda for Vichy's ideological crusade to remake France. Pétain's government, while still in Bordeaux, had signed an armistice with Germany on 22 June. According to its terms, France was divided into an Occupied Zone in the North, and along the Atlantic seaboard; and an Unoccupied Zone in the South. Since Bordeaux was, like Paris, situated in the Occupied Zone, the government took up quarters in the spa town of Vichy, whose numerous hotels provided ample accommodation for the ministers and their officials. The armistice said nothing about France's internal political arrangements in the Unoccupied Zone, but it was inevitable that the Third Republic would not survive the defeat. Meeting in the Vichy casino on 9 July, Parliament voted almost unanimously to accept a proposal by Pierre Laval that the constitution should be revised. As Laval said: '[A] great disaster like this cannot leave intact the institutions which brought it about.' On the next day, by a huge majority, Parliament voted to grant Marshal Pétain full powers to revise the constitution. Pétain almost immediately issued a number of constitutional acts which in effect gave him absolute power, and adjourned Parliament until further notice. The Vichy regime was born.

Many different political currents competed for power at Vichy, but all of them agreed on essentials. The new regime would be authoritarian and anti-democratic. The motto of the Republic—Liberty, Equality, Fraternity—was replaced by a new slogan: 'Work, Family, Fatherland'. Vichy, then, represented the victory of the opponents of the Republic, whether those who had always hated it or those who had turned against it because of the Popular Front. After the defeat, the Bishop of Drax was heard to declare: '[T]he cursed year for us was not 1940, that of our external defeat, but 1936, that of our internal defeat.' The triumph of the opponents of the Republic was, of course, only made possible by the defeat. On 28 May 1941, the economist Charles Rist noted in his diary: 'Mme Auboin tells me that after the Armistice she received a letter from a reactionary friend of hers containing the words: "At last we have victory".'[5] The Vichy regime's ideology was encapsulated in the phrase as the 'National Revolution'. It claimed to replace the materialistic liberal individualism of the Republic with the traditional values of a hierarchical society structured around organic 'natural' communities such as the region, family, and workplace. It condemned class struggle, and celebrated the peasant and the artisan. It proclaimed the need to punish and persecute certain groups that were identified as the enemies of France: Jews, Communists, and Freemasons. The Vichy regime argued that the defeat had revealed the decadence of the political values of the Republic. Only days after Reynaud's resignation Weygand had produced a memorandum setting down what he saw as the lessons of the defeat: '[T]he old order of things, a political regime made up of Masonic, capitalist and international ideas, has brought us where we stand. France has had enough of that.' 'We must not forget that we have been defeated and that every defeat has its price', commented the Vichy leader Admiral Darlan in September 1940.

Much of the discourse of Vichy was built around the themes of guilt (for the sins of the past), suffering (in the defeat and Exodus), and redemption (through obedience to the Marshal and the National Revolution). As Pétain put it: '[T]he spirit of enjoyment has prevailed over the spirit of sacrifice.' One Vichy propaganda documentary blamed the defeat on 'the English weekend, American bars, Russian choirs, and Argentinean tangos'. The Church was particularly prone to this kind of language. As Archbishop Gerlier of Lyon put it: '[V]ictorious we would probably have remained prisoners of our errors.' The Bishop of Toulouse was even more eloquent:

Have we suffered enough? Have we prayed enough? Have we repented for sixty years of national apostasy, sixty years during which the French spirit has suffered all the perversions of modern ideas . . . during which French morality has declined, during which anarchy has strangely developed. . . . For having chased God from the court, from the schools, from the nation, Lord we beg your forgiveness.[6]

In the immediate aftermath of defeat this kind of moralizing found a sympathetic hearing in the most unlikely quarters. André Gide, the author whose writing exemplified the kind of literature that Vichy judged immoral and decadent, criticized the 'sorry reign of indulgence' in his journal on 28 July 1940: 'softness, surrender, relaxation in grace and ease, so many charming qualities that were to lead us blindfolded to defeat'. As Blum noted from his prison cell: '[F]rom the beginning of time national calamity has

28. Vichy propaganda poster. On the left, Republican France undermined by democracy, speculation, anti-militarism, Freemasonry, Communism, pastis, bribery—with the Star of David floating above; on the right, Vichy's new France built on solid foundations of Family, Work, Fatherland—with the seven stars of the Marshal floating above

been linked with the idea of sin or error, and with its natural extension: contrition, expiation and redemption.'[7]

Vichy rested, however, on more than political reaction and revenge. The huge crowds who turned out to cheer Pétain on his frequent tours around the country showed that he was genuinely popular. This popularity rested partly on his legendary reputation as the victor of Verdun, but his speeches in 1940 genuinely touched a chord among the French people. The certainties that he offered in 1940 had some appeal to a population traumatized by the defeat and Exodus. Uprooted from their homes and separated from their families—for months afterwards the newspapers contained poignant advertisements from people trying to trace children and relatives whom they had lost—millions of French people had witnessed in person the disintegration of the nation and the collapse of the State. Often the authorities had been among the first to flee. From his first speech as premier Pétain had expressed his compassion for the refugees. His language of rootedness and authority, family and security, resonated with a nation traumatized by its recent experience of upheaval and dislocation. The defeat, then, provided Vichy with its moral authority; it was the foundation myth of the regime. When the regime seemed to be losing its popularity Pétain was quick to remind the French what he had saved them from. 'You have really short memories,' he announced in June 1941, 'remember the columns of refugees.'

Gradually Pétain used up the huge capital of goodwill that he had enjoyed in 1940 as the hardships of the Occupation pushed the sufferings of the defeat into the background. But what ultimately condemned Vichy to oblivion was its misreading of the international consequences of France's defeat. Most Vichy leaders assumed that France's defeat would soon be followed by a British surrender or defeat, and an end to the war. They had expected the armistice to be only the prelude to a peace treaty that would bring about a definitive settlement between France and Germany. Since the defeat of France seemed to ensure German hegemony over the European Continent, Vichy pursued a policy of 'collaboration' with its conqueror. In October 1940 Pétain met Hitler at the small town of Montoire-sur-le-Loire near Tours. He was photographed shaking Hitler's hand, and after the meeting he declared that he was 'entering upon the road of collaboration'. In 1941 the Vichy leader Admiral Darlan offered airbases to the Germans in the French colonial mandate of Syria. On one or two occasions the Vichy regime came to the brink of re-entering the war—this time on the side of Germany. This pro-German stance was partly driven by ideological affinity—Pierre Laval in June 1942 caused a sensation when he declared that he desired a German victory because it would represent the defeat of Russian Bolshevism—but even more by opportunism: Vichy believed that Germany had won the war. This judgement of course turned out to be Vichy's biggest mistake.

## 'Fulcrum of the Twentieth Century'

Vichy's narrow and Franco-centric view of the world failed to predict the massive consequences of the Fall of France for the future of the war. The war that had broken out in September 1939 had not been a world war but a European conflict involving France, Britain, Germany, and (briefly) Poland. It is at least possible that if the Allies had succeeded in holding off the initial German attack, a stalemate might have ensued, resulting in some kind of negotiated peace (it was not until January 1943 that the Allies adopted the principle of unconditional surrender). The Fall of France, however, transformed the international balance of power, sucking other powers into the conflict until by the end of 1941 the war had become a truly global one. De Gaulle had been right to proclaim from London that the Battle of France was only the first round in what would turn out to be a world war. The Fall of France was the end of the beginning, not the beginning of the end.

The consequences of the Fall of France for the war, and then the post-war course of international relations, were so dramatic that one historian has called it the 'fulcrum of the twentieth century'.[8] First off the mark to exploit the situation was Mussolini. Italy and Germany had been moving closer to each other since the later 1930s. On 18 March, Hitler and Mussolini had met at the Brenner Pass, and an Italian entry into the war seemed imminent. But Mussolini had not definitively burned his bridges with the democracies. He was urged against this course by his foreign minister, Count Ciano, and even more by the army Chief of Staff, Marshal Badoglio, who was only too aware of the inadequacies of the Italian armed forces. Badoglio told Mussolini that Italian intervention could only occur 'if the enemy was so prostrated as to justify such audacity'.[9] The startling German success in France seemed to have met this condition, and on 10 June Italy declared war on France. Mussolini's late entry into the war won him a tiny zone of occupation in south-east France, but more importantly it opened up a new Mediterranean theatre.

This posed a great threat to the British. Having lost the support of the French fleet, and facing a hostile Italy, the British now had to commit an important part of their naval strength to the Mediterranean, at the price of leaving their Far Eastern interests dangerously vulnerable. On 28 June, the British government informed the Australian and New Zealand governments that it would not in the foreseeable future be able to send a fleet to defend Singapore. None of this was lost on Japan which, like Italy, had been moving closer to Germany in the 1930s without however breaking entirely with the West.[10] Japan and Germany had signed an anti-Comintern Pact in November 1936, and there was a general desire among Japanese elites to expand Japanese influence in East Asia. This could only occur at the expense of the Western powers. But there were voices in the Japanese government urging caution, and these grew in influence at the end of 1939 after the signature of the Russo-German agreement. The defeat of France, however, shifted the argument back in favour of the pro-Axis camp. Quite apart from the increasing prestige of Germany and the weakening of British power in the Far East, the defeat of France also opened up a void in French Indo-China. In September Japan demanded free passage for its troops through Tonkin and the use of bases near Hanoi. The local representative of the Vichy regime, Admiral Decoux, had no choice but to accept, and Japanese troops moved into French Indo-China. On 27 September 1940, Germany, Italy, and Japan signed a Tripartite Pact in Berlin. The Fall of France had set in motion a radicalization of Japanese policy that was to lead in December 1941 to the fateful attack on America at Pearl Harbor.

While the German victory opened up possibilities and excited appetites in Italy and Japan, it caused corresponding alarm in Moscow. Stalin had been banking on a long conflict in the West, possibly ending in stalemate, certainly lasting long enough to allow the Soviet Union to build up its military strength. Now Hitler might turn against the Soviet Union at any moment. Stalin's fears were entirely justified. The ink on the armistice agreement with France was hardly dry before Hitler had ordered his armed forces to begin preparing an attack on the Soviet Union for the next year. The extraordinary success of the German campaign in France meant that there was no resistance from the German High Command, as there had been to Hitler's order to prepare an attack on France in 1939. The rapidity of the German victory had created a dangerous hubris among the German military, and on the part of Hitler himself a fatal conviction that he was a military genius who could never be wrong. This was to prove his ultimate undoing.

Stalin's immediate response to the Fall of France was to annex the Baltic States on 15 and 16 June, and to seize Bessarabia and the Bukovina from Rumania on 26 June. These measures were accompanied by the decision to speed up rearmament. Stalin's move into Bessarabia was intended to consolidate the Soviet position on the Black Sea littoral, and control of the mouth of the Danube. This worried Hitler, who saw the Balkans as a German sphere of interest, and it reinforced his conviction of the necessity to act against the Soviet Union as soon as possible. Thus were set in motion the decisions that would lead on 21 June 1941 to the German invasion of the Soviet Union.

The immediate reaction to the Fall of France by many British politicians was a kind of relief. Neville Chamberlain commented: '[W]e are at any rate free of the French who have been nothing but a liability to us.' Lord Hankey, who had been chairing the now defunct committee on building up long-term Franco-British cooperation, wrote: '[I]n a way it is almost a relief to be thrown back on the resources of the Empire and of America.'[11] Such comments revealed the pent-up resentment felt by many British observers at what was seen as France's weakness and betrayal. But there was no doubting that British survival now depended more than ever on American support. As the Chiefs of Staff noted as early as 25 May, Britain would only be able to fight on alone if the United States was 'willing to give us full economic and financial support, without which we do not think that we could continue the war with any chance of success'.

This required an important reorientation of British policy. Since 1919, Anglo-American relations had been far from cordial. The British had resented Wilson's pretensions to influence the peace despite having entered the war so late. America's refusal to cancel war debts was a running sore. In 1939, while hoping for American economic aid, the British remained wary of a greater American commitment. Chamberlain wrote in January 1940: 'I don't want the Americans to fight for us—we should have to pay too dearly for that if they had a right to be in on the peace terms.' But four months later, on 19 May, Chamberlain wrote: '[O]ur only hope, it seems to me, lies in Roosevelt and the USA.' Lord Halifax wrote to Hankey in July to tell him that the committee on Franco-British cooperation was now defunct and that 'it may well be that instead of studying closer union with France, we shall find ourselves contemplating the possibility of some sort of special arrangement with the USA'. Winning the closer support of America now became the central objective of British policy. It corresponded also to the personal and ideological affinities of Churchill. What gave this strategy a good chance of success was the fact that the Fall of France had also caused a panic in Washington. Massive military spending bills were rushed through Congress, and over the next year Roosevelt edged closer to the British, bringing the country to the brink of war with Germany even before the Japanese attack on Pearl Harbor.[12]

By the end of 1941, then, the European war had become a global one in which the massive power of America and the Soviet Union was soon to eclipse that of the other belligerents and lead inexorably to a new era of American–Soviet bipolarity after 1945. The Fall of France thus reveals itself in the medium term as a crucial moment in the eclipse of European power. Many of these developments would probably have occurred anyway. Even if France had remained in the war, it was likely that America would have joined the Allies ultimately. In that case America would certainly have emerged as the dominant force in the alliance. But without France the European balance in the alliance was dramatically weakened. The shift of British policy away from France also proved durable after 1945. In fact after the war there were those on both the British and French sides who hoped to rebuild closer links between the two countries. The French architects of the first stages of what was to become the Common Market certainly hoped to bring in the British, but by 1950 they had become convinced that this would not be possible. British ambivalence about European integration was certainly informed at some level by memories of 1940. The Fall of France helped to replace the Entente Cordiale, which had at some level informed British policy since 1904, by the Anglo-American 'special relationship' which has at some level informed it ever since.

## Gaullism and 1940

No one was more aware of this development, and ready to draw what he believed to be the appropriate conclusions, than General de Gaulle. De Gaulle was fond of repeating a phrase that Churchill allegedly expressed to him in 1944 during one of their particularly stormy encounters: '[I]f I have to choose between Europe and the open sea, between you and Roosevelt, I will always choose America.' The persistent suspicion that de Gaulle, and his successors, harboured towards the 'Anglo-Saxons' was born, to a considerable degree, out of the defeat. De Gaulle's two vetoes of British entry into the Common Market, in 1963 and 1967, were partly inspired by his belief that Britain would act as a kind of American Trojan horse in Europe.

In many other ways also, Gaullism, the political movement that has so marked the history of post-war France, was born out of the Fall of France and the lessons de Gaulle drew from it. 1940 is the Year I of 'Gaullism', markedly de Gaulle's first speech from London on 18 June. But de Gaulle already had a well-developed view of history by the time he arrived in London, and Gaullism resulted from the way he interpreted the events of 1940 in the light of his longer-term understanding of France's history. De Gaulle was born in 1890, and his vision of the world was rooted in late nineteenth-century romantic nationalism. As he later wrote on the first page of his war memoirs: '[A]ll my life I have had a certain idea of France.' The most fundamental conviction underlying that 'idea' was that 'France cannot be France without greatness'. Unfortunately de Gaulle, whose generation lived still in the shadow of the defeat of 1870, was all too aware that France was not always 'great'. He saw France's history as a vast epic of alternating moments of grandeur and decline, light and shade, glory and tragedy. The defeat of 1940 fitted easily into this millennial scheme, and allowed him to relativize its long-term importance.

From the particular circumstances of that defeat—both its causes and immediate consequences—de Gaulle drew two conclusions that are crucial to the development of Gaullism as a political doctrine: first, the need for a strong state; second, the need to preserve national independence. Unlike the politicians of Vichy, de Gaulle did not spend much time discussing the causes of the defeat. Since he wanted to argue that France was still a great nation with a great future, it would have been somewhat counter-productive to dwell on its weaknesses. For Vichy, which was ready to accept a more diminished role for France, this was less of a problem. Nor did de Gaulle spend much time in recriminations against those responsible for the defeat. He made his reasons for this clear in a letter written in 1943 to the journalist André Geraud, who had just published under the pseudonym Pertinax a two-volume attack on what he called 'The Gravediggers of France'. Géraud's book indicted almost the entire political and military establishment of the Third Republic—Gamelin, Weygand, Daladier, Laval, and so on—but de Gaulle wrote that it was wrong to be too severe: 'not that I deny their failure! But my feeling is that . . . [they] . . . suffered the effects of a deplorable general system that overwhelmed them. The fact is that it had become impossible truly to govern and to command in France because of the State's chronic paralysis.'[13] For de Gaulle, the most important fact about France's defeat was the weakness of the State that had turned a military failure into a national catastrophe. His War Memoirs dispatched President Lebrun with lapidary brevity: '[A]s chief of state he had lacked two things: he was not a chief and there was no state.'

When he returned to France in 1944 as Head of the Provisional Government, de Gaulle had not yet worked out in detail what kind of constitutional arrangements would guarantee the kind of state he believed to be necessary. Thus, he missed the opportunity to impose his ideas while still enjoying unrivalled popularity. It was only after his resignation in January 1946 that de Gaulle unveiled his constitutional proposals which provided for a strong President and weaker Parliament. His proposals were ignored because they went too much against the grain of France's Republican tradition. That tradition had emerged in the nineteenth century, in the shadow of Bonapartism, and was deeply suspicious of anything that smacked of authoritarianism. This suspicion had been reinforced by the recent experience of Vichy. Thus, the Fourth Republic, which emerged in 1947, was remarkably like its pre-1940 predecessor.

De Gaulle refused to have anything to do with this new Republic and set up a movement, the RPF, to advance his own ideas and bring about constitutional reform. The RPF was unsuccessful, and de Gaulle abandoned politics in 1953. But he finally had the chance to implement his proposals when he was called back to power in 1958 as a result of the crisis in Algeria. His new constitution was approved by a referendum in September 1958. The Fourth Republic was replaced by the Fifth, which still exists today. One of the most controversial provisions of the new constitution was Article 16, which allowed the President to assume emergency powers in case of crisis. De Gaulle himself applied this article in 1961 after an attempted army coup in Algeria. According to the Gaullist Michel Debré, the main architect of the new Constitution, de Gaulle insisted particularly on the importance of Article 16: '[H]e emphasized to us repeatedly that if the laws of 1875 [i.e. the constitution of the Third Republic] had provided for this right, President Lebrun would have decided to transfer the government to North Africa in June 1940 and France's situation would have been entirely different.'[14] After 1958, France, having had one of the weakest heads of state in Europe, was given one of the strongest.

The second moral that de Gaulle drew from the events of 1940 related to France's position in the world. Already during the war de Gaulle had begun to look to the future. He told Jean Monnet in June 1943 that: 'Anglo-Saxon domination in Europe was a growing threat and if it continued after the war France would have to turn to Germany or Russia.'[15] De Gaulle's entire foreign policy of the 1960s is contained in this sentence.

Another principle of foreign policy that de Gaulle derived from the Fall of France was the need as far as possible to conduct an independent foreign policy, and avoid dependence on any other power. This conviction was born partly out of the humiliating dependence of French policy on Britain in the 1930s, but even more out of de Gaulle's own experience in London during the war. For a man of de Gaulle's temperament and pride, it is almost impossible to measure the depths of humiliation he must have suffered through what he had witnessed in 1940 and through his complete dependence on the goodwill of the British. As one British observer (in fact Spears's wife) noted in 1940:

He felt the dishonour of his country as few men can feel anything, as Christ according to the Christian faith took on himself the sins of the world. I think he was like a man, during these days, who had been skinned alive and that the slightest contact with friendly wellmeaning people got him on the raw to such an extent that he wanted to bite. . . . The discomfort that I felt in his presence was due, I am certain, to the boiling misery and hatred inside him.[16]

De Gaulle spent much of the war fuming against the real or imaginary slights suffered at the hands of his allies. He never forgot—or forgave— the fact that he had not been invited to the Yalta Conference of February 1945. The moral was that no nation should ever count on the support of any other, and it inspired de Gaulle's decision to withdraw from NATO in 1966. It was for this reason also that de Gaulle gave prime importance to the development of a French nuclear weapon. He saw this as the only means by which smaller powers could achieve some semblance of equality with larger ones. In October 1945 he set up an Atomic Energy Commission (Commissariat à l'Énergie Atomique: CEA) to develop atomic research and technology.

The explosion of France's first atomic bomb over the Sahara on 12 February 1960 was hailed by de Gaulle, now back in power as President, as a great moment of national rejoicing. The satirical newspaper *Le Canard enchaîné* mocked his enthusiasm: 'this bomb has liberated France—what am I saying—it has liberated the French from a complex. It has liberated the old Gallic rooster that we all carry in our hearts and which hasn't dared to show itself since 1940. . . . This bomb, oh dear Frenchmen, is the most beautiful day of our lives.[17] Despite the opposition that de Gaulle's nuclear policy aroused at the time, after his departure no government, of right or left, has challenged the necessity of France's independent nuclear strike force (*force de frappe*). Implicitly they have accepted the logic of a speech made by de Gaulle immediately after the war: 'Vanquished today by mechanical force, we can vanquish tomorrow with superior mechanical force.'

29. De Gaulle's nuclear armour is mocked in the Communist *La Nouvelle Vie Ouvrière* on 8 January 1964. Wearing the Free French symbol, the cross of Lorraine, on his chain mail, he also has his 'nuclear head' [tête nucléaire], his 'strike force' [force de frappe], and his 'atomic shield' [bouclier atomique]

## National Renewal after 1945

There is no doubt that de Gaulle's achievement between 1958 and 1969 was an extraordinary one: he saved France from civil war, extricated it from Algeria, and provided ten years of unprecedented political stability and economic growth. Much of his legacy, so contested in his lifetime, has been untouched by his successors. But de Gaulle's success as President also owed a lot to the achievements of the Fourth Republic, despite his portrayal of it as twelve wasted and disastrous years. Visiting French cities in the early 1960s he would sometimes affect surprise at the speed with which they had been rebuilt after the war, rather as if the Fourth Republic had not existed. In fact the Fourth Republic may not have given France political stability, but it did lay the foundations of what have been called the *trente glorieuses*, the almost thirty years of extraordinary economic growth France enjoyed up to the middle of the 1970s. The causes of that growth are a matter of dispute. Many factors played a part, including the general growth in world trade, Marshall Aid, productivity increases, and so on. But there are two important, perhaps decisive, factors, which can be directly related to the impact of 1940: first, the role played in post-war France by a new technocratic elite of administrators committed in an almost mystical way to the idea of economic modernization; second, the development of European unity.

Writing after France's defeat in 1870, the philosopher Ernest Renan called on the French to undergo a complete intellectual overhaul. He commented that war was 'one of the conditions of progress, the lashing that prevents a country from falling asleep, by forcing self-satisfied mediocrity out of its apathy'.[18] In 1944, all political forces in France at the Liberation, divided on so many things, were united by the conviction that the defeat had revealed the profound mediocrity of France's elites. Indeed some Resistance denunciations of France's pre-war regime are all but indistinguishable from Vichyite ones. The Resistance saw itself as the new elite that would remake France, and overcome the decadence of the past. A key aspect of this analysis was the claim that France's pre-war bourgeoisie had been too egoistical and inward-looking, and that its industrialists had been the slave of 'Malthusian' values—preferring prudence to risk, saving to investment. Since liberal capitalism in France had revealed itself as so inadequate, it was necessary for the state to step in and provide the necessary dynamism. The idea that economic liberalism must be replaced by 'planning' was shared to some degree by most of the forces of the Resistance.

This ambition was embodied in a number of institutions that were set up, or profoundly reformed, at the Liberation. The École Nationale d'Administration (ENA) [National Administration School] was set up to train the administrators necessary for the success of a modern state. The Centre National de Recherche Scientifique (CNRS) [National Centre for Scientific Research], which had been created on the eve of the war, was overhauled and given a central role in promoting research and offering scientific advice to governments. The Commissariat Général du Plan [Planning Commission] was established to plan reconstruction and economic modernization. The origin of the Planning Commission was a memorandum presented to de Gaulle by Jean Monnet, warning that France had the choice between economic modernization or decadence. If France did not choose modernization, Monnet said, it risked being reduced to the rank of Portugal or Spain, living on past glory. At the Planning Commission, Monnet gathered around himself a group of young economists and administrators, some of whom had spent the war in America or Britain, others of whom had been in the Resistance. All were animated by the same sense of urgency about the necessity of modernization. How important the Planning Commission was to post-war growth is difficult to calculate, but at the very least it played a major role in transforming the mentalities of industrialists and economic policymakers. The planners became the apostles of the new religion of growth.

1940 was not the only factor in the emergence of this new mentality. Proposals for planning and managing the economy more effectively had been in the air since the 1930s. The most exhaustive historical study of the transformation of French economic policymaking sees it as a cumulative process in which a part was played by the Popular Front and even by some of the policies of the Vichy regime. The setting up of the ENA in 1945 had first been proposed by Blum's Popular Front government in 1936, but it had not managed to get the measure on the statute books. What made the defeat so important was that as a result of it the 'modernizers' became central to economic policy-making.

The second element that played a significant role in the success of the post-war French economy was the creation of the European Economic Community in 1957 after the signing of the Treaty of Rome. The origins of this go back to the beginning of Franco-German rapprochement in the late 1940s, and the setting up of the supranational Economic Coal and Steel Community between France, Germany, and four other countries in 1951. Here again the impact of the defeat was decisive, although of course there was no straight line leading from defeat in 1940 to reconciliation in 1950. It is true that some resisters were animated by a vague commitment to European federalism, but such ideas were never central to the Resistance, and their ideas had no influence on the policy of immediate post-war governments. On the contrary, in 1945 the whole idea of 'Europe' was somewhat tainted by its associations with Vichy, since many collaborators had claimed to be building a new 'Europe'. The policy of France's immediate post-war governments was not reconciliation with Germany but the destruction of German power once and for all. They wanted to break the country up and deprive it of the industrial powerhouse of the Ruhr. The unspoken assumption of Monnet's first plan was that France could draw on German coal resources.

Only when it became clear that France's former allies would not support such an approach to Germany did French governments decide to make a virtue of necessity and accept rapprochement with Germany. Since France could not destroy Germany, it had to find some way of living with it. The price of peaceful coexistence was that both countries would accept the need to sacrifice a degree of national sovereignty. This was the basis of the Coal and Steel Community. Even de Gaulle, so suspicious of any form of supranationalism, was pragmatic enough to accept and implement the Treaty of Rome when he returned to power in 1958. Later he made reconciliation with Germany one of the central planks of his foreign policy.

## 1940 and Colonial Nostalgia

The lessons of 1940 did not all point in one direction. While France was committed to modernizing its economy, it was also dragged into an enormously costly and divisive series of colonial wars, first in Indo-China (1947–54) and then in Algeria (1954–62). There is no doubt that the process of decolonization in France was massively complicated by the legacy of 1940. In Britain, where the empire had traditionally loomed larger in the national consciousness, decolonization was considerably less traumatic. For many people in France after 1945, 'Empire' functioned as a sort of compensation for the humiliation of 1940. It represented all that was left of France's claim to be a great power. Already in 1938, after Munich, many commentators had seized on the idea of the Empire as a way of softening the blow suffered by French prestige.

The significance of the Empire grew immeasurably after 1940. It was one of Vichy's main assets, evidence that France still counted, even if half the mainland was occupied by the Germans. De Gaulle had also banked on the Empire, hoping that it would rally to him. In fact only French Equatorial

Africa passed into the Gaullist camp in 1940, but even this gave de Gaulle a base of sorts outside London. Then in 1943, once the Allies had conquered North Africa from Vichy, de Gaulle was able to set up his government there. The whole Free French epic was intimately bound up with the Empire. Few people believed that the Empire could continue unchanged after the upheavals of the war. There were endless discussions in 1945 about transforming the Empire into a so-called 'French Union'. De Gaulle issued a famous call for reform in his 1944 'Brazzaville declaration'. But all these reforms were about finding ways to bind the colonial populations more closely to France, preserving the future of the Empire rather than preparing its demise. When the French army was defeated by the Vietnamese nationalists at the battle of Dien Bien Phu in 1954, the event was seen as a devastating humiliation (and just to underline the point, Paul Reynaud was a member of the government in power at the time). In some people's minds this defeat only made it all the more urgent to hang on to French Algeria at almost any price. Algeria was the revenge for both 1940 and 1954.

By the mid-1950s, however, an increasing number of politicians, at both ends of the political spectrum, had started to question the viability of trying to hold on to the Empire. For such people Dien Bien Phu came almost as a relief, since it ended a war that was becoming ruinous for the country. As a result of the Indo-China war, between 1952 and 1954 military spending took up one-third of the budget, and represented a higher percentage of national revenue than it had even in 1938. Was it not becoming clear that, far from enhancing and augmenting French power, the Empire was in fact draining it, and acting as an obstacle to the economic modernization that was a much better guarantee of real power? By 1954 such ideas were sufficiently widely shared for the Prime Minister, Pierre Mendès France, to extricate France from Indo-China without much dissent.

The argument had to be fought out all over again when the Algerian war began in 1954. The withdrawal from Algeria was to be far more traumatic than the abandonment of Indo-China. This was partly because the territory was technically not a colony but part of France, and because there was a large European settler population. But the biggest problem in Algeria was the army, and here we return again to the legacy of 1940. The war had subtly affected France's relationship with its army. After 1945 the army as a whole was no longer felt to represent the nation in the way that it had, despite the importance of pacifism, after 1918. Figures such as Foch and Pétain had been national heroes, almost demigods, and the prestige of the army had never been higher. After 1945, although the French army that de

Gaulle reconstituted in North Africa had played an important role in the Italian campaign, the hero of the hour was the Resistance. The army emerged from the war partially detached from the nation.

Many of the post-war generation of professional soldiers who fought in the colonies had come into the army through the adventure of the Free French, which had emerged in revolt against the legal French state. Thus, these men were socialized into an army career whilst lacking the French army's traditional respect for civilian authority. Their sense of alienation from the State was accentuated by years of fighting in Indo-China, far from France, and they were convinced that the politicians were letting them down. Where the image of the army in the inter-war years had centred upon the *poilu*, representative of the nation in arms, after 1945 it increasingly centred upon the paratrooper—member of a tough professional elite contemptuous of the softness of the civilian. In these circumstances it is easy to see how many soldiers in Algeria could feel that in rebelling against the French government they were being loyal to the true France, as de Gaulle had been when he rebelled against the government in 1940.

Twice the military in Algeria defied the government in Paris. On the first occasion, in May 1958, the result was to bring de Gaulle back to power. The second rebellion, in April 1961, was against de Gaulle himself once it was clear that he was preparing to give up Algeria. In the end, de Gaulle was able to ride out the military rebellion in Algeria precisely because these soldiers had become so disconnected from the nation that their defiance of the government in Algeria received no support from the mass of ordinary conscripts. Algeria acquired independence, and from that moment de Gaulle was free to pursue his wider foreign policy ambitions. Once de Gaulle had accepted Algerian independence in 1962, it is remarkable how quickly France seemed to adapt to a post-colonial existence. This was, of course, helped by the rapid economic growth of the 1960s, but also by de Gaulle's skill at turning the process of modernization into a kind of epic adventure. In June 1960 he told the French: '[W]e must transform our old country of France into a new country, and it must marry its epoch. . . . France must become a great industrial state or resign itself to decline.' 1940 was never explicitly mentioned in his many speeches on this theme, but the message was clear enough.

## 1940 Today

In the 1960s, then, France seemed finally to have put the defeat behind it. But it may be that the relative absence of references to 1940—compared to the ever more obsessive concern with Vichy—represented a refusal, or a reluctance, to confront the realities of declining French power (despite the successes of the *trente glorieuses*). This has become clearer in the years since de Gaulle's death. At one level, Gaullism was about drawing lessons from 1940; at another it was about pretending that 1940 had not happened, or at least denying that it had any significant implications for France's place in the world. France could—and indeed must—still be 'great' (de Gaulle's favourite word). De Gaulle probably knew himself that this was not possible. Once he commented that he had written the 'last pages of our greatness'. De Gaulle described his policy during the war as one of bluff, throwing dust in the Allies' eyes so that they might be blinded into thinking that France still counted for more than it did. This is what he went on doing throughout the Fifth Republic, and because he was a prodigiously effective showman, he was remarkably successful. But the Gaullist conjuring trick could not last forever. After de Gaulle's departure it became increasingly hard to sustain the illusion of French influence—partly because the economic crisis of the 1970s brought about an end to economic growth, partly because de Gaulle's successors lacked his charisma. In the 1980s, the mood of France became extraordinarily pessimistic and inward-looking. There was much agonizing about threats to French identity and the dangers that globalization posed to French cultural 'exceptionalism'. The success of the right-wing Front National in France since 1983 has certainly owed something to this ambient cultural pessimism. The Front's appeal was partly built around a rhetoric of combating the imagined decadence of the French nation.

Perhaps, then, France is only facing up belatedly and obliquely to the full implications of 1940 for the place of France in the world. This book has, of course, sought to argue against some of the more 'catastrophist' interpretations of the Third Republic and against the idea that the defeat was unavoidable. But there is no doubt that the defeat was the military translation of a shift in the balance of world power away from France and Europe. The defeat of 1940 may not have been inevitable, but the longer-term decline of French power probably was. If this conclusion is right, it may follow that Gaullism drew quite inappropriate conclusions from 1940: it condemned a regime that had served France well in many respects, but refused to accept the geopolitical realities underlying France's decline. The evident disillusion felt by much of the French population with its current political institutions suggests that de Gaulle's vision of the State has less and less appeal. On the other hand, one could argue the contrary view: that despite the trauma of the memory of 1940, despite the somewhat exaggerated and superficial pessimism of the 1980s, the most striking feature of France in the second half of the twentieth century, after the terrible bloodletting of the First World War, has been its capacity for survival and reinvention, its resilience, the continuing attraction of its culture. It is hard enough to understand the past, and historians should be modest about understanding the present, let alone trying to predict the future. The debate on the consequences of 1940 is surely still open. As the Chinese leader Chou En-lai once commented when he was asked in the 1960s to judge the consequences of the French Revolution: 'it is too early to say'.

# Guide to Further Reading

Unless otherwise stated, all French books are published in Paris and English ones in London. Where an English translation of a French work exists, it is this version that I have cited.

## GENERAL STUDIES

The best overall study of the Fall of France is J.-L. Crémieux-Brilhac, *Les Français de l'an 40*, i. *La Guerre oui ou non?* ii. *Ouvriers et soldats* (1990). On almost all the individual topic areas covered below, he has something important to say. L. Mysyrowicz, *Autopsie d'une défaite: Les Origines de l'effondrement militaire français de 1940* (Lausanne, 1973) is useful, especially on the 1930s.

For an overview of the historical literature, J. C. Cairns, 'Along the Road Back to France, 1940', *American Historical Review*, 64/3 (1959), 583–605 and 'Some Recent Historians and the "Strange Defeat" of 1940', *Journal of Modern History*, 46 (1974), 60–85 offer many insights and a survey of the literature at the time they were written; M. Alexander, 'The Fall of France', *Journal of Strategic Studies*, 13/1 (1990), 10–44 is an excellent overview of the literature as it stood in 1990.

There are some recent collections of articles on all aspects of 1940, where most of the more recent historiographical views can be found: J. Blatt (ed.), *The French Defeat of 1940: Reassessments* (Providence, R.I., 1998); M. Vaïsse (ed.), *Mai–juin 1940: Défaite française, victoire allemande, sous l'oeil des historiens étrangers* (2000); C. Levisse-Touzé (ed.), *La Campagne de 1940* (2001); B. Bond and M. Taylor (eds.), *The Battle of France and Flanders 1940: Sixty Years on* (2001). E. May, *Strange Victory: Hitler's Conquest of France* (New York, 2000) is a stimulating book that pushes revisionism to its limits (if not indeed beyond them). It is particularly good on the German side.

Immediately after the defeat, a number of instant histories by well-placed eyewitnesses appeared. These works, which fall somewhere between memoir, history, and polemic, have lots of inside information and anecdotes, but must obviously be used with care: A. Maurois, *Why France Fell* (1940); Pertinax [André Géraud], *The Gravediggers of France: Gamelin, Daladier, Reynaud and Laval* (New York, 1944); E. Bois, *Truth on the Tragedy of France* (1941); P. Lazareff, *De Munich à Vichy* (New York, 1944); P. Cot, *Triumph of Treason* (New York, 1944). In a class of its own (but only appearing after the war) is M. Bloch, *Strange Defeat* (Eng. trans. New York, 1968).

## DIARIES AND JOURNALS

The two most interesting diaries by leading French protagonists are: P. Baudouin, *Private Diaries: March 1940–January 1941* (1948) and P. de Villelume, *Journal d'une défaite 23 août 1939–16 juin 1940* (1976). They were both leading members of the pro-armistice faction, and very close to the centre of power. It is possible that Baudouin doctored his diary after 1945. Other quite informative diaries by leading French politicians are J. Bardoux, *Journal d'un témoin de la troisième, 1 septembre 1939–15 juillet 1940* (1957), and J. Jeanneney, *Journal Politique: septembre 1939–juillet 1942* (1972). Jeanneney's diary is superbly edited by the historian Jean-Noel Jeanneney, his grandson. A. de Monzie, *Ci-devant* (1941), gives the views of an Italophile member of both the Daladier and Reynaud governments. H. Queuille, *Journal de guerre: 7 septembre 1939–8 juin 1940* (Limoges, 1993) is the diary of another minister who was also in both governments, but his comments are very brief. Neither Reynaud nor Daladier kept diaries while in office, but they both did so while in captivity during the Occupation, and these contain a lot of reflections on 1940. See E. Daladier, *Prison Journal 1940–1945* (Boulder, Colo., 1995), and P. Reynaud, *Carnets de captivité, 1941–1945* (1997). One also picks up quite a bit of the atmosphere of the Phoney War from the diaries of the economist Charles Rist: C. Rist, *Une Saison gâtée: Journal de guerre et de l'Occupation* (1983). Although it does not cover the war itself, Weygand's notebook is also worth consulting to get an insight into his mind. It is published as '*Le Journal' du Général Weygand, 1929–1935*, ed. F. Guelton (Montpellier, 1998).

For French diaries that describe events seen from 'below', see: J.-P. Sartre, *War Diaries: Notebooks from a Phoney War, November 1939–March 1940* (1984); D. Barlone, *A French Officer's Diary (23 August 1939–1 October 1940)* (Cambridge, 1942); G. Sadoul, *Journal de guerre (2 septembre 1939–20 juillet 1940)* (1994 edn.); F. Grenier, *Journal de la drôle de guerre (septembre 1939–juillet 1940)* (1969); G. Friedmann, *Journal de guerre 1939–1940* (1987); R. Balbaud, *Cette drôle de guerre: Alsace–Lorraine–Belgique–Dunkerque* (London, 1941).

On the British side, there are several very frank diaries by leading military and diplomatic figures: *Chief of Staff: The Diaries of Lieutenant-General Sir Henry Pownall*, ed. B. Bond (1972); *The Ironside Diaries, 1937–1940*, ed. R. MacLeod and D. Kelly (1962); *War Diaries of Field Marshal Lord Alanbrooke*, ed. A. Danchev and D. Todman (2001); *The Diplomatic Diaries of Oliver Harvey, 1937–1940*, ed. J. Harvey (1970); *The Diaries of Sir Alexander Cadogan, O.M., 1938–1945*, ed. D. Dilks (1971).

## MEMOIRS

Over the years Reynaud produced three versions of his memoirs. One version is available in English as *In the Thick of the Fight 1930–1945* (1955). M. Weygand, *Recalled to Service* (1952), the third volume of Weygand's memoirs, deals with his period as generalissimo. It is as anti-British as one would expect, and very critical of the Republic for having failed to prepare France adequately for war. None of Gamelin's three volumes of memoirs, *Servir* (1946–7), are available in English. A. Beaufre, *1940: The Fall of France* (1965) is a vivid account of the Fall of France as seen by a young officer. J. Chauvel, *Commentaire* (1971) recounts the events as seen by a young diplomat. The Fall of France figures, of course, in the memoirs of both de Gaulle and Churchill. See W. S. Churchill, *The Second World War*, ii. *Their Finest Hour* (1949) and C. de Gaulle, *War Memoirs*, i. *Call to Honour* (1955). In a class of their own are the two volumes of General Spears's memoirs, *Assignment to Catastrophe* (London, 1954). Not only was their author at the centre of events, but his account of them is a literary masterpiece.

Two interesting memoirs by French soldiers are G. Folcher, *Marching to Captivity: The War Diaries of a French Peasant, 1939–1945* (1996), and P.-A. Lesort, *Quelques jours de mai–juin 40: Mémoire, témoignage, histoire* (1992). Lesort's book, mixing his diaries and letters of the period with his subsequent memories, is a highly intelligent reflection on 1940.

## BIOGRAPHIES

On the main French protagonists, the best books are: E. de Réau, *Édouard Daladier* (1993); P. Bankwitz, *Maxime Weygand and Civil–Military Relations in Modern France* (Cambridge, Mass., 1967); G. Sherwood, *Georges Mandel and the Third Republic* (Stanford, Calif., 1970); P. le Goyet, *Le Mystère Gamelin* (1976). On Gamelin, see also M. Alexander, 'Maurice Gamelin and the Defeat of France', in B. Bond (ed.), *Fallen Stars: Eleven Studies of Twentieth Century Military Disasters* (1991), 107–40. Reynaud still awaits his biographer.

On the main British protagonists, see M. Gilbert, *Finest Hour: Winston S. Churchill 1939–1941* (1983); J. Colville, *Man of Valour: The Life of Field Marshal the Viscount Gort* (1972); M. Egremont, *Under Two Flags: The Life of Major General Sir Edward Spears* (1997).

## INTER-WAR FRENCH POLITICS

The historical literature on this subject is enormous. J. Jackson, *France: The Dark Years 1940–1944* (Oxford, 2001) surveys the inter-war years in the light of 1940. On the Popular Front, see J. Jackson, *The Popular Front in France: Defending Democracy 1934–1938* (Cambridge, 1988). On inter-war Fascism in France, see K. Passmore, *From Liberalism to Fascism: The Right in a French Province, 1928–1939* (Cambridge, 1997). R. Remond (ed.), *Édouard Daladier, chef de gouvernement* (1977), and *La France et les Français en 1938–1939* (1978) contains the proceedings of an important conference that transformed our view of the Daladier government and hence of the last two years of the Third Republic. On inter-war French pacifism, N. Ingram, *The Politics of Dissent: Pacifism in France 1919–1939* (Oxford, 1991) takes a slightly narrow approach, but is useful nonetheless.

# FOREIGN POLICY AND DEFENCE PLANNING IN THE INTER-WAR YEARS

The relevant chapters of J. Doise and M. Vaïsse, *Diplomatie et outil militaire 1871–1991* (1997) provide a good overview. So does R. Doughty, 'The Illusion of Security: France 1919–1940', in W. Murray et al. (eds.), *The Making of Strategy: Rulers, States and War* (1994), 466–97.

The most important 'revisionist' accounts are: M. Alexander, *The Republic in Danger: General Maurice Gamelin and the Politics of French Defence* (Cambridge, 1992) and R. Young, *In Command of France: French Foreign Policy and Military Planning, 1933–1940* (Cambridge, Mass., 1978) and *France and the Origins of the Second World War* (New York, 1996). In the same spirit is P. Jackson, *France and the Nazi Menace: Intelligence and Policy-Making 1933–1939* (Oxford, 2000), whose scope is wider than the title of the book suggests.

More negative perspectives on the late Third Republic include: J.-B. Duroselle, *La Décadence (1932–1939)* (1979); A. Adamthwaite, *France and the Coming of the Second World War* (1977); and N. Jordan, *The Popular Front and Central Europe: The Dilemmas of French Impotence* (Cambridge, 1992). A short version of Jordan's argument can be found in Jordan, 'The Cut-Price War on the Peripheries: The French General Staff, the Rhineland and Czechoslovakia', in R. Boyce and E. Robertson (eds.), *Paths to War: New Essays on the Origins of the Second World War* (1989), 128–66. S. Schuker, 'France and the Remilitarization of the Rhineland, 1936', *French Historical Studies* (1986), 299–338 is an important discussion of this alleged 'turning-point' in inter-war international relations.

On the issue of the Soviet alliance, see J. Haslam, *The Soviet Union and the Struggle for Collective Security in Europe 1933–1939* (1984), and P. Buffotot, 'The French High Command and the Franco-Soviet Alliance', *Journal of Strategic Studies* (1982), 546–60. M. Carley, *1939: The Alliance that Never Was and the Coming of World War II* (1999) presents too Manichaean a view to be convincing.

On the Maginot Line, see J. Hughes, *To the Maginot Line: The Politics of French Military Preparation in the 1920s* (Cambridge, Mass., 1971), and M. Alexander, 'In Defence of the Maginot Line', in R. Boyce (ed.), *French Foreign and Defence Policy, 1918–1940* (1998), 164–94.

## THE ARMED FORCES

For a general survey of the French armed forces, R. Doughty, 'The French Armed Forces, 1918–1940' in A. Millett and W. Murray (eds.), *Military Effectiveness*, ii. *The Interwar Years* (Boston, 1988) is a good place to start.

On French military thinking in the 1930s, see: R. Doughty, *The Seeds of Disaster: The Development of French Army Doctrine, 1919–1939* (Hamden, Conn., 1985); H. Dutailly, *Les Problèmes de l'armée de terre française (1935–1939)* (1980); J. R. Tournoux, *Haut-Commandement: Gouvernement et défense des frontières du Nord et de l'Est, 1919–1939* (1960); B. Posen, *The Sources of Military Doctrine: France, Britain and Germany* (Ithaca,

NY, 1984); R. Young, 'Preparations for Defeat: French War Doctrine in the Inter-war Period', *Journal of European Studies* (1972), 155–72; E. Kiesling, *Arming against Hitler: France and the Limits of Military Planning* (Lawrence, Kan., 1996); E. Kiesling, ' "If it ain't broke, don't fix it" ': French Military Doctrine between the Wars', *War in History*, 3 (1996), 208–12.

For a critique of de Gaulle's contribution, see B. Bond and M. Alexander, 'Liddell Hart and de Gaulle: The Doctrines of Limited Liability and Mobile Defence', in P. Paret (ed.), *Makers of Modern Strategy* (Princeton, 1986), 598–623.

On French rearmament, see R. Stolfi, 'Equipment for Victory in France in 1940', *History* (1970), 1–20. R. Frankenstein, *Le Prix du réarmement français, 1935–1939* (1982) shows the strains that were caused in France by the financing of rearmament. On tanks, the latest book is G. Saint-Martin, *L'Armé blindée française, Mai–juin 1940! Les Blindés dans la tourmente* (1998).

On the French airforce see: P. Fridenson, *La France et la Grande Bretagne face aux problèmes aériens 1935–mai 1940* (1976); P. Facon, *L'Armée de l'air dans la tourmente* (1997); C. Christienne, 'L'Industrie aéronautique française de septembre 1939 à juin 1940', *Receuil d'articles et d'études, 1974–1975* (1977), 142–65; Charles Christienne et al., *Histoire de l'aviation française: L'armée de l'Air, 1928–1980* (1981). On air doctrine, see R. Young, 'The Strategic Dream: French Air Doctrine in the Inter-War Period', *Journal of Contemporary History*, 9/4 (1974), 57–76.

## FRANCO-BRITISH RELATIONS

For the general background, see J. C. Cairns, 'A Nation of Shopkeepers in Search of a Suitable France, 1919–1940', *AHR* 79 (1974), 710–43; P. M. H. Bell, *France and Britain 1900–1940: Entente and Estrangement* (1996); *Les Relations franco-britanniques de 1935 à 1939*, ed. Comité d'Histoire de la Deuxième Guerre Mondiale (1975).

For the relationship of the Allies in the Phoney War, see the many contributions to the collective volume *Français et Britanniques dans la drôle de guerre*, ed. Comité d'Histoire de la Deuxième Guerre Mondiale (1979); F. Bédarida, *La Stratégie secrète de la drôle de guerre: Le Conseil suprême interallié, septembre 1939–avril 1940* (1979), which publishes the full minutes of the Supreme War Council during the Phoney War with excellent commentaries; D. Dilks, 'The Twilight War and the Fall of France: Chamberlain and Churchill in 1940', in D. Dilks (ed.), *Retreat from Power* (1982), 36–65; R. A. C. Parker, 'Britain, France and Scandinavia, 1939–1940', *History* (1976), 369–87; D. Johnson, 'Britain and France in 1940', *Transactions of the Royal Historical Society* (1972), 141–57.

To follow the Franco-British relationship through to the defeat, see J. C. Cairns, 'Great Britain and the Fall of France: A Study in Allied Disunity', *Journal of Modern History* 27/4 (1955), 365–409; P. M. H. Bell, *A Certain Eventuality* (1974); E. Gates, *The End of the Affair: The Collapse of the Anglo-French Alliance, 1939–1940* (1981).

## THE PHONEY WAR

F. Fonvielle-Alquier, *The French and the Phoney War* (1973) is a bit impressionistic, but there is little else in English; G. Rossi-Landi, *La Drôle de guerre: La vie politique en France 2 septembre 1939–10 mai 1940* (1971) is narrow but useful; H.-J. Heimsoeth, *Der Zusammenbruch der Dritten Französischen Republik: Frankreich während der 'Drôle de guerre'* (Bonn, 1990) is probably the best overall study of French politics in the Phoney War. Our understanding of the Phoney War will be much enhanced by T. Imlay's forthcoming book *Facing the Second World War: Strategy, Politics and Economics in Britain and France, 1938–1940* (Oxford, May 2003). Some of his conclusions are previewed in T. Imlay, 'France and the Phoney War, 1939–1940', in R. Boyce (ed.), *French Foreign and Defence Policy, 1918–1940* (1998), 261–82. For Allied military planning, see J. O. Richardson, 'French Plans for Allied Attacks on the Caucasus', *French Historical Studies* (1973), 130–56. For the Norwegian expedition, see F. Kersaudy, *Norway 1940* (1990). (See also the contributions of Bédarida and Parker cited in the previous section.)

For the problem of Belgium, see B. Bond, *Britain, France and Belgium, 1939–1940* (1990 edn.); J. Vanwelkenhuyzen, *Neutralité armée: La Politique militaire de la Belgique pendant la Drôle de guerre* (Brussels, 1979); and M. Alexander, 'The French General Staff's Co-operation with Neutral Belgium, 1936–1940', *Journal of Strategic Studies*, 14/4 (1991), 413–27.

## GERMANY

On German planning, see K.-H. Frieser, *Blitzkrieg-Legende: Der Westfeldzug 1940*, 2 vols. (Munich, 1996) and B. Posen, *The Sources of Military Doctrine: France, Britain and Germany* (Ithaca, NY, 1984). L. Deighton, *Blitzkrieg: From the Rise of Hitler to the Fall of Dunkirk* (1979) is extremely readable; R. L. Dinardo, *Mechanized Juggernaut or Military Anachronism? Horses and the German Army of World War II* (New York, 1991) shows the German army in an unfamiliar light. For the German airforce, see W. Murray, *Strategy for Defeat: The Luftwaffe 1933–1945* (1983). B. H. Liddell Hart, *The Other Side of the Hill* (1951) is a famous book in which the German generals give their side of the story.

## THE BATTLE

On the course of the battle, the most readable narrative is A. Horne, *To Lose a Battle: France 1940* (1969). J. Gunsburg, *Divided and Conquered: The French High Command and the Defeat of France* (Westport, Conn., 1979) is a trenchant 'revisionist' account. A. Goutard, *The Battle of France 1940* (1958) was an excellent pioneering study that still repays reading. P. Rocolle, *La Guerre de 1940*, 2 vols. (1990) is the best recent French account of the battle, but it is very much the war seen from above. The most detailed account of the Sedan crossing is R. Doughty, *The Breaking Point: Sedan and the Fall of France* (Hamden, Conn., 1990). On the Dyle Plan, see the classic article of D. Alexander, 'The Repercussions of the Breda Variant', *French Historical Studies* (1973), 459–88. On the role of the BEF, see L. Ellis, *The War in France and Flanders 1939–1940* (1953). For quite a stimulating essay on the causes of defeat, see B. Lee, 'Strategy, Arms and the Collapse of France', in R. Langhorne (ed.), *Diplomacy and Intelligence during the Second World War* (1985), 43–67.

On the combatants, see Jean Delmas, Paul Devautour, Eric Lefèvre, *Mai–juin 40: Les Combattants de l'honneur* (1980); L. Menu, *Lumières sur les ruines: les combattants de 1940 réhabilités* (1953); M. Alexander, ' "No Taste for the Fight?": French Combat Performance in 1940 and the Politics of the Fall of France', in P. Addison and A. Calder (eds.), *Time to Kill: The Soldiers' Experience of War in the West, 1939–1945* (1997), 167–76; J. Vidalenc, 'Les Divisions de série "B" dans l'armée française dans la campagne de France', *Revue historique des armées*, 4 (1980), 106–26.

## THE LEGACY OF 1940

A. Shennan, *The Fall of France 1940* (2000) is an excellent essay on the consequences of the Fall of France. For the experience of the prisoners of war, see C. Lewin, *Le Retour des prisonniers de guerre français, naissance et développement de la FNPG* (1997). D. Reynolds, 'Fulcrum of the Twentieth Century?', *International Affairs*, 66/2 (1990), 325–50 is a stimulating article on the international fall-out from the Fall of France.

# Notes

## INTRODUCTION

1. R. MacLeod and D. Kelly, eds., *The Ironside Diaries* (1962), 204.
2. L. Werth, *Trente jours* (1992 edn.), 30.
3. A. Shennan, *The Fall of France, 1940* (2000), 165–6.
4. R. West, *Black Lamb and Grey Falcon* (1941), ii. 510.
5. *Khrushchev Remembers*, i (1977 edn.), 191.
6. *Fullness of Days* (1957), 215.
7. *Flight to Arras* (Eng. trans. 1942).
8. L. Tolstoy, *War and Peace* (OUP, 1983 edn.), 1069.

## CHAPTER 1

1. J. Chauvel, *Commentaire: De Vienne à Alger* (1971), 95–7.
2. W. S. Churchill, *The Second World War*, ii. *Their Finest Hour* (1949), 40–4.
3. F. Delpla, *Les Papiers secrets du général Doumenc (1939–1940)*, (1991), 206.
4. P. le Goyet, *Le Mystère Gamelin* (1976).
5. The Bibis was a modified version with heavier protection—60mm instead of 40mm and weighing 31.5 tons instead of 25 tons.
6. It was called Plan V because there had been two abortive Plans, III and IV.
7. *Les Événements survenus en France de 1933 à 1945* (1951–2), i; 67.
8. Indeed the adjective 'light' was now a misnomer, and if they were still called DLM it was to distinguish them from the *divisions marocaines* (Moroccan Divisions), designated as DMs, and from the *divisions motorisées* (Motorized Infantry Divisions), designated as DIMs.
9. Because there were not enough SOMUA tanks the DLMs were equipped half with these and half with another medium tank, the Hotchkiss 39 (H39).
10. G. Saint-Martin, *L'Armée blindée française. Mai–juin 1940* (1998), 18, 35. E. Kiesling, *Arming against Hitler: France and the Limits of Military Planning* (1996), 162.
11. R. Doughty, *The Breaking Point: Sedan and the Fall of France, 1940* (Hamdon, Conn. 1990), 132.
12. *The Halder Diaries*, iii (Washington, 1950), 75; E. May, *Strange Victory: Hitler's Conquest of France* (2000), 284.

NOTES

13. M. Gamelin, *Servir* (1946), ii. 128.
14. M. Alexander, 'Prophet Without Honour? The French High Command and Pierre Taittinger's Report on the Ardennes Defences, March 1940', *War and Society*, 4:1 (1986), 53–77.
15. Le Goyet, *Le Mystère*, 250.
16. XVI Panzer Corps (3rd and 4th Panzer Divisions) of General Erich Hoepner.
17. 1st, 2nd, and 10th.
18. 6th division of General Kempf and 8th of General Kuntzen.
19. 5th and 7th (Rommel).
20. May, *Strange Victory*, 419.
21. B. H. Liddell Hart, *The Other Side of the Hill* (1951), 169. The general was Blumentritt.
22. Doughty, *Breaking Point*, 100.
23. Ibid. 155–6.
24. A. Beaufre, *The Fall of France* (1967), 189.
25. D. Richards and H. Saunders, *The Royal Air Force, 1939–1945*, i. *The Fight at Odds* (1953), 120.
26. For an example of this, see the fate of the 61DI on page 177 below.
27. A. Horne, *To Lose a Battle* (1969), 301.
28. J. Minart, *P. C. Vincennes: Secteur 4*, ii (1945), 148.
29. Beaufre, *The Fall*, 188. The exact details of this occasion are much disputed, and some authors dismiss Beaufre's account, claiming even that Gamelin had left before lunch. But a careful cross-referencing of all available sources does seem to suggest he was present, even if in its detail Beaufre's account is somewhat too exuberant.
30. M. Gamelin, *Servir iii, La Guerre (September 1939–19 Mai 1940)*, iii. (1947), 435.

CHAPTER 2

1. See above, p. 56.
2. M. Weygand, *Recalled to Service* (1952), 59.
3. R. van Overstraeten, *Albert I–Léopold III: Vingt ans de politique militaire belge, 1920–1940* (1948), 655–6.
4. R. Young, 'The Aftermath of Munich: The Course of French Diplomacy', *French Historical Studies*, (1973), 305–22, 308.
5. Quotations in this paragraph from: J. C. Cairns, 'A Nation of Shopkeepers in Search of a Suitable France, 1919–1940', *American Historical Review*, 79 (1974), 710–43, 711, 713, 718, 722; B. Bond, *Britain, France and Belgium, 1939–1940* (1990), 8; P. M. H. Bell, *France and Britain, 1900–1940: Entente and Estrangement* (1996), 130.
6. Cairns, 'A Nation', 741; H. Nicolson, *Diaries and Letters 1939–1945* (1967), 298–9; Bond, *Britain, France*, 14.
7. O. Bullitt, *For the President: Personal and Secret Correspondence between Franklin D. Roosevelt and William C. Bullitt* (1973), 310 (6 Feb. 1939).
8. J. Zay, *Carnets secrets* (1942), 53–4. The minister was Mandel.
9. M. Carley, *The Alliance that Never Was and the Coming of World War II* (1999), 169.
10. G. Bonnet, *Défense de la paix, ii. Fin d'une Europe* (1948), 277.

11. J. Haslam, *The Soviet Union and the Struggle for Collective Security in Europe 1933–1939* (1984), 228.

12. M. Alexander, *The Republic in Danger: General Maurice Gamelin and the Politics of French Defence 1935–1940* (1993), 303.

13. Ibid. 311.

14. *The Diplomatic Diaries of Oliver Harvey, 1937–1940*, ed. J. Harvey (1970), 329–30 (13 Nov. 1939).

15. N. Jordan, *The Popular Front and Central Europe: The Dilemmas of French Impotence, 1918–1940* (1992), 297.

16. *Chief of Staff: The Diaries of Lieutenant-General Sir Henry Pownall*, ed. B. Bond (1972), 178 (hereinafter *Pownall Diaries*).

17. J. R. Colville, *Man of Valour: Field-Marshal Lord Gort* (1972), 177–8.

18. *Pownall Diaries*, 244 (12 Oct. 1939).

19. There were three TA divisions, which were still incomplete and remained behind the lines.

20. *Ironside Diaries*, 77.

21. Colville, *Man of Valour*, 137–8; *War Diaries of Field Marshal Lord Alanbrooke*, ed. A. Danchev and D. Todman (2001), 7; *Pownall Diaries*, 249.

22. *Ironside Diaries*, 200; *Pownall Diaries*, 243; *War Diaries of Alanbrooke*, 4.

23. Cairns, 'A Nation', 739; D. Johnson, 'Britain and France in 1940', *Transactions of the Royal Historical Society* (1972), 141–57, 148–9.

24. Bullitt, *For the President*, 370 (3 Sept. 1939).

25. *The Diaries of Sir Alexander Cadogan, O.M., 1938–1945*, ed. D. Dilks (1971), 218.

26. *Ironside Diaries*, 173 (20 Dec. 1939).

27. *Ironside Diaries*, 215, 226; *Cadogan Diaries*, 262.

28. Letter to Hilda, 30/3/40; PRO/FO 800/312, Campbell to Halifax, 12 Feb. 1940; *Ironside Diaries*, 234–5.

29. P. Baudouin, *Private Diaries: March 1940-Jan. 1941* (1948), 41.

30. PRO/FO 800/312, Campbell to Halifax, 29 Apr. 1940; F. F. Bédarida, *La Stratégie secrète de la drôle de guerre: Le Conseil suprême interallié, septembre 1939–avril 1940* (1979), 526.

31. Bond, *Britain, France*, 67; *Pownall Diaries*, 323.

32. *Ironside Diaries*, 321; *Pownall Diaries*, 323–4.

33. G. Chapman, *Why France Collapsed* (1968), 186.

34. E. L. Spears, *Assignment to Catastrophe* (1954), i. 184.

35. *Pownall Diaries*, 333.

36. P. de Villelume, *Journal d'une défaite, 23 août 1939–16 juin 1940* (1976), 350.

37. J. Vanwelkenhuyzen, *Pleins feux sur le désastre* (1995), 304–5.

38. Bond, *Britain, France*, 92.

39. Delpla, *Papiers de Doumenc*, 278; Bond, *Britain, France*, 97 n. 28.

40. Baudouin, *Private Diaries*, 76; Villelume, *Journal*, 370; J. Cairns, 'The French View of Dunkirk' in B. Bond and M. Taylor (eds.), *The Battle of France and Flanders 1940: Sixty Years on* (2001), 87–109, 90.

41. Cairns, 'The French View', 95.

42. Baudouin, *Private Diaries*, 73.

43. Spears, *Assignment*, ii. 19, 171; Churchill, *Finest Hour*, 97.

NOTES

## CHAPTER 3

1. A. Werth, *The Last Days of Paris* (1940), 144–5.
2. P. Reynaud, *La France a sauvé l'Europe* (1947), ii., 315.
3. Baudouin, *Private Diaries*, 47.
4. P. Reynaud, *In the Thick of the Fight 1930–1945* (1955), 504.
5. R. Aron, *Histoire de Vichy 1940–1944* (1954), 21.
6. P. Lazareff, *De Munich à Vichy* (1944), 32–3.
7. C. Micaud, *The French Right and Nazi Germany 1933–39* (1943), 120.
8. Zay, *Carnets secrets*, 58.
9. Harvey, *Diplomatic Diaries*, 223, 250.
10. Villelume, *Journal*, 42, 70, 74; J. Jeanneney, *Journal Politique: Septembre 1939–juillet 1942* (1972), 23; Bullitt, *For the President*, 373 (16 Sept. 1939).
11. H. Nicolson, *Diaries and Letters 1939–1945* (1967), 42.
12. PRO/FO 371/22913, Phipps to Halifax, 23 Oct. 1940.
13. P. Reynaud, *Finances de guerre* (1940).
14. Harvey, *Diplomatic Diaries*, 342.
15. *The Ciano Diaries 1939–1943* (1945/6), 238.
16. Villelume, *Journal*, 248 (24 Mar. 1940).
17. P. Reynaud, *Carnets de captivité, 1941–1945* (1997), 72.
18. M. Alexander, 'The Fall of France', *Journal of Strategic Studies*, 13/1 (1990), 10–44, 26.
19. H. Queuille, *Journal de guerre: 7 septembre 1939–8 juin 1940* (1993), 281; A. de Monzie, *Ci-devant* (1941), 214.
20. See above, p. 83.
21. Harvey, *Diplomatic Diaries*, 347 (7 Apr. 1940), 349 (14 Apr. 1940).
22. Villelume, *Journal*, 43 (25 Sept. 1939).
23. Baudouin, *Private Diaries*, 17.
24. See above, p. 86.
25. *'Le Journal' du général Weygand, 1929–1935*, ed. F. Guelton (1998), 233, 303.
26. E. Gates, *The End of the Affair: The Collapse of the Anglo-French Alliance, 1939–1940* (1981), 139.
27. Baudouin, *Private Diaries*, 57–8.
28. Bullitt, *For the President*, 434, 441.
29. A. Fabre Luce, *Journal de France, mars 1939–juillet 1940* (1940), 313.
30. J. C. Cairns, 'Great Britain and the Fall of France: A Study in Allied Disunity', *Journal of Modern History*, 27/4 (1955), 365–409, 382.
31. Villelume, *Journal*, 403–4 (11 June 1940).
32. PRO/Fo371/24310 C7125/65/17.
33. Baudouin, *Private Diaries*, 57, 79.
34. Spears, *Assignment*, ii., 148.
35. Spears, *Assignment*, ii., 229.
36. Ibid., ii. 222; Baudouin, *Private Diaries*, 108–9.
37. PRO/PREM 188/6, Spears to Churchill, 27 May 1940.
38. Bullitt, *For the President*, 452–4.
39. W. Shirer, *The Collapse of the Third Republic: An Inquiry into the Fall of France in 1940* (1969), 813; A. Maurois, *Why France Fell* (1940), 69.

## CHAPTER 4

1. P. Pétain, *Discours aux Français* (1989), 57–8.
2. G. Friedmann, *Journal de guerre 1939–1940* (1987), 273, 305.
3. G. Sadoul, *Journal de guerre (2 septembre 1939–20 juillet 1940)* (1994 edn.), 352.
4. Gamelin, *Servir*, iii. 425.
5. Bullitt, *For the President*, 368 (8 Sept. 1940); Sadoul, *Journal*, 44.
6. G. Folcher, *Marching to Captivity: The War Diaries of a French Peasant, 1939–1945* (1996), 12, 36.
7. Friedmann, *Journal*, 40, 76–7.
8. H. Clout, *After the Ruins: Restoring the Countryside of Northern France after the Great War* (1996), 3, 19.
9. J.-L. Crémieux-Brilhac, *Les Français de l'an 40*, i. *La Guerre oui ou non?* (1990), 59; Bullitt, *For the President*, 368; PRO/F0371 22918, 2 Nov. 1939.
10. Zouaves were a colonial regiment, but made up of white conscripts only.
11. Roger Escarpit, *Carnets d'outre siècle*, (1989), 232; J.-P. Sartre, *War Diaries: Notebooks from a Phoney War, November 1939–March 1940* (1984), 222; Friedmann, *Journal*, 46, talks of living in a 'petit milieu replié' (a small, inward-looking world).
12. Crémieux-Brilhac, *Les Français de l'an 40*, ii. *Ouvriers et soldats* (1990), 527.
13. Friedmann, *Journal*, 173 (16 Feb. 1940).
14. Sartre, *War Diaries*, 46, 224–5; F. Grenier, *Journal de la drôle de guerre (septembre 1939–juillet 1940)* (1969), 85–8; Sadoul, *Journal*, 84–7, 121.
15. Crémieux-Brilhac, *Ouvriers et soldats*, 433.
16. Facon, 135–6.
17. J.-P. Sartre, *Carnets de la drôle de guerre: Septembre 1939–mars 1940* (1995), 50–1 (24 Sept. 1939) (Sartre's Phoney War diaries for September and October are not available in English); Folcher, *Marching*, 286; Sadoul, *Journal*, 101, 123, 139.
18. H.-J. Heimsoeth, *Der Zusammenbruch der Dritten Französischen Republik: Frankreich während der 'Drôle de guerre'* (1990), 339.
19. Sartre, *War Diaries*, 356; Crémieux-Brilhac, *Ouvriers et soldats*, 518–21.
20. The analysis here and in the next six paragraphs draws heavily on E. Kiesling, *Arming against Hitler*.
21. The longer service was introduced as a result of the 'hollow years' in which, owing to the effects of the First World War, there was a demographic shortfall.
22. Kiesling, *Arming against Hitler*, 114.
23. See above, p. 48; and below, p. 171 ff.
24. Paul-André Lesort, *Quelques jours de mai–juin 40: Mémoire, témoignage, histoire* (1992), 105–6, 111.
25. C. Paillat, *Le Désastre de 1940*, ii. *La Guerre immobile* (1984), 40, 327.
26. A. Bryant, *The Turn of the Tide 1939–1943* (1957), 71.
27. Crémieux-Brilhac, *Ouvriers et soldats*, 545–6.
28. M. Alexander, ' "No Taste for the Fight?": French Combat Performance in 1940 and the Politics of the Fall of France', in P. Addison and A. Calder (eds.), *Time to Kill: The Soldiers' Experience of War in the West, 1939–1945* (1997), 167–76, 166.
29. See above, p. 50.
30. Horne, *To Lose a Battle*, 248–9.
31. R. Balbaud, *Cette drôle de guerre: Alsace–Lorraine–Belgique–Dunkerque* (1941), 49.

32. Horne, *To Lose a Battle*, 247.
33. Ibid. 250.
34. E. Ruby, *Sedan, terre d'épreuve* (1948), 38.
35. Crémieux-Brilhac, *Ouvriers et soldats*, 585.
36. See above, pp. 47–48.
37. Lesort, *Quelques jours*, 64, 84, 160–1.
38. Folcher, *Marching*, 82, 84, 73, 75.
39. See above, p. 38.
40. Balbaud, *Cette drôle de guerre*, 98.
41. Ibid. 48.
42. Folcher, *Marching*, 99, 101.
43. A. Shennan, *The Fall of France 1940* (2000), 8.
44. N. Dombrowski, 'Beyond The Battlefield: The Civilian Exodus of 1940', Ph.D. thesis (New York, 1995), 166.
45. On memories of atrocities in 1914, J. Horne and A. Kramer, *German Atrocities, 1914* (2001), 375–410.
46. J.-J. Becker, *1914: Comment les Français sont entrés dans la guerre* (1977), 554.
47. Crémieux-Brilhac, *Ouvriers et soldats*, 635–43.
48. J.-J. Arzalier, 'La Campagne de mai–juin 1940: Les Pertes?', in C. Levisse-Touzé (ed.), *La Campagne de 1940* (2001), 427–47. He deducts, for example, about 15,000 civilian deaths and 30,000–40,000 deaths of POWs in captivity—though presumably many of these might have died as a result of wounds incurred during the fighting.
49. *Documents on German Foreign Policy 1918–1945*, D, IX (1956), No. 317. Conversely, Hitler did also remark to General Juan Vigon on 16 June that the French and British soldiers were worse in 1940 than in 1914. Note also the positive contemporary German comments on the fighting qualities of the French soldier in Heimsoeth, *Der Zusammenbruch*, 11 n. 6.
50. PRO/FO371/24311 C7451/65/17.

CHAPTER 5

1. B. Lyon, 'Marc Bloch: Did He Repudiate *Annales* History?', *Journal of Medieval History*, 11 (1985), 181–91, 187–9.
2. R. de Aylana and P. Braudel, *Les Ambitions de l'histoire* (1997), 12; F. Braudel, 'Personal Testimony', *Journal of Modern History*, 44/4 (1972), 448–67, 454.
3. M. Alexander, 'The French View', in Bond and Taylor, *The Battle of France*, 181–205, 194.
4. Horne, *To Lose a Battle*, 29, 59.
5. J. C. Cairns, 'Some Recent Historians and the "Strange Defeat" of 1940', *Journal of Modern History*, 46 (1974), 60–85, 81.
6. Saint-Martin, *L'Armée blindée*, p. xviii.
7. S. Berstein, *La France des années 30* (1993), 169.
8. G.-H. Soutou, 'Introduction', in Levisse-Touzé (ed.), *La Campagne*, 21–37, 21.
9. P. Vidal-Naquet, *Les Juifs, la mémoire et le présent* (1991), 87.
10. Becker, *1914*.
11. J. B. Duroselle, *L'Abîme, 1939–1945* (1982), 51.

12. On Gort and Lanrezac, see E. L. Spears, *Liaison 1914: A Narrative of the Great Retreat* (1930).

13 *War Begins at Home* by Mass Observation, edited and arranged by Tom Harrison and Charles Madge (1940), 80–100.

14 S. Nicholas, *The Echo of War: Home Front Propaganda and the Wartime BBC 1939–1945* (1996), 31–54.

15. I. McLaine, *Ministry of Morale: Home Front Morale and the Ministry of Information in World War II* (1972), 42.

16. *War Begins at Home*, 177, 183; *The Diary of Beatrice Webb*, iv. *1924–1943* (1985), 443.

17. R. Griffiths, *Patriotism Perverted: Captain Ramsay, the Right Club and British Antisemitism 1939–1940* (1998), 34–65.

18. *Cadogan Diaries*, 220.

19. C. King, *With Malice Towards None. A War Diary* (1970); J. Mearsheimer, *Liddell Hart and the Weight of History* (1988), 154–6.

20 Nicolson, *Diaries 1939–1945*, 44–5.

21. King, *With Malice Towards None*, 14.

22. M. Gilbert, *Finest Hour: Winston S. Churchill 1939–1941* (1983), 190.

23. 'Édouard Daladier: La Conduite de la guerre et les prémices de la défaite', *Historical Reflections/Réflexions Historiques*, 22/1 (1996), 91–115, 102.

24 D. Thorpe, *Alec Douglas Home* (1996), 102; *Chips: The Diaries of Sir Henry Channon*, ed. R. Rhodes James (1967), 249–50; J. Colville, *The Fringes of Power: Downing Street Diaries* (1985), 141; K. Jefferys, *The Churchill Coalition and Wartime Politics 1940–1945* (1991), 48.

25. *Cadogan Diaries*, 287.

26. The most perceptive discussions of this debate are D. Reynolds, 'Churchill and the British Decision to Fight on in 1940: Right Policy Wrong Reasons', in R. Langhorne, *Diplomacy and Intelligence during the Second World War* (1985), 147–67; and Reynolds, 'Churchill the Appeaser? Between Hitler, Roosevelt and Stalin in World War Two' in M. Dockrill and B. McKercher (eds.), *Diplomacy and World Power: Studies in British Foreign Policy, 1890–1950* (1996), 197–220.

27. *The Second World War Diary of Hugh Dalton*, ed. B. Pimlott (1986).

28. Reynolds, 'Churchill and the Decision to Fight on', 149.

29. King, *With Malice Towards None*, 55.

30. A. J. Sylvester, *Life with Lloyd George: The Diary of A. J. Sylvester* (1975), 281; T. Munch-Petersen, '"Common Sense not Bravado": The Butler–Prytz Interview of 17 June 1940', *Scandia*, 52/1 (1986), 73–114.

31. *Cadogan Diaries*, 80 (2 July 1940); C. Ponting, *1940: Myth and Reality* (1990), 116–17; A. Roberts, *The Holy Fox: A Biography of Lord Halifax* (1991), 250.

32. Roberts, *The Holy Fox*, 186.

33. D. French, *Raising Churchill's Army: The British Army and the War against Germany, 1919–1945* (2000), 122, 126, 177.

34. PRO/FO 371 24310/C5767 (15 Apr.); PRO/FO 800/312 (1 May).

35. Jordan, *The Popular Front*, 5.

36. P. Jackson, 'Intelligence and the End of Appeasement', in R. Boyce (ed.), *French Foreign and Defence Policy, 1918–1940* (1998), 234–60, 252.

37. *Ironside Diaries*, 313.

38. K.-H. Frieser, *Blitzkrieg-Legende: Der Westfeldzug 1940*, 2 vols. (1996). His thesis is

summarized by him in 'La Légende de la "Blitzkrieg"', in M. Vaïsse (ed.), *Mai–juin 1940 Défaite française, victoire allemande, sous l'oeil des historiens étrangers* (2000), 75–86.
39 W. Shirer, *Berlin Diary: The Journal of a Foreign Correspondent 1934–1941* (1941), 152, 162; R. Overy and A. Wheatcroft, *The Road to War* (1989), 60; W. Diest et al., *Germany and the Second World War*, i (1990), 120–1.
40. May, *Strange Victory*, 368.
41. Vanwelkenhuyzen, *Pleins feux*, 87.
42. Balbaud, *Drôle de guerre*, 96.
43. French, *Raising Churchill's Army*, 178.
44. R. Prioux, *Souvenirs de guerre* (1947), 86–96.
45. Alan Brooke, *War Diaries*, 68.
46. M. Howard, *The Franco-Prussian War: The German Invasion of France, 1870–1871* (1961), 1.
47. H. Dutailly, *Les Problèmes de l'armée de terre française* (1980), 180.
48. *'Le Journal' du Général Weygand*, 65.
49. R. Aron, *Memoirs: Fifty Years of Political Reflection* (1990), 106–7.

## CHAPTER 6

1. P. Péan, *Une Jeunesse française, François Mitterrand, 1934–1947* (1994), 113.
2. F. Mitterrand, *L'Abeille et l'architecte* (1978), 281.
3. S. Hoffmann, 'The Trauma of 1940' in J. Blatt (ed.), *The French Defeat of 1940: Reassessments* (1998), 354–70, 356.
4. C. Lewin, *Le Retour des prisonniers de guerre français, naissance et développement de la FNPG* (1997), 91, 295 n. 126, n. 129.
5. C. Rist, *Une Saison gâtée: Journal de guerre et de l'Occupation* (1983), 165.
6. Heimsoeth, *Der Zusammenbruch*, 19 n. 32.
7. L. Blum, *For all Mankind* (1946), 24–5.
8. D. Reynolds, 'Fulcrum of the Twentieth Century?', *International Affairs*, 66/2 (1990), 325–50. This section owes much to Reynolds's analysis.
9. Overy and Wheatcroft, *Road to War*, 179.
10. See A. Best, *Britain, Japan and Pearl Harbor: Avoiding War in East Asia* (1995).
11. M. Dockrill, *British Establishment Perspectives on France 1936–1940* (1999), 157.
12. Reynolds, 'Fulcrum', 22; D. Reynolds, *The Creation of the Anglo-American Alliance 1937–1941* (1981), 101.
13. Shennan, *Fall of France*, 78.
14. Ibid. 165.
15. E. Roussel, *Charles de Gaulle* (2002), 364–5.
16. M. Borden, *Journey Down a Blind Alley* (1946), 113–15.
17. Quoted in G. Hecht, *The Radiance of France: Nuclear Power and National Identity after 1945* (1998), 232.
18. Shennan, *Fall of France*, 166.

# Index

capitulation of 93–4
Dyle Plan 25–30, 37–8
encirclement of 59
neutrality 63, 75–7, 220
refugees 174
Belin, René 113
Bell, Clive 204
Benoist-Méchin, Jacques 190
Béraud, Henri 68
Bérenger, Henry 121
Bergery, Gaston 124
Berstein, Serge 196
Biddle, Anthony 140
Billotte, General Gaston 23, 28, 33, 38, 42,
    60–1, 85–8, 220, 223
Blanchard, General 33, 34, 37, 38–9, 40, 85,
    86–7
    as Allied coordinator 88, 89, 91–2, 94
    collapse of 224
    Gort's scathing opinion of 98
Blitzkrieg 31–2, 215–6
Bloch, Marc 185–7, 191, 204, 222, 224
Blum, Léon 109, 110, 112, 113, 115, 116, 124, 150,
    188, 211, 233–4, 244
Bonnet, Georges 64, 69, 73, 113, 115, 116, 117,
    121, 205
Bordeaux 136, 232
Bossuet, Bishop 68
Bouthillier, Yves 134–5
Brasillach, Robert 112
Braudel, Fernand 190–1
Briand, Aristide 213, 214
Britain 226
    appeasers in 203–5, 208
    on Belgian capitulation 93–4
    bomber support in France 42, 48
    Dunkirk evacuation 94–7
    France and 66–71, 79–85, 97–100, 135,
        198–9, 214–5
    historians analysis of fall of France
        192–3
    morale 201, 210–1
    negotiations with Soviet Union 72–4
    pacifism 203–4
    possible approach to Italy 132–3
    pro-Nazi sympathizers 202–3
    propaganda 200–1

reorientation of foreign policy 238–9
response to French armistice plan 137–8
Reynaud and 127
Turkey and 71 *see also* BEF (British
    Expeditionary Force)
Brittain, Vera 204
Brittany 134
Brocard, General 50
Brocket, Lord 202, 203
Brooke, General Alan 78, 79, 160, 220, 224
Bruneau, General 52
Buccleuch, Duke of 202, 203
Bulgaria 71
Bullitt, William 70, 80, 120, 133, 136, 140, 145,
    151
Bulson panic 166–7
Butler, R. B. 205, 206, 209

Cadogan, Sir Alexander 80, 81, 84, 203–4,
    207, 209
Cagoule (clandestine organizations
    group) 110
Caillaux, Madame Joseph 198
Cain, Julien 155
Cairns, John 193
Cambon, Jules 213
Campbell, Sir Ronald 70, 82, 84, 180, 182,
    211
Campinchi, César 132
Cangé, Chateau of 103–4, 105, 135–6
Caquot, Albert 19
Carroll, C. E. 202
casualty rates 179–80
Catholicism 107
Catroux, General 100
Chamberlain, Neville 67, 69, 80, 84, 98, 133,
    206, 207
    on American support 238
    appeasement 205
    Daladier's opinion of 70
    on Fall of France 237
    loyalty towards successor 211
    negotiations with Soviet Union 73
    popularity on return from Munich 149
    on Reynaud 82
    visit to Rome 71
Channon, 'Chips' 69, 206

Printed and bound by CPI Group (UK) Ltd, Croydon, CR0 4YY